A LONG SLOW AFFAIR OF THE HEART

Bruce Ansley has written for radio, television, newspapers and magazines for a very long time. His last book was *Stoned on Duty*. He is still married, has three sons, and lives in Christchurch and Golden Bay.

A Long Slow Affair of the Heart

An Adventure on the French Canals

BRUCE ANSLEY

Longacre Press

Acknowledgements:
I thank Glenn Busch and Trish Allen, who inspired this journey, helped us along the way, put up with the fallout, and took many of the photographs.

ISBN 978 1 877460 21 0

First published by Longacre Press, 2008
30 Moray Place, Dunedin, New Zealand

A catalogue record for this book is available from the National Library of New Zealand.

The quotation on page 27 is reproduced with permission from the *Listener*

The quotation on page 41 is taken from *South Sea Vagabonds* (1939) by John Wray (Wellington: A.H. and A.W. Reed, 2nd and rev. edn, 1952)

Book and cover design by Christine Buess
Cover photograph by Glenn Busch
Printed by Astra Print, Wellington

www.longacre.co.nz

For Sally (of course)

Chapter One

I don't know when it changed. No shadow flickered in the bright landscape of our new life. One moment we were in a traveller's tale of escape and adventure and the romance of journeys in another world. The next, it turned into a story of love, and a marriage trembling on the edge, and how hard it is to live life well.

We knew nothing of this, that March morning when we arrived in Holland.

I whimpered in the grey air outside Schipol airport, Amsterdam. The Singapore Airlines flight had touched down at six a.m. We were tired. We cannot sleep on long flights. I am claustrophobic and Sally is scared. I fight panic as the tiny space around me fills with papers, passports, books, tickets, forms, pens, headphones, tables, towels, food and those strange personality changes which afflict people on aeroplanes, causing them to confess serial adultery to neighbours, or fossick around endlessly in overhead lockers. Sally worries clots are forming in our deepest veins which will kill us in our tight economy class seats, and if they do not, that a wing will fall off and we'll die anyway.

We knew it was six a.m. because the pilot had said so. He sounded the hour with an American's certainty, but as many of his compatriots had established in countries we had only that morning flown over, he might have been mistaken. This could have been Amsterdam, or it might have been anywhere dark, and cold, and foggy, such as Hamilton.

For a moment I hoped it *was* Hamilton.

I'd dreamed of throwing in my job, of going to Holland, buying a boat, sailing it first to Belgium then France, of living on the French canals for a year or two. Sally had imagined villages and flowers and peace. But the trouble with dreams is not so much their coming true as the chill kiss of truth when they do.

The fourteen-hour flight from Singapore had wrecked my internal calendar and clock. Like my phone, and my watch, they needed re-setting, and I couldn't be bothered with any of them.

Had the American pilot, like his leader, taken a wrong turn? Of course he had not. This was indisputably liberal Holland. To get into the country I answered a single question: why was I there?

I was on holiday, I replied, not wanting to complicate matters. Have a good time, said the immigration official, waving me through. His mate glanced at Sally's European Union passport (Sally had been born in England) and skipped the questions altogether.

The Netherlands lay outside: cold, grey, flat, like our mood. I dug out my mobile with no great hope of connecting to anyone, but surprisingly it worked. A man in the car lease office answered. He'd got up early for us, he said, and he'd been waiting. His office was in a hotel, and we'd find the hotel's shuttle bus right outside the airport.

We rode to the hotel with our two pilots as fellow-passengers, peering out of the windows at concrete and cars and morning mist. The American captain talked deals. He knew about property prices, and shares, and where best to buy automobiles. His co-pilot watched him through hooded eyes and said nothing.

The car lease man was German but said he'd always wanted to live in Amsterdam with his Brazilian wife, and when he got this job only last January all his dreams came true. All of this I learned on our way up the stairs. I envied him the simplicity of his dream. Perhaps that was the secret.

His name was Flores, which meant flowers in Spanish he said, and was evidence of the Spanish influence in both Germany and Holland, a history stretching over so many centuries that it would take quite a long time to explain but he had the time if I did.

Let's talk about it on the way back down the stairs to the car, I said, and departed around the time Sephardic Jews first arrived from Spain and Portugal in 1492 with only around 500 years to go until we were fully up to date.

It was eight a.m. Dismal. Huge trucks were racing by on a nearby motorway along which we had to travel in a leased Peugeot so tiny I looked around for a remote control.

The dream hadn't mentioned this.

Now I was a man without a job in a strange city.

It had seemed very fine when I'd awoken one autumn morning in our Sumner home with a wonderful, excellent idea. I'd throw in my job, do something so different, so bold, that it would change our lives, throw the cards in the air and the heck where they landed. Outside the window yellow leaves were dripping off the cherry tree, the old wattle was gathering strength for its winter show. Change is good, they whispered, the time is right.

I yearned for adventure; but adventure is so contrary you spend a lot more time thinking about it than doing.

Easy, I supposed, if you'd been born Sir Edmund Hillary. For people like him adventures bloomed like crocuses in spring. As soon as a very high mountain appeared, or a pole, or a long river or something of that kind, you simply set out to climb it, or drive to it, or sail up it in the most dangerous way possible, certainly the most uncomfortable one, and everyone knew you'd had an exciting time.

Unfortunately there was a downside, as any number of heroes from Robert Falcon Scott to Rob Hall could testify if only they were in a position to.

Downside was not a mountaineering expression. It sprang from another kind of adventure whose Everest was the boardroom, where men and women in suits clambered after power and money and some became heroes also, even if mainly among their own. I preferred Hillary's clean run and respect for humanity.

But none of that was any help to the rest of us, the men and women over the garden fence who wanted to spike their lives a little, seek something different, find a bit of fun or even that hideously overworked term, a challenge.

Mostly, adventures were things someone else had. You read about them, or watched them on television, and those were probably best of all. Real adventures were uncomfortable, and could be dangerous, and might be best not approached by the unarmed citizen.

Some time ago I listened to a man called Alistair, whom I knew vaguely as a neighbour, talking on radio about a very big adventure. He'd been sailing down from the Suez Canal in his large motorboat when he spied what could only have been pirates zooming towards them in a speedboat.

Dear god. What were they to do? The pirate ship signalled them to stop, which they did. Then they saw the baddies leaning over the stern of their boat. They slowly realised they were looking at deliverance: the pursuing boat had fouled the fishing lines they'd been trailing, and the lines were now wrapped tightly around its propellers. Slowly the two boats drifted apart, and when they were a decent distance off they quietly chugged away, leaving the pirates rather than themselves dead in the water.

I could see it all as he spoke: their white-and-varnished ship in the blue gulf waters, the blazing sun, the pirates in their rakish vessel doubtless in red headscarves. The story had everything: heat, danger, excitement, the triumph of good over evil, or at least a tidy escape.

Much later I met Alistair in a restaurant. 'What an adventure!' I said. 'Not if you were there,' he replied. 'We were terrified.'

Terror was not part of your own script when you were imagining these things. Terror was best left entirely alone, along with boredom, worry, squabbling, exhaustion, discomfort, hardship, possibly death. They were all nicely filtered out by an imagination which saw only fun and excitement.

The idea, then, was to pick an adventure which had maximum potential for fun and excitement and minimum possibility of boredom, discomfort or death. That was not so easy. Even for fifteen seconds of excitement on a hydroslide you had to battle the traffic, climb an awful lot of stairs then wait in a queue with a bunch of very noisy kids. A fortnight in Bali or a bus trip around Europe were all very well, involving nothing more ferocious than a travel agent, but you still had to pack yourself in to an aeroplane (see boredom, discomfort above), then pass the time when you reached your destination (see squabbling, exhaustion etc.).

I quickly ruled out anything too dangerous on the grounds that Sally wouldn't go, although the truth was that she was much braver than I. She just could not see the fun in boredom, discomfort or death. She would have been happy watching the surf down the street, or planting a peach tree, or telephoning our twin sons Sam and Simon. But she was prepared to forego those things and go along with me — god knew why.

Sally suggested driving around Australia. I'd done a little of that, once. I'd driven from Sydney to Canberra and back with my four brothers and sister, in a van.

We'd turned off the motorway to have a beer in a small town, where the pub was laced with verandahs and the locals stopped talking when we walked in, as if the video shop stocked only old westerns. So we had a beer or two, and as we were leaving someone started screaming.

It turned out to be me, because there was a huge, hairy spider on the footpath, advancing towards the van, and one little hop on those legs would carry it right into the vehicle to where, in fact, we were huddling in a corner like sheep in a pen.

All five brothers and one sister were scared of spiders. Our father had returned from fighting in the Solomons during the war with a horror of the creatures which he faithfully passed on to us. World War Two, to his kids, had eight legs and a nasty bite.

A small boy, attracted by the screaming, came out of the pub. The other patrons either couldn't be bothered, or were worried about leaving their beer, or just thought screaming was what Kiwis did. He checked the spider, which, I fancied, eyed him right back. 'Sheeitt,' he said. 'It's just a tarantula.'

Just? The last time a van left the town in such a hurry was when the pub ran out of beer. We were not slowed even by the discovery that the town had an off-ramp from the motorway, but no on-ramp. We simply reversed up the off-ramp.

The only other time I'd attempted a long-ish trip in Australia, I'd set out for Hall's Creek from Kununnara. After a couple of hours I was so bored by the red earth and drab trees I was nearly comatose. I turned around and went back. Australia, for me, was off the list. 'Later,' I promised Sally.

We could live in Golden Bay, and that seemed quite a good idea. Our little green and blue tin bach stood beside the yellow sand of a bay whose clear water cooled our bodies, warmed our hearts and provided dinners of scallops, mussels and flounder when I roused myself enough to get them. A natural harbour opened to one side, and I could sit at the table in the living room and watch my boat rising and falling on the tide. Sally planted lilies and lettuce and wafted around the garden in her red-and-yellow lavalavas like a butterfly.

When we were in Golden Bay among its gentle community we could think of no life more perfect. We wondered why we ever wanted to do anything else: could there be too much loveliness, too much perfection? Yet when winter came and the house and garden grew dark at five p.m. the night seemed very long. Paradise had one cinema, a small library, and only a few cafés braving the off-season when the community hunkered down.

Perhaps we could go and live in my brother's house in Brittany. His house stood in the tiny hamlet of Le Bois Meen, near St Malo. We'd lived there once, for a few weeks, and we loved it. Getting up in the morning, strolling around to Madame at the boulangerie for baguettes and croissants, breakfast in the garden, perhaps a dip at Dinard or a drink in Dinan, a chat with the neighbours (Sally, who had never learned French, had much less trouble chatting than I, who had), the happy gurgle of the first glass from a bottle of Bordeaux. *C'est la vie*!

Where was the adventure in that? Well, I once heard Alan Duff say that looking at the first blank sheet of paper, knowing he'd just signed a contract for three novels, was a true act of courage, and I believed it. I could write, couldn't I? The only difference, after all, was that Duff had a contract and oh, perhaps a little talent.

The idea was alluring. But my brother, although endlessly welcoming, might jib at an announcement that we were taking over his house for quite a long time. Perhaps instead we could learn to play bridge, or telephone the Inland Revenue Department, exceed our credit card limit, park on the yellow line, ask a mechanic to take a quick look at our car, extend the kitchen or order tea in a café. All of those were risky, and all had their downside. But they lacked something, didn't they?

I supposed, in the end, it was best just to watch murder, mayhem and ripping yarns on television, and when you got sick of the six o'clock news, reach for the off-switch (see heroic etc. above). That seemed a bit tame. All right. We'd quit working. Then we'd go to Holland and buy a canal boat and spend a year living on the French canals and perhaps sail on the Mediterranean Sea; that's more like it, we thought.

At eight a.m. in the Netherlands romance curdles and dreams go sour. Tackling the motorway in our toy car was rather like putting to sea on a Lilo, except that death seemed certain to be more immediate. Looked at from the Peugeot's point of view, we were the lucky ones. The car had to go from brand new to 120 kilometres per hour in the space of five minutes. It had to endure outraged honkings as its terrified driver dodged this way and that. It had to shut its eyes and pray when calamity seemed inevitable, and would not have been reassured to know that its contents were doing the same.

Like storm-tossed debris on a beach, we were washed up in the village of Aalsmere, where I confessed to a passerby that I was lost. 'You cannot be lost in such a small country,' he replied. 'Here no one is lost.' Sure enough, neither were we. He pointed to a lane. 'Down there.'

A short distance along a narrow road near the lake, we disembarked, walked along the side of a little creek and met our first … shipbroker. So we thought. He proved to be a friend of our first broker. Our first broker had been admitted to hospital, where he was likely to remain for some time, and his friend had stepped into the breach. The first broker's friend was a thin man with wispy grey hair, a scholarly manner and a forbidding attitude. 'We want,' we said, 'a boat suitable for canals, and perhaps even the sea, one we can live on for a year, maybe two.'

He frowned. 'Have some coffee,' he said, walking up a gangplank to a little office built on a floating pontoon. It wobbled under our weight.

He was much better at making coffee than selling boats. Unlike almost everyone in the Netherlands, who seemed born knowing a stern gland from a sea-cock, boats clearly puzzled him. He scarcely knew his bow from stern, much less his koelkast from a boegshroef. Even I knew one was a fridge and the other a bow-thruster, although I wasn't sure which was which.

Outside, the foredeck and outboard motor arm were the only items of a runabout above water. A huge Dutch barge, partly converted for living, looked as if it might soon snuggle down beside it. Might we, I asked, have a look at one or two boats, preferably afloat? 'Have some more coffee,' he replied, hopefully. In marine terms, caffeine overload hove onto the horizon rather than the blue boat we thought might suit us.

'The blue boat?' he said at last, as if surprised that we were there for some other reason than his excellent coffee. 'Certainly.' He picked up a bunch of keys and strode confidently to the green boat nearby. 'No?' A spread of the hands. He was doing his best, but buyers were so difficult.

'This one,' I said, going to the blue boat and tapping it firmly on its stern. 'Ah.' He unlocked it and in we went.

We were learning lesson number one about Dutch boats. They seemed huge. Perhaps on the glistening blue waters of the Hauraki Gulf in summer, or the vast (by Dutch standards) green expanses of the Marlborough Sounds, they might have shrunk a little. In the tight marinas within Holland's narrow waterways they became massive, like cows in farm sheds. A twelve metre boat assumed the proportions of a Devonport ferry. A fourteen metre vessel looked ready to take paying passengers to the Bahamas. A sixteen metre boat — well, stand by Monaco.

Lesson number two was they were almost always steel. The Dutch worked with steel as New Zealanders used *pinus radiata*. Any properly brought-up Dutch child moved straight from potty-training to arc welding. By the time they were teething they could roll, form and rivet.

Wooden boats were treated as museum pieces and otherwise regarded with suspicion. Fibreglass, New Zealand's favourite boating material, was a stupid foreign invention with no place in decent society. Proper Dutch boats were steel: big, heavy things which you certainly did not want to trip over.

Third, the Dutch were the best of marine photographers. Their pictures could make a pile of rust look ready to take on the North Sea, carrying its crew in centrally-heated luxury. We were about to learn all three lessons at once.

The blue boat was enormous. As we looked at it I heard a sharp intake of breath from Sally, as if she'd been imagining a family saloon and come across a bus. 'It's so big,' she whispered.

It was so seriously steel that I stubbed my toe just thinking about it. The builder had been quite careful with curves but every now and then he'd evidently gone for coffee, forgotten where he'd left off, come back and headed in an entirely different direction. Rusty stains leaked from knocks in the paintwork. The whole boat was covered in green mould from Holland's wet winter. None of this was visible in the neat photographs we had admired on the internet back in New Zealand.

'You came a bit early,' said our broker's friend unconvincingly. 'I was about to start cleaning it down. A good scrub and it'll look much better.' Perhaps not that much better, we thought, heading inside.

We were to become familiar with the smell of boats locked up for the winter. They had an odour of old cabbage and lost summers. Diesel fuel fermented in the bilges. This one had a tincture of desolation. It had two single bunks in a little V-shaped cabin in the bow, or front. Behind that was a dinette on one side and a galley, or kitchen, on the other. Then came the saloon, a boat's living room, with one of the two steering positions (the other was on the deck at the back). Right in the stern was a big cabin with two single beds. We wanted a double bed, and by then had not learned lesson number four: every boat is a compromise.

Worse, this boat had no shower. We wanted one of those. French marinas sometimes offered showers, but charged for them. We wanted to save money and a long walk and given the sometimes lengthy gaps between showers, we needed our own. We imagined ourselves sniffing anxiously, uncertain whether that occasional whiff was the chicken in the fridge or something going off much closer to home.

This was a large boat, thirteen and a half metres. Why anyone would spend the amount of money needed to build a boat like that, without a shower, was one of the mysteries of the Netherlands we never quite resolved, for we were to find that in the matter of showers the Dutch were whimsical. Quite big boats often had none. Rather small boats might have two.

But it was not time wasted. We had taken the first step to lesson number five, the most important of all: trust your instincts. First impressions counted. If the boat failed that first test, we were to find that no amount of rationalising made up for it. Not trusting our instincts almost led us unto disaster later. In the meantime, however, our instincts told us first that the boat was not going to be our home for the next year or two, and on a more feral level, it stank.

So we moved on to the next boat, a few berths further on. I'd been studying this boat on the internet for months. It seemed perfect, for one outstanding reason: it was a classic, and I loved classic boats. My own little motor-sailer at home was designed by the wonderful Athol Burns and built in 1966. It was planked in kauri and had more ribs than Eve ever contemplated. Sally refused to set foot on it. If she could avoid looking at it — not easy, since it was moored in Golden Bay within sight of our dining table — she would. If she had to describe our bay there would be a black hole at one end of it. She thought it smelly and a thorough waste of time. Both were quite true.

I'd drooled over boats, lived for them since I was a kid and had put to sea in a banana box. I'd discovered two things about boats immediately. First, if they can go wrong they will. Second, nothing in boating is cheap because if it is, it sinks. The third thing I found out was that boats, like porn, are fantasies best kept to yourself. I lugged the sodden crate home and asked my dad to put a point on one end and fill in the holes. To my delight he spent several hours obliging.

When he'd finished I picked it up and set off on what I intended to be its maiden voyage as a real boat rather than a mere banana box.

'Where are you going?' he demanded, the beginnings of alarm in his voice.

'Down to the beach.'

'My god,' he said, 'not in that thing.'

He seized his hammer once more and began knocking it back to the banana box which, he said, at least he could stand on so it would come in handy for something. Delight turned to despair, but the box served me as well as it had its bananas. It gave me nagging rights which I exercised so thoroughly that next Christmas, I came down the stairs to find the most amazing present I have ever had: a boat! Not just any old boat. A brand-new one, built by my dad and my Uncle Jock, who was a carpenter. For the first time I saw the perfect beauty of stem fitting keel, frames holding planking to voluptuous curves ending in a transom whose metaphor I was far too young to appreciate.

It didn't work, of course. It was too heavy, too narrow, too small. Its bottom planking split in the sun. 'Cover it in wet sacks,' said my dad. 'It'll soon come right.' But I'd discovered yet another thing about boats. They were so beautiful I didn't really care whether they were good or bad. I loved looking at them, and I admired this one until it had rotted into a pile of mould.

Later I built a kayak out of wood and some sort of sacking which the shop said was cheap but every bit as good as canvas. It was not. It leaked, always. I built an oil-drum raft, a racing catamaran, bought a R-class yacht, a clinker dinghy, a surfboard, a fine X-class yacht which I saw lying in someone's front garden with grass growing through its bottom and spent at least three times longer restoring than it would have taken to build a new one. I took my new girlfriend Sally out sailing on Otago Harbour in that glorious boat. She got wet and accused me of using her as a fender to prevent my varnished topsides crashing into an iron piling. I thought it a sacrifice any woman would be proud to make. She got over it but I learned another of those endless truths about boats: women are at best resigned to them, or at least all who sail in them.

So this classic boat lying in its funny little marina not far from Amsterdam definitely started from behind. I had spent a lot of time working on Sally. Oh all right, lying to her. I'd told her how roomy the vessel was, how beautifully built by van Lent, one of Holland's leading builders of luxury craft; how maintaining its varnish would take only a couple of hours every six months, possibly every year; how it would certainly appreciate in value and could quite easily make us a fortune. The last argument was difficult to sustain with a straight face because no boat I had ever owned had made us so much as a cent; rather, every one of them had cost us dearly.

This boat had been on the market for at least three years, and even the rankest optimist might conclude that it was hardly being rushed by buyers tearing open their cheque-books as they ran. It was a disaster, of course, varnish so hideously water-stained my estimate of a couple of hours work multiplied by a factor of, oh, a thousand or so. Its teak decks looked forlorn, its paintwork forsaken. Bits of interior lay around inside. We didn't even bother unlocking its doors.

'It's cheap,' the broker's friend said. 'Make an offer.' His tone suggested any offer. But the boat may lie there still, mould dripping over its curves, its splendid design a trap for smitten Kiwis looking for a cheap doer-upper.

I was not dismayed. In fact, I was delighted. After just one day I knew I was onto something here, something good, unusual, wonderful. Ask yourself this question: how often do you go out with a load of money to buy yourself a hideously extravagant toy? Or: how did he get a load of money in the first place? The answer to the first was, of course, never; to the second, the money was a legacy Sally had received from her mother, which she'd rashly decided to invest in her husband's later-life crisis.

If you're a bloke, you might rephrase the situation like this: how often do you get licence to do nothing else but cruise this way and that, looking at anything you like as long as it floats, in company with a woman who isn't viewing this as some peculiar blokey addiction but is, as they say in the world of boats, on board?

Like sex, it was exquisite for him, and she quite liked it too. When I drew this analogy for my friend Tom, he sent an acid addendum back from New Zealand: like sex, he said, it didn't happen all that often either.

The weather was perfect. Our friends Glenn Busch and Trish Allen had been in Holland a month later when they'd bought their canal boat a few years before. The cold had riven their bones.

When Glenn found a parka in a second-hand shop back in Christchurch, he bought it for me immediately. 'You'll need it, mate,' he said. It was a remarkable garment, made by Ralph Lauren. Oh, how the mighty price had fallen, to twenty dollars. It could have warmed a Mac truck. When I put it on I looked like a cartoon Eskimo. Sally said it made a mountain out of a molehill and I agreed that it certainly occupied more than its fair share of a bus seat. It was like carrying my own home around with me, warm and worn and comfy. But too big. When I came to pack it, the parka needed a suitcase all of its own. I could have worn it onto the plane, but the airlines were then contemplating excess fares for obese people, and I feared this might tip the balance. An economy class seat just wasn't big enough for both of us.

Instead, I went out and bought a state of the art fleece jacket from Earth Sea Sky, a wonderful Kiwi-made thing, light as a feather and quite at home in Colombo Street or up a mountain. Sally bought merino jackets and fleece and lots of polyprop shirts and long johns for both of us, and with ski hats and gloves we felt outfitted for the worst the Netherlands could heave at us.

The weather turned out to be as shocking as we expected, but for a different reason. The sun shone from a clear sky; well, as clear as it gets in the Netherlands, which is like a nice blue day in New Zealand only with the curtains drawn. 'We have not had a proper winter,' Mr Flores had said, happily. 'You are very lucky.' Blue day followed blue. The temperature one Sunday reached twenty degrees. The winter gear hung in the wardrobe as a reproach. The Dutch celebrated by walking everywhere, especially right in front of our little Peugeot. They took to their bicycles in vast numbers. They celebrated their good fortune endlessly.

Every night on television the news on global warming grew darker. Every day the Dutch mood grew brighter. I asked Jan Jellema, whose boat I was then visiting, whether he felt threatened in such a low country with the sea rising outside. He looked at me as if I'd come down in the last shower, even if that had fallen quite some time ago. 'No,' he said. 'I don't worry a bit. The Dutch have been fighting the sea for centuries.' Of course he was right. The place was as much water as land. Dykes were so common I scarcely noticed them any more.

With more than sixteen million people jammed into a space much smaller than Canterbury the entire nation would have sunk into the mud under the sheer weight of humanity if they'd treated flooding as, say, people in the Bay of Plenty did: an act visited upon them rarely enough for them to hope that next time it would go somewhere else. The Dutch were so used to keeping the sea out of their living rooms that what did another few centimetres matter to them? If only they'd colonised Bangladesh instead of their East Indies, that country's troubles might have vanished from the six o'clock news.

So, in the Netherlands this March, there was no apprehension among either the Dutch or ourselves. The Dutch turned their pale faces to the sun, or where they felt the sun might be behind the haze. We put away our long johns and went looking for boats in the warm.

We'd gone to Holland to buy our boat because the market was huge, the country was small, and most people spoke English. The Dutch loved boats almost as much as they did bicycles. They had millions of them. Water comprised a quarter of the country, and boats were jammed into every wet bit. The Dutch ran boats as New Zealanders ran sheep. The real problem here was not in finding a boat, for you could not miss them; it was finding the right boat.

People had tried various methods. Glenn and Trish went off to Holland with essentially just a single boat in mind. They had seen it advertised on the internet. When that one was disappointing they set off in their hire car, staying in B&Bs in the places their search took them. Eventually they found their lovely boat, a turn of the twentieth century milk carrier converted for living, through a small ad in one of the boating magazines. A couple from Auckland hired a broker to search for them, and he found them a boat, a barge, in just two days. Our own technique was to watch the boats advertised on the internet, get a feel for the market, then compile a list of possibilities before we boarded our plane.

Then I stumbled across a website used by the Dutch to advertise their holiday homes for rent. We found a warm, bright one-bedroomed cottage in Schoorl, a nice little village on the edge of a national park in north Holland. Behind the village lay the biggest sand dunes in all the Netherlands, some of them almost sixty metres high. We could sit in a café and watch families climb to the top of a huge sand dune then march down again, like the grand old Duke of York's ten thousand men. The sand hills rolled down to the North Sea, a brownish-grey place that on a good day might be called bracing, although I preferred bleak. Still, the Dutch loved it, and like people everywhere went down to the sea in droves and stood, rugged-up, staring over the wild surf.

Not far down the road was the town of Alkmaar, a fine tenth-century town which was the first city in the Netherlands to be freed from Spanish occupation in the sixteenth century after withstanding a siege whose last day was still celebrated each year. 'Victory begins in Alkmaar,' cried the locals, and in an office near Schipol I could hear Mr Flores rubbing his hands. Alkmaar's houses sometimes rose straight from the canals, like a stumpy Venice. On sunny afternoons when the brokers' yards were closed, or we had time, we would sit and watch the Dutch ambling by, for this was a nation of quiet pleasures.

Between Schoorl and Amsterdam lay tulip fields, and the famous Keukenhof Gardens, striping the land in brilliant colours. Schoorl was not a popular boating area — not, that is, in the usual sense, for of course there were canals and boats everywhere. The brokers' yards, though, were to the south, and east, or across the long causeway over the mouth of the Isselmeer, the shallow sea running down to Amsterdam. The country was so small it took, at most, a couple of hours to reach the boatyards in any direction, and we didn't have to spend time looking for a place to stay. We could come home as late as we liked, sloth out and watch forty channels on the television, encountering perhaps the sole benefit of New Zealand's mono-lingual education: we understood hardly any of them, so cutting down the number of channels we had to curse at.

Still, our landlady was hardly any more cosmopolitan. 'You came from New Zealand?' she asked, doubtfully. She stared at our tiny Peugeot. 'Did you drive?'

Oh, there was another reason for buying a boat in Holland, pure Kiwi: boats were reputed to be cheaper there. Here lay the universal truth about boats however: usually they were cheap for a reason. With boats, probably more than anything else, you get what you paid for. Holland's bustling market might keep its prices below other countries'. Certainly I looked at boats and imagined them selling in Auckland for far more than the asking price here. But if the boat seemed too good to be true, then even in Holland it was. The boats at the top of our list quickly dropped off. Some were unsuitable. Some were in other places, such as the south of France, or Belgium. Some were just awful.

We weren't in the market for a barge. Instead, we wanted a steel cruiser, big enough to live aboard for months, even years. We thought of spending the first year on the French canals, the second drifting down the wide river leading south. We might nip out into the Mediterranean, we told each other, perhaps to Marseilles, even to the French Riviera.

If we got that far, why not to Spain? We breathed deeply and smelled suntan oil. So we drew another list, of non-tradeable essentials. The boat had to have: a double bed, a good living space, a shower, a place for friends and family to stay, and an after-deck to sit on in the evenings watching the world turn rosy through the bottom of a wine glass.

Naturally, these were the qualities we began to renege on when we saw boats which might otherwise fit. 'Well, I wouldn't mind sleeping in single beds for a while. It's only for a year or two.' (Not me.) Or, 'How many people are going to stay with us anyway?' (Me.)

The boat heading our list seemed perfect on all counts. It was a Valk cruiser, a fine make. Panelled in mahogany with a teak deck and rakish bow. Lo, when we turned up at the yard, it had just been repainted too. New stainless steel railings glinted in the afternoon sun. Sally wanted to make an offer on the spot. But when we collected the keys and went below, oh dear. Its fine wooden floors were buckled. It stank. Mess was everywhere. I lifted the engine room hatch. Something gurgled far below.

And the price had just gone up.

'Well,' said the broker, 'the owner went bankrupt. The boat was lying around going to rack and ruin. So we bought it ourselves. We had to take off the teak deck. It was beyond repair. We've already spent thirteen thousand Euro (twenty-six thousand dollars) on it. You won't have to spend much more. New upholstery, well, a couple of thousand, canopies — they're only cloth after all — a bit of work on the wiring, the engine doesn't sound too bad ... but we've spent so much, you offer me only five hundred Euro less than the asking price, I won't take it.' Five hundred Euros? I was thinking 5,000, at least. So we moved on, quickly. Over the next week we looked at big boats, small ones, the ordinary, the flawed and the downright boring. Creatures of grace and beauty proved to be of dubious virtue. Our list of essentials was so compromised it refused to appear in public. Until, finally, we had a short list of two: Beauty and the Beast.

The Beauty was a varnished jewel, kept inside a huge gloomy shed where dark water lapped around hundreds of boats. Its owner, Jan Jellema, had it painted and revarnished every three years. It was an immaculate Super van Craft named *Alcyon*. Jan had visited Christchurch that January. 'It is a very pretty city,' he said politely. He had just sold his business and was buying another boat, of the same make but much bigger.

We fell in love with his boat at first sight, of course. Yes, it had disadvantages. The shower was primitive. The main sleeping cabin was low, so it didn't interfere with the vessel's fine lines, and you climbed into bed doubled up in the interests of good design. Jan, a huge man, climbed into his bunk to show how easy it was, and lay there like a whale that had found its way into a bookshelf. Yet you could forgive anything of something so splendid.

Jan had a nice line in responses. Anything I asked him he shrugged his shoulders and said, 'I don't know. Dirck/Hendrick/Johannes/Jens looks after that.'

At night we discussed the boat rather in the way we'd talked of buying one of Sally's favourite paintings, an old, sick man holding a cat. It wasn't at all what I'd imagined living with but we loved it, so that was that. We arranged a second visit. This time Jan had his boat displayed on the jetty outside. It glittered nicely in the weak afternoon sun. His wife and son were there too. They stood to attention as they were introduced, as if for inspection. The son, with the weary patience of youth, explained to us that diesel engines did not run on petrol.

The imminent parting with a large sum of money focuses the mind, like death, and we crawled over the boat metre by metre. It was like inspecting a grand piano. Beautifully-polished pieces of mahogany swung open on silent hinges, revealing yet more mahogany inside. Finely-cast bronze fittings held coats and towels, kept things shut. Best of all, its teak after-deck featured a banquette, upholstered in rich red, crossing the entire width of the stern.

'I won't take anything less than the asking price,' said Jan. Why should he for such a splendid thing, we thought? Every desiring organ within us wanted to pour money into his outstretched hands. But we'd discovered, well, not faults, because how could they exist in this lovely craft? No, issues.

The engine leaked a lot of oil. The shower was unusable because while it streamed water into the boat in the way showers are supposed to do, there was no way of getting the water out again. 'I've never used it,' Jan shrugged. The gas water heating proved obsolete. 'I don't use hot water either,' he said.

We did, though. We visited a nearby boat builder. Lots of talking and measuring went on. He announced he could fit a new shower pan with pump, and a new boiler to heat the water, for about $4,000. Possible, we thought. But while I was talking to the boat builder, Sally was deep in conversation with one of his clients, a man working on his fine new cruiser. 'I had a Super van Craft,' he told her. 'I took it to France. Within three months, in the heat, the varnish was ruined. The boat looked a wreck. You must keep them inside, in a boatshed. You must not buy one. There is only one boat you must buy, and that is an Altena, like mine here.' His hand flapped at half a million Euros worth of boat.

It was a telling blow. Ours was a flawed beauty. A rich person's boat.

'I'm very sad,' I texted Glenn and Trish that night, 'and Sally suicidal.' 'Me too,' Glenn wrote back. 'Find another one or I jump.'

That left the Beast. She was a solid lump of metal, seventeen tonnes of steel and gear. She was a Beachcraft, owned by Dirck, whose surname we never quite discovered. Dirck skippered one of the huge barges plying the rivers and canals. He seemed to be an on-call skipper, for he never knew where he'd be next, or for how long he'd be away. At least, that was his story.

He was a good-looking man in his mid-thirties on the run from his ex-wife.

He talked of her lawyers as the dark pursuers, and gave the impression he was always aware of who was behind him. He was funny, furtive. We never knew whether to trust him or not.

He kept his boat in the small town of Alblasserdam, between Rotterdam and Utrecht. She was a blocky beast. No one would ever call her pretty. Utilitarian, with a touch of workboat, and a very long way from the *Alcyon*. 'Why am I selling her?' said Dirck. 'Because I now have a girlfriend who has a boat, and because I need the money.' Both stories seemed entirely plausible. Lots of women skipper boats in Holland. His girlfriend's boat, the *Yvette*, was moored not far away, a fine ship, much better than Dirck's, and Dirck definitely looked short of cash.

Whoever had fitted out his boat started from the back with a magnificent after-cabin, all in white, containing twin beds and a huge wardrobe. Next came a household-size shower and a capacious toilet, then a big saloon, followed by a newly installed, well-crafted kitchen with a brand-new stove complete with oven, a good fridge, and a dinette opposite. Alas, the forecabin paid the penalty for all of this. It was little more than a slot in the wall in front of the kitchen, like a letterbox where you might post your guests. But, we told ourselves with that rationalising now so familiar over our tortured list of must-haves, how much do you owe guests anyway?

New gear was everywhere, pumps, stoves, engine-room equipment, even a new four-blade propeller instead of the usual three-blade. 'For better manoeuvring,' said Dirck, looking as if he knew all about manoeuvres.

But Sally had noticed a whole lot of things that escaped me. She had a much better eye for detail, and a vastly improved feel for what was right. I might wax over a water pump while she was waning over a settee which, she pointed out, had come from someone's lounge and had simply been chopped off to fit. And the dinette cushions had come from another boat. And the mattresses in the back bedroom were brand new but the room was panelled in what seemed to be melamine.

We asked Dirck where he kept the ship's papers, the documentation of its gear, receipts and lots of reassuring print. He looked nonplussed. He rooted around and emerged with a couple of tatty bits of paper. 'Ah,' he said. 'No receipts. I pay cash. Cheaper. Under the table.' Or off the back of a truck, we thought.

Sally asked, 'And how will anyone, such as authorities in this country and others, know this is our boat?' Dirck laughed at this. 'Because it *is* your boat,' he said.

We would have to pay for it by telegraphic transfer of funds from New Zealand to Holland and for that Dirck needed a bank account.

'Is a problem,' he said, and his face appealed to us as reasonable, understanding people. 'I pay no tax. This money appears in my bank, I get caught.' He seemed to glance over his shoulder, catch a glimpse of a grey suit. The taxman, his wife's lawyers, they were all the same to Dirck: tormentors. 'Well, we don't carry this amount of money in cash,' said Sally who, I felt, was starting to sympathise with the ex-wife.

Another problem appeared. Dirck had sold the boat to someone else. They'd paid a deposit, and were to settle in six weeks. 'But I don't know whether they will,' said Dirck, with the scent of immediate cash strong in his nostrils. 'I get rid of them.' 'We'll let you know by five o'clock,' said Sally. 'You get everything sorted out by then.'

It was now three p.m. We drove off. Neither of us felt good. The boat stacked up well, but didn't feel right. Both of us had learned to trust that feeling more than any engineer's report. The boat, like Dirck, had a strong dash of bodgie. It was called the *Nothing*. Any good boat deserved a better name than that. We decided we had time to visit another yard.

Chapter Two

Sally hunched over the map.

Sally did not drive. She had a driver's licence, but she had a problem which her examiners had missed: she could not tell right from left. This made driving quite interesting. If you needed to turn right, and she turned left, matters could become fraught. They'd become even trickier if you wanted to go somewhere in particular. We might be driving from Christchurch to Picton, or even from Wellington to Taihape, and Sally would insist that we were driving the wrong way because we hadn't passed through Ashburton yet. For her, Swahili was easier to read than a map. Maps were kaleidoscopes.

Now, here in Holland, something had clicked into place. She could read a map. Not just read it, but follow its tricks and whims and work out the best way through the maze. 'Not this way,' she'd say briskly. 'Take the A-28 until we get to Harderwijk, then the N302.' Or, 'This is Exit 17. We need Exit 21.' Lois Lane must have felt the same way the first time she realised Clark Kent was not hopping into the telephone box just for the fun of it, and all that blue and red and yellow suddenly made sense.

Moreover, Sally now knew her right from her left. 'Keep to the right,' she'd say, avoiding disaster several times as I absent-mindedly tootled off on the wrong side of the road. With this new Sally beside me I felt I could tackle the universe, or at least navigate the motorways, roads and country lanes between Alblasserdam and Alem, a tiny village beside a broad inlet leading off the River Maas. There, along a long avenue of trees bursting into leaf, lay the Jachthaven de Maas.

It was lunchtime in the yachthaven. No one was about. I wandered around the little marina and saw our boat immediately.

She had a jaunty bow and a proper look, and through her windows I could see finely-crafted teak furniture. She was an Altena, built by a good firm still run by the same family. So I fetched Sally who read the name *River Queen* on her side, and she was as good as sold. The name was OK, I thought, but I'm not going to wear the T-shirt.

Ricardo Bosma, the broker, turned up, recognised the smitten looks and called the owner who came immediately. 'I've been to New Zealand sixteen times,' said Leen Bakker, a retired seaman who peered at the world through a face full of deep cracks and crannies. 'You come from the South Island? I know where Bluff is. Why do you want to come to Europe when you live in such a beautiful country?' It was the age-old question for Kiwis, although none of us knew the answer; besides, we were more interested in his boat.

We did everything wrong, of course. We should have thought it over, but we had Dirck's deadline hanging over us. We should not have trusted Leen, or Ricardo, but we did. We should have made our offer conditional on a full survey, rather than the limited one we thought was enough. We should have mulled, and considered, and prodded and poked, and come and gone, and feigned reluctance. Instead, I called Dirck and told him we weren't buying his boat after all. He didn't sound surprised. More slings and arrows from outrageous fortune.

Then we went ahead and bought the *River Queen*, for around $135,000 at the day's exchange rate and including various fees and charges.

We trusted our instincts. And Leen and Ricardo did everything they said they would. And we got a proper set of ship's papers, and Leen's old deck shoes, and his coffee-maker, blackened by countless cups. We never regretted any of it, and the *River Queen* never missed a beat.

Leen shook hands and wished us well. I recited the old adage to him: 'They say the two happiest days in boat-owners' lives are the day they buy the boat, and the day they sell it. So we're probably the three happiest people in all of Alem today.' 'Ah,' he said. 'I am perhaps not so happy.'

We were all set for adventure.

It had all begun when they gave me a new neck and I knew something had to be done.

I'd picked up the latest copy of the magazine where I'd worked for more than twenty years, the *Listener*, and turned to the editorial. It was about Auckland's snarled traffic, and began:

> I can report both as a pedestrian and a South Islander that if there's one thing worse than being stuck in Auckland, it is being marooned there without a car. It is slightly worse even than being trapped there with a car, for then, as you crawl over the harbour bridge in lines of belching traffic, angry drivers and cybercreatures whose cellphones seem surgically implanted, you know the true meaning of being caught between the devil and the deep blue sea.

The title said: 'Foot Slagging'. I liked the rest of it too, but that was because I'd written it. Then I saw my picture above the byline. I didn't like it. I should have known.

Pamela Stirling, the editor, had called a few days previously.

She'd said that the picture they were using over those editorials was wonderful, fabulous, but she wasn't sure about the black T-shirt. I believed she was being remarkably restrained. Combined with a shaven head, a feeble sneer and a red complexion colour-coded with hung-over eyes, I looked the kind of person who should be reported to police immediately and not otherwise approached.

Stirling believed in the miracle of photo-shop. I replied that I didn't give a bugger and why didn't she get photo-shop to give me some hair and a tan while she was about it?

Oh, foolish bravado. In the next issue I appeared still bald and red-eyed with the slimy grin but possessing a complexion as khaki as the second expeditionary force. The black T-shirt had gone all right but was replaced by a striped blue shirt I knew was owned by Tim Watkin, then the deputy editor. Moreover, the shirt was open at the top, so they'd thrown in his neck as well.

Now, Watkin was an upright fellow, a good quarter-century younger than I, and in other circumstances his neck might have been a prized item. In the present situation, however, it looked rather like those fairground photographs where you shoved your head through a hole above Dan Carter's body.

I stared at the photograph for a long time. I was quite attached to my neck actually, and had spent a lot of my working life saving it. But I remembered Tom Scott saying he knew that Prime Minister Rob Muldoon was on his way out when his TV colour changed from khaki to yellow. I was going from pink to khaki. What could it mean? Like traffic lights, that I was ready for the off? Something had to be done about my life, and I was the man to do it.

I thought about my long career in journalism. It had been lovely, adventurous. It had taken me around the world many times. I'd covered Moscow's bungling efforts to stage the Olympics, the Commonwealth Games in Edinburgh, the America's Cup in Auckland and Valencia. I'd had a midsummer swim in the Antarctic. I'd met the King of Spain in Madrid, Ian Paisley in Belfast, Nelson Mandela in Kuala Lumpur, Prince Charles in Wellington. I'd won fellowships to both Cambridge and Oxford Universities, where I'd learned to drink sherry, pole punts, eat bony trout and dream in dusty libraries.

I'd worked in radio and television and written for the television programmes *A Week of It* and *McPhail and Gadsby*, but print was my favourite. Earlier I'd hacked for the notorious *Sun* in London, pulling night shifts in Fleet Street, been London-based feature writer for a big chain of provincial newspapers, and had come back to New Zealand determined to live my life the way I wanted to.

I didn't fancy ever using that tired old line of politicians and executives when someone finally found them out: I didn't want to spend more time with my family then, I wanted to do it now. My job had to fit around my life, not vice versa. So I became a columnist for the Christchurch daily, *The Star*, then moved to Wellington with the *Listener*.

I'd always loved the *Listener*. When I was young, editors like Monte Holcroft, Alexander McLeod, Ian Cross, Tony Reid and David Beatson were national news. They presided over a mighty journal, in every sense. When the *Listener* said something, it remained said. When the *Listener* pronounced, the pronouncement was writ in stone. When it declared something to be good, then that object was so elevated in public esteem it became immediately iconic. When the *Listener* touched the shoulder of a budding artist, or writer, or media savant, the nation bowed before them.

Its writers were stars themselves: Cross, Reid, Tom Scott, Helen Paske, Sue Macaulay, Geoff Chapple, Gordon Campbell. At its height, more than

400,000 people bought the *Listener* each week, passed it on to spouses, relatives, children, patients, customers. Half the nation was in thrall to its heavy type, or at the very least, its television listings. It was huge. The aged and infirm could scarcely lift it, much less open its broad pages. Caught in the wind, a *Listener* was as powerful as a galleon scudding in the trades. A single page could wrap fish and chips for a large family, including friends and relatives.

When such a discerning eye descended upon a mortal journalist, who could not pass through those pearly gates? Not me. I sniffed fame. I quit my job and moved my family, my wife Sally and twin sons Sam and Simon to Wellington, persuaded the magazine it needed a South Island office, moved back to Christchurch and did what I liked doing most: writing stories about people, where they lived, how they lived.

I wrote about the biggest land swap of all time: high-country cockies giving up their mountaintops to the conservation estate in exchange for freehold title to public land. I stumbled over land claims on the East Coast in the vanguard of the modern Māori land claims movement. I wrote about group hysteria and mass panic over the alleged offences of the so-called paedophile Peter Ellis, still the most dangerously unjust conviction in the country after Rex Haig's, whose story first appeared under my byline in the *Listener*. I covered rock and roll contests in Lower Hutt, poodle clipping in Papanui, sheep rustling in South Canterbury, gang fights in Timaru, country music awards in Gore, oyster-opening in Bluff, property panic in Stewart Island, gold rushes on the West Coast, kōtuku squabbles in Whataroa. I wrote about Ed Hillary, Tim Wallis, Colin Meads, Helen Clark, Todd Blackadder, Bub Bridger, Cilla McQueen. I puzzled over Rick Mayne's revolutionary new engine, which came to him in a vision as he sat in a jail cell and never ran and despite this, attracted millions of dollars from droves.

I'd had a lovely, adventurous time. But times had changed, as times do. The print industry was in the throes of yet another revolution, and print journalism with it. Magazines were caught between falling sales and boardroom banalities which ignored a fundamental truth: you had to be good at what you did.

At its best, the *Listener* was what any decent magazine with an intelligent readership was: it questioned accepted wisdom, declined to accept face value. Often, it simply took the piss. Its touch of subversion was handy. No one ever lost readers through being sharp, and well-written. In an increasingly conservative age, though, it was taking on the colours of its environment, however drab.

Listener readers stubbornly remained the same as they'd always been: older, intelligent, critical, curious and not easily fooled. But that was exactly the demographic coming to be regarded in the industry as dinosaurs who joined libraries, switched off lights and never watched *Survivor* on TV, much less attended away-days or cared a jot about mission statements.

A succession of good writers became disillusioned, went elsewhere or were pushed. The survivors tackled health, property, lifestyle with as many celebrities as were desperate enough to show their faces.

I seldom left the office now, no longer met and talked to people in person. I telephoned them. Bald, beautiful, shrewish, perceptive, smart, stupid, rotting teeth or artificial limbs were synthesised by Telecom and presented to me in one neat, uniform package. I was sick to death of focus groups and surveys, of circulation graphs and budget projections, of marketeers whose idea of a good read was a text message. I was tired of the ten steps to happiness and the insider's guide to becoming a more beautiful you.

Perhaps I'd become an old fart. I didn't care. I was filled with self-loathing and bored to boot. My neck was the wrong demographic. And I was getting … older.

I'd discovered that the only copy of Elizabeth Jane Howard's *Casting Off* in the local library was in large print. That might seem unimportant. But a large print book is not the same as a normal print edition. It might as well contain a different story. Perhaps an eye scanned a whole page before it started on the particular, the reason you could always spot the letter Z on a page. That would explain why reading stories on the internet was unsatisfying. Large print took up so much space that you could only scan half as much and the anticipation was much reduced, but the real issue was this: reading an Elizabeth Jane Howard novel in large print was like, well, not saying 'like' in every sentence. It signalled senility. An Elizabeth Jane Howard in large print was the Zimmer frame of literature.

Oh dear, life was so elliptical.

As kids we'd spent much of our time trying to look older, to impress partners, to be cool, to get into bars, to buy cigarettes from the local dairy. Looking eighteen was one thing, although now I couldn't believe *anyone* was eighteen; I wouldn't have sold any of them so much as a can of Pepsi.

Looking twenty-one was something else. That took much more than a dark night and a scowl. And if you couldn't look twenty-one you might as well give up and join the Guides.

After thirty you headed off in the opposite direction and spent the next three decades trying to look younger. Men wore their shirts over their trousers instead of inside them as god intended. Women fretted over body shapes which added up to a whole lot more than the figure eight.

David Round, a former neighbour in the tiny Banks Peninsula community of Port Levy, claimed to be thirty-seven for several years (and looked it, moreover) until one day he took the gullible by surprise and threw a fiftieth birthday party. I knew a woman in Wellington who was the longest-serving forty-two-year-old in the history of the capital city, although almost certainly not the nation.

Middle age became life's longest period. It lasted a great deal longer than any other era, every bit as long as the golden age of Byzantium. It ran from around forty-five, which everyone knew as more or less the end of adolescence, until the mid-eighties or even longer if you could still tell lies without losing your teeth. In the process it eclipsed the second-longest period of your life, the mid-fifties, which could stretch from fifty-four until you picked up the pension.

The chronologically-challenged, however, might suffer a setback in their early sixties. They were torn between vanity and frugality, swept this way and that by ego on one side and outright meanness on the other.

What did you say, for example, when you bought a movie ticket and were handed a half-price one for seniors? Indignation was not only pointless, but costly.

The previous autumn we'd called at the Maruia hot springs deep in the passes that divide east and west coasts of the South Island. Sally bought two tickets, a full-priced adult ticket for herself and a discount, senior one for me, although I was a good five years short of the mark. I maintained a craven silence throughout this transaction.

Far, far worse, the woman behind the counter, whom I judged to have been of the bewitching age, glanced at me incuriously. Did she object? Did she threaten to call the police and complain of dishonesty, even of fraud? She did not. She handed over the tickets, took the money and ordered us to have a nice day. She might even have helped me down the steps had I asked. A stitch in time saved, well, five dollars in this case.

But the real cost of buying time was far, far higher. I'd met people who, like Glenn and Trish, spent much of their time living on canals in Europe. They were well into the so-called third age. But they were fit, and active, and they loved the adventure of what they were doing, and they not only looked young, but expectant. Life no longer owed them; it was paying.

One day my doctor was talking to me in that distracted way while hacking away at his computer. I asked what he was doing. He said he was drawing up a risk list for me. He said that given my own and my family's medical histories, there were a few issues in my life. He seemed to have been typing for a long time. Tolkien could have whacked out a couple of chapters by the time he finally looked up. Come and see me again in three months, he said. Over my dead body, I thought. Then, given the circumstances, changed it to, *I'm not going down that path if I can help it.*

But life was adding up for me.

The calculation — family, health, job and everything else — came out to this: from now on I paid for my mistakes in the most valuable currency of all, time. I had to make a break for it.

Sally however did not. She had had the sense to leave her job as a department head in a polytechnic several years before. She gave up work completely. Her life had been bountiful ever since. She was a happy woman, a living, smiling advertisement for throwing away a life she did not want for a life she did. She did not need a new one. Yet without so much as an audible sigh she abandoned peace and tranquillity and went along with me.

We drove to our little bach in Golden Bay and thought about it. We swam in the clear green sea, lay on the sand. We walked in the bush, stood under white waterfalls with the noise of cold water scouring our minds.

The hardest part of escaping was what to escape *to*. Sally wanted to grow lavender; if, that was, we needed to do anything at all. Imagine, she said, the fields of purple running down to the stream; although we had no fields, and no stream, and experience had taught us both that romance was the first to flee from dreams which involved working the land. We discussed, mulled, argued and at the end of that summer we were no closer to deciding what we wanted to do.

One wet Saturday in autumn I sat before my computer pretending to work. I was searching the internet for a quote on the weather, one of those platitudes about silver linings or what follows the rain, which in a Christchurch autumn is usually the cold.

I thought of Glenn and Trish, who lived in a shippy old house over the hill in the port of Lyttelton. They were more than canal boating enthusiasts. They were evangelists. I thought it would be a fine idea if they went into business with us, on the French canals. Thirty seconds of earnest research on the internet turned up the ideal vessel, a huge Dutch barge divided into two apartments. We could rent one of them to canal travellers and live in the other, see? Glenn did not.

For a start, he said, he had this job, teaching photography at Canterbury University, and Trish worked as a Family Court counsellor, and they both liked their work, and their house likewise, and he wasn't about to chuck everything away and trip around after some flake with a life crisis.

Actually, he was much too nice to say any of that. A man of succinct vocabulary, he summed my plan up in a word: no. But he sent me a clutch of websites. They were all in Dutch, but I got the drift. They offered boats for sale. Thousands of them. I opened one of the sites and everything fell into place. We'd buy a canal boat, live *la vie Française* amid splendid villages and smooth water and baguettes and berets. It would be an affair of the heart. And we'd come back and live in Golden Bay for two or three months in the New Zealand sun when in Europe the cold winds blew.

I wasn't the rat leaving the sinking ship. I was the rat looking for a new one. I felt like the Grinch at Christmas, getting his incredibly good idea. I explained it to Sally as Thomas might have explained the electric light to Mrs Edison. Sally had the money, her mother's legacy, enough to buy the boat and live on it for the first year. Or enough to do all sorts of things she might have thought worthwhile, other than her husband's current neurosis.

'Great,' she said. 'Let's do it.'

We sat with Glenn and Trish in their house above the harbour, talking it over in the evening quiet. A comfy smell of roast chicken filled the room.

Mate, he said, you'll love it.

They'd invited a friend around for dinner. The friend had bought a canal boat and kept it in France. Mate, said the friend, you'll love it.

Sally grilled Trish. 'Will I like it?'

'Mate,' said Trish, 'you'll love it.'

The wood fire made us content, for a storm was brawling outside. We watched from the warm as it hurled across the harbour. The grey sky shrouded the hills until only the lights of Diamond Harbour told us of people in their own living rooms, perhaps dreaming their dreams too, and I felt satisfied that everything was in its proper place, all right.

Chapter Three

We'd been in Holland two weeks when we became the proud new owners and de facto skippers of the *River Queen*. I felt vaguely Bogart-ish. Sally felt … well, the way you feel when your partner wakes up one day wanting to throw away the weekly pay cheque, leave your beloved house and abandon your family, friends and country for as far ahead as you could see.

We weren't even sure where we'd be going, except that it was a long way: a giant loop to Paris would cover three countries, 1,560 kilometres and 376 locks. Or we might go down to the south of France and the Mediterranean, fewer locks but breathtaking. Who knew? We only had to ready the *River Queen* and the journey would begin.

We loaded our expanding baggage into the little Peugeot, said goodbye to the lovely Schoorl, and took up our new address in the Jachthaven de Maas, Alem.

Living in marinas was one of my passions. I loved the gentle movement, the clinking, slapping, gurgling sound of boats at rest, the ranks of them lined up for inspection while their owners were absent and so unable to look indignantly from portholes as I prowled around.

The Jachthaven de Maas was unusual. Foreigners had lived there before, but so few of them they were all known by name, and people at the marina could recount their sailing history, or where in the world they could be found at this very moment.

The marina lay in a pool at the end of a branch off the River Maas, some forty kilometres south of Utrecht. It was owned by the Bosma family. Mrs Bosma, dark, attractive, looked after the office, wielded power saws and paintbrushes, and in her spare time crewed on a fast, open sailing boat. Mr Bosma, dark, attractive, floated hither and yon, and in his spare time skippered an extremely fast open boat full of laughing passengers on the River Maas. The two of them lived on a brightly painted tugboat reached by a winding path and rustic bridge.

Carlos, the younger son, was studying to be a barge captain. He lived on a small converted barge with his girlfriend, who was a waitress in the café floating on a huge pontoon in the marina. Ricardo, the older, lived with his girlfriend on a much bigger barge, immaculately kept, moored beside his parents. He spent much of his time with the red-haired Patric, who was about his age, twenty-three, and was mechanic and general fix-it man. The two got along in the way young men do.

Patric drove an old Citröen limousine, Ricardo a Mercedes.

Ricardo: I like his car. Pity it's French.

Patric: If I want to drive in a Mercedes, I take a taxi.

The Jachthaven de Maas lay below an imposing church in the tiny village of Alem, whose industrial pottery museum hinted at a former life. Now it was quiet, so still that walking in its streets in the evenings we'd be startled by the appearance of a human being. Even the church door seemed permanently locked. Apart from the marina the village had only two functioning businesses when we got there. One, the grocery store, closed down the day after we arrived, leaving the other, the local pub. This seldom opened and when it did, accommodated some event or another, such as a male choir, or a flower show. It too had been about to close its doors forever, until a local man took it over and saved it. He had a job in another town, so it opened only two or three nights a week, and sometimes at weekends.

The job of entertaining locals fell to the marina café. Except for lunchtimes on fine days, the pickings seemed to be slim, until we discovered that it didn't really start to spark until after ten p.m. Then, the various inhabitants of the marina would go for schnapps and a chat, for the yachthaven had quite a lot of permanent residents.

Some lived on luxurious motor launches which would have fitted right into the Riviera. One couple spent weekends aboard a huge white fibreglass construction with curved glass and engines which blasted the peace of

Saturday mornings and suggested great speed, although on the slow rivers and canals of the Netherlands its pace obviously reverberated only in the minds of its owners.

She was bright blonde, one of those thin Dutch woman so youthful we suspected they were trophy brides until close up they proved to be as carefully maintained as, in this case, the immaculate cruiser. He also was older than his apparent years; he dressed in tight white pants and yellow T-shirts, which he shed as the sun came up to reveal a sunbed tan and a finely-shaped little paunch. The white leather banquettes on their vessel's sundeck were reserved for their two ferocious Alsatians, whose black snouts hung over the rails as we passed, snarling and barking and delighting their owners. They were our introduction to European dogs. Most European boats kept dogs.

Dogs smell and the boats were small. Most of them reeked. Once I knew a man who lived on a boat in the Lyttelton marina, with a cocker spaniel. He locked his dog in the cabin when he went to work, and in the evenings when he returned home he'd unlock the cabin door and exclaim, 'Oh, you dirty dog, oh, you filthy mutt, oh, oh, oh.' Everyone sided with the dog, whose options were limited. Canal boaties would have agreed, then invited you in to admire the mess. Rover was so tidy, they'd say. Always behind the chair.

I had nothing against dogs. We'd owned a few. A golden Labrador, which could dive for rocks, and dig to Spain, and my favourite, a border collie named Tim which wanted to work sheep, usually when no one wanted him to. They were real dogs. We'd also looked after my son Sam's black pug Lulu and, like many European dogs we encountered, we weren't sure whether the pug was a dog at all. She had started as a tiny ball with bug eyes on the sides of her head, and as she grew bigger her eyes moved to the front. We were surprised to see she had legs. She wore a collar studded with diamonds, fake we hoped, and ran around on our wooden floors sounding like a legion of fairies in high heels. She refused to sleep in a separate room, wanted to climb into bed with us and even kept to her own end of it, sometimes.

She made us laugh, until I discovered things had changed in the world of dogs; when we took her for a walk we were expected to pick up doggy-do and store it in plastic bags, under pain of censure by the beady-eyed. On the spot I resolved never to own another. She was a great licker — her mouth wasn't big enough for her long tongue, so a bit of it always hung out — and a vibrant snorer, but if you told her to shut up, she'd stop snoring and start licking, which was just as noisy. I should have been fully prepared for European dogs, but I was not. Soon I longed for a New Zealand cockie with a back-country voice and a big stick.

Only a few yards along a pontoon from the fabulous white fibreglass confection in the Jachthaven de Maas, a couple of old men lived in a rowing boat. At least, they seemed to live in it, for they were there in the mornings when we got up, and still there when it grew dark. In between those times, and probably outside them too, they fished. They sat with flasks and food stacked between them, talking amiably and catching nothing all day, and when it rained, as it seldom did that fine spring ('You are so lucky,' they said), they hoisted a makeshift canopy above their heads and fished on.

The first person we met in the marina was an elegant man from Luxembourg. He was slim and his English was perfect. He was kindly and talkative, in his late sixties and like so many men and women of that age we met on the canals, he looked fit, healthy and happy. Everything about his boat was immaculate, its paintwork unmarked, covers like new, equipment ready for the ocean crossing he told us he'd never made. The boat's name was Benny. Their dog was named Benny too. We called them Mr and Mrs Benny.

They'd drive from Luxembourg, some four hours away, and live in the marina for a week or two at a time, sitting on their little back deck in complete harmony. Mr Benny had been born in Alem, and this was the closest he'd got to coming home.

Benny the dog dictated the tempo. He was a foul-tempered arthritic beast whose origins lay somewhere between spaniel and springer. One morning I met them on the jetty and went to pat the dog. 'No, no!' screamed Mrs Benny. 'Is not possible!' The dog looked disappointed. Probably it had been looking forward to a piece of me.

On Saturdays the Dutch owners of the tjalks and barges and old patrol boats and tugs and cruisers climbed aboard their vessels and hosed and mopped and cleaned then arranged furniture on the decks or the pontoons and spent the rest of the weekend chatting to visitors and friends. Occasionally they would even take their boats out onto the river, handling them with the ease the Dutch do, watched critically by their neighbours. Like creatures from *The Wind and the Willows* they simply liked being on the water, or in it, and they would have chirruped agreement with Ratty: there was nothing, absolutely nothing, half so much worth doing as simply messing around in boats.

On the next pontoon lay a small cruiser whose owners, he short and friendly, she in a wheelchair, appeared punctually on Saturday mornings and scrubbed inside and out. Then they sat on the jetty and entertained. She presided from her chair.

One morning I finished scrubbing the side of the *River Queen* and turned it around to work on the other side. Casual tasks could be fatal, I found, if you took them casually. Today I did. I threw off the lines and began manoeuvring.

The boat wouldn't respond. Each time it left the pontoon it wanted to spring back in again. It felt as if it was on an elastic band. It was.

My neighbour had been watching with as much forbearance as she could manage. She could stand no more. Her aluminium stick tapped sharply on my stainless steel rail. 'The cable!' Her voice rapped briskly as her stick. We were tethered by our power cord. Sheepishly I unplugged and set off again. I turned the boat end for end, backed into its space. I was doing well, I thought; no, brilliantly.

Scarcely had the last word sprung to mind when the *Queen* went off on her own, as boats do when they feel their crew is growing complacent. The stern made a bid for freedom, swinging away from the pontoon.

My neighbour sat to attention. The boat spoke to her, along the lines of 'throw down thy sticks and walk'. She sprang from her wheelchair, grabbed a line and pulled eleven tonnes of steel into its mooring as effortlessly as she'd lifted her glass. Then she settled back into the chair and waved away my thanks.

I took cover on the after-deck and watched a small boy paddling across the chocolate-brown water of the marina. What might a New Zealand mother or father have done when their small son set sail on a plastic blow-up jet-ski upon waters whose colour suggested that residents of the marina were not on good terms with holding tanks for sewage, the boy armed with a broom as his only means of propulsion? The great New Zealand love of adventure would have come to a screeching halt, the only question being which would have screeched louder, halt or parents.

Our immediate neighbours were Vielm and Renee. Vielm was an IT consultant. He wrote computer programmes. He wrote them the way composers create music, or novelists weave stories. 'It is an art,' he said. 'Look, I show you.' He passed his hand over his computer screen smoothly as a conjuror, although the hand was much quicker than the eye, for I was wrecked on the first few … Were they really words?

Vielm and Renee lived aboard a houseboat. 'Wrong,' he said, 'it is a ship. It has an engine.' Its controls were pure PlayStation. Little levers and buttons rather than a steering wheel directed it this way and that while a screen told you what you were doing. Instead of anchors it had hydraulic legs which emerged from the ship's bottom and secured it to the riverbed.

Gauges, screens, and gyros adorned its insides but still it looked like suburbia-on-sea. It had two bedrooms upstairs and two living rooms down with a kitchen and bathroom from a period which seemed much later in the twenty-first century.

'I love new stuff,' said Vielm. He drove a new Cadillac four-wheel-drive.

Renee didn't say very much at all, except 'Pouf', when something distasteful such as Thatcherism, or childbirth, came up in conversation.

Vielm had left his wife with the St Bernard dog, sold his company, and taken up with Renee four months ago. She'd left god-knew-what, but whatever that was, it hung in the air like the smell of manure that hovered over Holland. She drank tea endlessly.

Vielm showed us pictures of his holiday in the Maldives. He showed us lots of other pictures too. Computers have replaced photo albums and slide shows, but they're every bit as boring. His overseas holidays were over, he said. Now he could not take long flights because they did not allow him to smoke. 'They were talking about halting smoking in cafés,' he said. 'In cafés! They might as well ban wine from bars.'

He rolled himself another. So did Renee. 'Pouf,' she said. But less than a year later even France banned smoking in cafés. Pouf!

During the day we worked on the boat. At first there seemed little to do.

I looked over Sally's shoulder as she wrote home: 'It's a lovely blue day and the boat is even better than we realised. A good clean, some paint and inside a rub down with teak oil and she, the *River Queen*, will be nearly as good as new.'

Something had to be done. Yes, it was a lovely blue day. The Dutch were having an unusually good spring, as they told us almost every day: 'You are very lucky,' said Vielm. The best, finest, sunniest spring they'd ever had was developing.

But that wasn't the way boats worked was it?

Here was one of life's vexing questions. Why do blokes love working on boats but loathe toiling on houses, even if it is exactly the same job? Or, why do women admire blokes working on houses, yet detest them working on boats? The answer, I thought, was because boats symbolised everything men, or some of them, desired: freedom, adventure, simplicity, self-sufficiency, order (not listed among most men's instincts, but regarded as a desirable option, like airbags on cars), and boats were so shapely too. Most of all, they represented potential — what you might do if only life gave you a shot at it. Houses were the hum-drum, the routine, the intransigent, the grindstone for the nose, the burden (for houses had mortgages, whereas boats possessed only loans). For many unfortunate women, boats were the competition. Fundamental to owning a boat was resolving this tension. Unresolved, it hung over matrimony like the high divorce rate to which it made such a contribution.

I knew all this because I had owned quite a few boats.

Sally asked which was the best book I'd ever read. *South Sea Vagabonds*, I said. I read it when I was twelve and it influenced my life forever. John Wray, the author, got the sack for dreaming on the job. What was he to do? He had no money, for it was about the time of the Great Depression. So he borrowed a boat, went out on the Hauraki Gulf, collected old kauri logs from beaches, towed them home, sawed them up and made his own boat. He picked tar off roads, scrounged spars and sails from a wreck, made fastenings out of No. 8 fencing wire, picked an old engine out of a paddock. From all of these he created a boat so fine that it was still as new more than seventy years later. He named it the *Ngataki*, and set sail for the Pacific Islands with his mates.

He began with:

> … this book is written primarily for dreamers … for the man who works in a city office and dreams about sparkling blue waters and coconut palms and white sails bellying to the warm trade winds … I was a dreamer once, but now my dreams have come true, and I am satisfied and happy.

What boy could resist something like that? The book was almost a parody on New Zealanders, or at least New Zealand men. Yet it fixed in me a quintessential love of country, self-sufficiency, the notion that you could do whatever you wanted, adventure, laughter, light-heartedness, the Kiwi belief that things were only dangerous for people from other countries. It even showed me how to pronounce 'Ng', which Wray believed every New Zealander knew; but obviously he'd never visited the South Island.

I spent the next three years scouring the beaches of Pegasus Bay and Kaikoura, searching for old kauri logs. I had no idea what one looked like, and as one piece of driftwood is very similar to the next, I was disappointed all of the time. Only the thought that such minor setbacks would never have deterred Wray kept me going, until someone pointed out that kauri didn't grow naturally this far south, and even if it did, and people were careless enough to let logs float out to sea, they would be carried north by the current.

My search for No. 8 wire was much more successful. There was a lot of wire in the South Island, even after I'd taken quite a bit of it, and several farmers must have stroked their grizzled chins over mysterious gaps in their fences and muttered about townies.

Vessels do not sail on No. 8 wire alone, however, and it took me quite a long time first to understand then acquire that fundamental, essential ingredient of boats: money. But this raised another cruel maritime trick. Usually you worked to make money to spend. But with boats it was the other way round. You spent money to work.

We had five boats at home: two sea kayaks, a small dinghy, an open sailing boat, and the old motor-sailer. The kayaks were excellent vessels. They represented adventure, even though no one took them much further than the nearby lagoon. The point was, they were capable of much longer voyages, and with a little proper dreaming, they could be envisaged cruising the cerulean waters of the Abel Tasman National Park, or exploring the islands of the Gulf. More immediately, they were made of plastic, so when they'd finished roaming for the day (the trip to the other side of the lagoon and back, damned tide) they could be left entirely alone.

The little dinghy bustled to and fro and made no demands on anyone. The bigger sailing dinghy was used for everything: dredging for scallops, fishing for snapper (a grandiose term for hopelessly, happily, heaving a line over the side), rowing energetically, even sailing. It cost $1,500 complete with trailer and in terms of dollars per hours used must have represented the best value in the history of boating, certainly in my own.

Which puzzled Sally. Why, she asked, would I then spend endless hours working on my venerable motor-sailer, which hardly ever got used and chewed money like an alligator? Naturally, if I had a good answer I'd have trotted it out. Nothing sprang to mind.

I mentioned that it was allegedly a motor-sailer. This implied that it sailed. Yet the verb hardly suited the ponderous way it heaved through the ocean, not so much cleaving the seas as chopping them into little pieces and flinging them all over the place. Someone once described its motion as that of a brick dunny under sail. I felt such insults keenly, and anyway, the dear thing hardly ever sailed, for it was always being worked upon.

No sooner was one part of it painted than another demanded attention by shedding the paint painstakingly and recently applied. It differed from the Sydney Harbour Bridge in two respects: the painters of that structure actually finished at one end before they had to start again at the other, and the bridge sailed better.

The engine might once have powered a charabanc but always started first go and chugged away happily. It splashed muck around its engine room like a pig in a sty, and took far, far longer to clean up. Then there was the deck to be re-caulked, and the compressor to be overhauled, and the steering to be renewed, and the toilet to be put right for oh, the thousandth time, and none of these jobs were brief, because no matter how simple they appeared the boat somehow converted them into advanced callisthenics. All of this meant many happy hours spent covered in paint, or oil, or substances only boat-owners knew about.

Countless hours for me, for blokes, of course, didn't count. Sally counted, in both senses. Why, she asked? Like most of life's great questions, there was only one answer. Dunno.

So did the *River Queen* need only a mop and a sponge? Improbable. No, impossible. I was sure I could do better than that. Yep, here was a little rust poking through the paint. Underneath the floor were a few jobs the surveyor reckoned needed to be done.

Around and about were things that needed attention, for the very best maintenance reasons of course, or even renewed, because as Ricardo said, often, better it was done here in Holland than … France. He made that country sound like the black hole of boat maintenance, where the simplest task turned nasty and complicated under the twin obstacles of French intransigence and a language only the cunning natives could speak. And if it were done in Holland, best it were done right here in the Jachthaven de Maas, of course. Our bill at the yard's chandlery grew alarmingly: paint, brushes, rollers, ropes, fenders, new engine hoses, oil, grease, a new fridge control, fuel, a dozen other items. The hardware store in the neighbouring town soon knew me by name, Bruis.

Ricardo told me how to paint in the rain, an essential Dutch ploy: you threw a bucket of water over the wet paint, he said. That way the rain didn't pit the paint, and it would dry off all right. I cringed at the thought.

We didn't have to paint in the rain, though. The weather stayed fine. 'You are very lucky,' said Ricardo.

In the evenings we drank dark Bordeaux or rode the bicycles we'd bought from a repair shop under the big railway station in S-Hertogenbosch where commuters stacked thousands of bikes on racks each day. We jammed them into the tiny Peugeot, a task so unlikely a suspicious old man called the *politie*. The cops arrived promptly but we must have seemed impossible thieves, for they merely eyed us from the car windows and left.

We pedalled around the streams and rivers under avenues of trees along with cavalcades of Dutch on the solid upright bikes ridden by everyone from the very young to the quite old. It was very peaceful.

Dutch living rooms with soft lights and plump furniture lay open to the street. 'They are intended for you to look inside,' said Vielm, 'but you should not look too long. It is not polite.'

We bought blue and white china, bowls for fruit, vases for flowers. Sally bought a nubile white Asiatic orchid in a pot and pink begonias in a blue bowl. They became our good friends.

Stern grey herons watched the water intently from the banks. We saw a stork eating a frog with its arms and legs spread out like a baby's. Sally tripped and fell hard against a companionway step, bruising her shin badly. It hurt a lot. She felt depressed and a little homesick.

We went into S-Hertogenbosch and bought foam rubber to soften our mattress. It was expensive. We bought it from a little upholstery shop in a cellar. It seemed down at heel, but when the owner learned we needed the foam rubber for a boat he showed us a picture of his own: a very costly classic launch whose polished woodwork reflected the sunlight.

The surveyor came to check that the work he'd recommended, quite minor, had been done properly. His name was Coen, and he was in his late twenties. 'Some think I am too young,' he said.

Well, he was gnarly on the inside. He had inspected the boat so closely he found a hidden hose clip whose tightening screw might have damaged the adjacent exhaust cover. Later I searched for an hour before I found it again. He found a nut under the engine that needed tightening. Ricardo couldn't find that one at all.

We had coffee in the café. Coen told us a story about a beautiful old tug lying amid a clutch of ancient ships just outside the marina. They'd had trouble with a boat they were inspecting and found themselves with buckets-full of dirty oil. Where should they put it? They spotted the old tug, then marked for demolition, sneaked alongside and poured the oil through a porthole, confidently expecting the whole business to be towed away and scrapped.

But the tug wasn't demolished. It was historic. A fund was got up to save it. The man I bought the *River Queen* from, Leen Bakker, was one of the group formed to preserve it. Some time later Coen asked Leen how the restoration work was going. 'Slowly,' said Leen. 'The inside was filthy. For some reason it was covered in old oil.'

Coen felt the burden of a protective state lying heavily on his shoulders.

'There are too many people who live on welfare here. Young people like me must pay for it. We pay taxes, taxes, taxes.'

You heard the same in every country, I suggested, sensing even from this distance the moans of those New Zealanders who firmly believed they were among the most heavily-taxed nations in the world, an opinion easily held if they'd never been further than a Bali resort.

Coen shrugged. 'Here it is different.'

I paid for the coffee.

Then we ran the boat up the river at full speed. We ran it down again. Coen pronounced himself satisfied. 'You have a DAF engine,' he said. 'They are very good.' (The DAF was Dutch-built). 'Your boat is good. You should just go.'

'Yes,' Sally said. 'Let's just go.'

Just … *go*?

That was the thing about Sally. She made up her mind and went for it. If you were to throw in your job etc., etc., a partner like Sally was very handy. I was dodging the potholes and peering down the abyss but Sally took them all in one great leap of faith.

I was not a decisive man. When I wanted to do something, usually I couldn't decide what it was I wanted to do. When it eventually came to me, anxiety kicked in. I was an anxious man. I worried up a storm on Sunday evenings, when the past week seemed a waste of time and the coming one impossible. On Sunday evenings I would sit in my little puddle of gloom, knowing that disaster was dusting itself off, dressing up and cleaning its teeth ready for tomorrow.

Sally believed my anxiety was groundless, a stupid quirk that complicated the proper business of life, which was living as happily as possible. She was brought up in a neat little family — mum, dad and two daughters — whose enjoyment of life was undisturbed by the crises that regularly struck my own. If I now feared disaster would strike at any moment, it was with good reason: growing up, disaster *did* strike at any moment, sometimes saving all the to-ing and fro-ing and just hanging around for a while.

Six kids, the beach, assorted vehicles ranging from mopeds to hot rods, never enough money, always far too much exuberance: this was disaster's home, and I was surprised it ever left to go anywhere else. Life was chaotic, always; injuries were so common only broken bones won any attention and then only if you needed crutches. Disappearances were routine, once resulting in two nationwide searches for one of my brothers; and you could never, *never* find anything.

So I and my brothers and sister grew up with the certainty that sooner or later we'd wind up living under the bridge, if only we could find it.

All of us married orderly people. Sooner or later we found partners who liked clean houses; paid power bills on time; insisted on mealtimes; never drove unregistered cars nor ran out of toilet paper; threw away underpants with holes in them; knew which day of the week it was; answered the telephone; never spent money they didn't have, and always, always flushed the toilet. They kept chaos at bay, and when it dared make an appearance they made it wipe its feet and sit on the sofa, and after a while it looked at its watch, muttered politely about the time and left.

One look at Sally and I knew chaos didn't stand a chance.

We met while she was still at university and I was working for the *Otago Daily Times*. A friend had entrusted his wife to me, to escort to a Dunedin party.

His wife was attractive and I was busy doing what any good friend would do in the circumstances: I plotted to make off with her just as soon as I could swing it. Anything less would have been an insult to the lady, my friend's taste in women, and the behaviour expected of a young reporter, even if the dear old *ODT* ran more to sobriety than sleaze.

'I hope you're going to talk to me,' said a voice at my elbow, 'because I told that guy over there I had to go and say hello.' I was inclined to sulk, but you did not ignore Sally. When she came by for a chat, you chatted, or at the very least mumbled until your testosterone-clouded vision cleared enough to change targets. When it did I noticed that the interloper wasn't too dusty herself. In fact, as I warmed to the task, I thought she was stunning. She was nicely tanned, with short dark hair and a wonderful smile and hazel eyes with sparks in them. She wore a short blue dress with white spots. My ego swelled like a third-grade rugby player's bladder at an away game.

One proper look at her and I knew chaos didn't stand a chance. I fell in love immediately and abandoned my charge. After all, that's what friends were for.

I turned all my charm upon her, although in truth that cupboard was as bare as my later promise concerning all my worldly goods.

Yet Sally was interested enough to walk home with me, and I was helped in the charm job by my staunchest ally, my dog Henry. Henry was a golden Labrador bought as a gun dog by the corner grocer. Henry was not keen on guns. When he heard one, he went the other way. The grocer gave him to me. Guns and I were all the same to Henry for a while. He often went away and hid. He and the dog ranger were on first-name terms.

Now Henry was waiting outside with a can of Fido in his mouth and the kind of reproachful look in his eye that I had so narrowly avoided back at the bash.

Henry was the clincher. His foresight fascinated Sally. He gave her a cheery hello, as much as he was able with his mouth full, and off we went to my flat. Sally looked at the décor: Hugh Hefner meets Woolworths. What's a nice dog like you doing in a place like this? she asked Henry, and left.

Two days later I took her for a ride on my Triumph Thunderbird motorbike, which had a goldflake petrol tank and lots of chrome. We blasted along Kaikorai Valley Road on a crisp autumn night. She got bronchitis and was in bed for a week.

That was March. In May we decided to marry, not so much a leap of faith on her part as an act of lunacy.

I couldn't believe my luck. She was finishing her studies at a university which had told me never to darken its doors again. She liked Bob Dylan, I liked Pink Floyd. She loved people and wanted to help, I was a professional sceptic. She came from an orderly family with a nice house on the hill, I sprang from confusion. She was sure of herself, my psyche showed the pin-holes of borer.

No one gave tuppence for our chances, but we loved each other. Why else would she do it? Her flatmates were busily pledging their troths to doctors, dentists, lawyers, accountants. She planned to marry someone whose weekly wage could be blown in one good night in the City Hotel's bar, and often was, until I threw in my job (not for the last time).

I had bigger fish to fry. Tonnes of them in fact, for I planned to become, not the lawyer I had once set out to be, nor even the reporter I was pretending to be, but a sturdy fisherman, of the kind who, when you were tucked up in blankets snug and warm, was riding out the storm. My partner Ian and I planned to ride it out to Fiordland, and make our fortune catching crayfish.

But first, as Mrs Beaton might have said had she chosen a more aromatic vocation, find your boat. Ours was then a pile of steel in a Dunedin boat builder's yard. It had to be converted to a thing of beauty by skilled, experienced, hardworking men, and me.

It was an exciting prospect. I, however, was not.

Look at it from Sally's point of view. She was taking on an unemployed bodgie who by then had been thrown out of not one but two universities on the grounds of laziness, whose only asset was a motorbike which gave her bronchitis, and who for months brought his work home with him in the form of paint, oil, rust and lots of body odour. My hands were scarred and calloused from the steel work, I was usually covered with paint so durable it took months to wear off, dirt was ingrained in every pore. I was scared of touching Sally's perfect skin for fear of spoiling it. Sally seemed everything I was not: intelligent, thoughtful, considerate, resolute and of course, unscarred. My shambles orbited around her core like space rubble.

Also, I was broke, for as boats do, this one was taking much longer and costing far, far more than we ever thought possible. We were in debt not just up to our necks but well into the airspace above. I ran out of money. Some friends, David and Anne McPhail, took me in, fed me and gave me somewhere to sleep.

They say that just when you think things can get no worse, they do; and they did. We decided it was time for me to meet Sally's parents in Christchurch. Sally had already met mine. My mother had been in tears because my father had accused my brother's friend of being a drug dealer, and decided to pulp him with a golf club.

Sally had called her mum and dad and told them the good news: she'd met a man and was going to marry him. No, he wasn't a doctor. Her sister had married one of those. He was a journalist. No, not like that awful Brian Edwards (whom her mother, somehow or other, had met, and disliked intensely). Well, actually, he wasn't a journalist right now either. He was a fisherman. Well, in fact, he wasn't a fisherman just now, exactly…

With an entrée like that, it just had to get better didn't it? Well, didn't it?

For me this was the natural order of things. For her parents it was something else altogether. A reporter was bad enough. A fisherman was worse. An unemployed fisherman ran the needle right off the scale of undesirable sons-in-law.

I'd traded in the motorbike for a turquoise Rover, now repainted an impressive black which I felt lent a certain gravitas so far missing from my make-up. I loved the car. It was the most luxurious thing I'd ever owned. The engine muttered in a genteel sort of way, the tyres hummed, the woodwork glowed softly in the light, the dashboard shone and tinkled like a cocktail cabinet. The effect was of a drinks party in a kennel.

We arrived in the Garden City in good time for the dinner that Sally's mother was preparing for the occasion. But first, I had to call at my home in rumbustious New Brighton, close to the sea. Then, on the way to Sally's home in Sumner, also beside the sea but more affluent, I had to drive onto the big car park we called the Ramp.

This was traditional. The Ramp was one of the formative influences of my childhood. My brothers, my friends and I had spent more time there than almost anywhere, including university. It was one of the reasons I'd been evicted from that institution, which had foolishly timed its examinations for October when the wild nor'west surf was, unlike them, not to be missed.

When you weren't in the surf, you were hoping to be, so it had to be studied endlessly, and the best place to do that was the Ramp. Beside it stood the surf club, where my father and his brothers and nephews (but not his sons) featured in the gilt-lettered lists of office-holders hung solemnly on walls. Surfboard riding was not popular with clubbies in those days: it was considered subversive, took young people away from the proper business of beach patrols and competitions which seemed to me to involve far too much marching about and standing to attention, not to mention lots of hard work.

At night, when we could no longer see the surf from the Ramp, we sat there in old cars with our girlfriends. So it was illogical and possibly illegal to pass the Ramp without driving up for a gink at the surf, and the old Rover's wheels turned onto it as if on rails.

I sat for a while genuflecting while Sally looked at her watch and worried about being late for dinner. But I was a responsible fellow now. I drove off, with a last look over my shoulder at the surf — my undoing, for since I'd last been there the authorities had planted a large post in the carriageway, and the Rover barrelled straight into it.

I'd always felt the car was built like a tank, but it was no match for the post, which now stuck up from the bonnet in a position which should have been occupied exclusively by the engine. The switches and levers which jutted everywhere usually changed gear, operated windscreen wipers and so on. Right then they were impaling Sally. Switches had become spikes, levers cudgels.

She wasn't badly hurt, but she certainly looked as if she was. Blood trickled from several cuts on her forehead and face. The skin had been taken off her knees by a previously benign heater. One arm had been grazed by a door handle with no previous criminal record. She looked a mess.

'I'll take you straight to the doctor,' I said decisively.

'No,' she said, probably tight-lipped but it was hard to tell through the blood. 'I. Want. To. Go. Home.'

'Well,' I thought, not aloud. 'No accounting for it.'

I ran around the corner to my home. All of the five brothers had friends. All of the friends stayed in the house from time to time. Quite long times, sometimes.

Usually their cars littered the yard, my mum and dad appealing for us to pick them all up and put them away. I'd borrow one, take Sally home, and we'd all have a nice drink, once she'd stopped bleeding. But only one car sat on the front lawn that day.

The car was an old Holden. It belonged to a friend of my brother's who'd come to visit, and stayed. It was painted black, but its owner had relieved the tedium with long red and orange flames painted along both sides. Take it, he offered, and with no option, I did.

The car started with a clamour and set off with an even louder one. Straight pipes, I heard him yell after me, in case I imagined Holdens emerged from the factory sounding like World War Two. It roared in a way which, when they heard it approaching, made the fathers of daughters sit bolt upright in bed and reach for weapons.

I blatted back to the car park, packed the battered Sally into the passenger's seat (I thought I heard a faint 'oh no') and drove to her parents' house up a hill which brought out the best in the car's acoustics.

Her mum and dad were sitting outside on their terrace, admiring their splendid view of the city. Alarm turned to horror as the Holden turned into their drive.

Sally opened the car door and spilled into view. They looked aghast at her bloodstained face, gory knees, bruised arm. Her mother trundled down the drive with the stoic expression of a wartime stretcher-bearer and bore away her bleeding daughter for emergency surgery inside. Her father surveyed the wheels. 'Quite good cars these Holdens,' he said.

All right, I knew I had some work to do with my prospective in-laws. But look on the bright side, I thought. At least I had a decent excuse for being late for dinner.

We finished the fishing boat just in time to save me from penury, painted her bright orange ('You'll thank me if we ever need to get rescued,' said Ian, prophetically) and christened her the *Nina* with the cheapest bottle of wine we could find. We filled the hold with brawn pie which was supposed to be good for us. I had a couple of teeth pulled just in case. ('Rinse with salt and water,' the dentist advised. 'It's as good a treatment for teeth as anything, and much cheaper than me.')

Sally asked when we'd be back.

In the autumn, I said.

Well, wouldn't that be a good time to be married, she said.

Yes, I said, and we set off for Fiordland with Sally and Anne and David waving goodbye from Taiaroa Head, Sally sadly (I think) and the McPhails gaily (I think) as I'd been living in their spare bedroom and sponging on their hospitality for months.

We steamed around Puysegur Point into Preservation Inlet and Chalky Sound, where we caught crayfish, packed their tails into big plastic bags which we stored in our freezer, went off eating crayfish in three days flat (not a record among crayfishermen), complained about the freezer-load of food we'd brought which soon all tasted like seaweed, got sick of blue cod, ate only the cheeks of groper and put the rest of those fine fish into the pots as bait, cursed the sandflies and soon, each other. At night the ship's radio picked up the hit parade: '*I beg your pardon, I never promised you a rose garden....*'

For months we stayed there, seldom setting foot on land, rafting up with other boats at night, setting off each morning before dawn, living a surreal life in the deep, still water and primeval bush of the farthest, quietest part of all New Zealand.

In the southern latitudes night didn't fall so much as frolic in the dusk for a while and if you were out at sea then for ages there'd be enough light in the sky to show the outline of Stewart Island, Rakiura, isle of glowing skies. We sheltered in Preservation Inlet, where fishermen rafted their boats at night and told stories of a river of gold, the purest gold in the world, between Coal and Steep-to islands where no one could reach it. The lost lode.

Australia was six days by good boat from there, Auckland seven days.

The crayfish boom was just ending; that is, in the New Zealand way they'd been fished almost to exhaustion, never to recover in the same numbers. The work was wild and exhilarating. Occasional slips showed rock polished smooth by glaciers. The heavy, sweet smell of honeydew hung over the bush. Beaches white as dreams fringed the black water. Pale green kina shells jewelled in white lay on the sand like Fabergé eggs.

Europeans had lived here only a few years after Cook's third voyage. Under the bush lay remains of old civilisations where people once hacked a living until they were beaten, and the forest mended its scars. Bits of an old timber railway could still be seen at Sandy Point. The finely-crafted long brick chimney of the Tarawera mine rested in the bush with its big iron driving wheel nearby. In Cuttle Cove there was a little plaque for the whaling station there from 1829–36. It didn't say anything about a gold mine, although nearby a shaft went deep into the mountain through solid rock branching two ways with a great cavern in the middle and driven with god knows what effort.

Just a few steps off a beach you might find the remains of a stamping battery, or a railway beneath the bush canopy. Hut sites were marked by old bottles, a few bricks, a heap of rusting iron. Life must have been dark and hard for those people who slaved in the mountain's bowels by day and squatted in primitive huts by night.

Not far from where twentieth-century entrepreneurs built a luxurious lodge, incongruous in the wilderness, Māori had sheltered in cave networks. Stone walls still marked living and sleeping areas. The mounds of calcified middens remained on floors alongside tool-working areas, escape routes and waka slipways. In 1877 the scout Walter Traill discovered the body of the Ngāi Tahu chief Tarewai entombed in limestone in a cave not far from Cuttle Cove. The chief had been mortally wounded in an attack on the Kati Mamoe's last stronghold at nearby Matuira.

On fine days we could see the mysterious Solander Islands at the entrance to Foveaux Strait, with their story of the sailor accused of sleeping with a sailing ship captain's wife and marooned there on the rocks. The ship sailed on to Timaru where the real culprit promptly absconded with the missus. Heartbroken, the captain sailed for London and it was three years before a passing ship rescued the very hairy castaway.

We left this magical place one fine morning when the Puysegur Point light was still flashing. It was three weeks before my wedding day. A small fleet of fishing boats, held up by weeks of bad weather, popped from Preservation Inlet like corks. We skirted the white water of the Marshall Rocks into Foveaux Strait, passed reefs glittering black in the morning sun, steamed by the dark V of Big River draining the thin Lake Hakapoua, the Knife and Steel and the low Long Point, and saw the jelly mould shape of the Solanders faint on the horizon.

We creamed smoothly over great rollers left over from one of the fierce storms which swept Foveaux Strait, running down their backs and pausing for a moment in their valleys before the next picked us up and we surged forward again, the deck stacked high with steel craypots.

Yet something strange was happening. Each time we ran down the face of a wave, the boat listed, more and more, until it tipped dangerously at the bottom and threatened to turn side-on.

We checked the pots. Nothing had shifted. Maybe it was the load, said Ian. In the refrigerated hold lay stacks of frozen crayfish tails in their plastic bags. I left him in the wheelhouse and checked the deck. The heavy steel hatch cover was buried beneath crayfish pots. I lifted them away, stacked them as best I could, raised the hatch cover and the insulated metal plug below it and wedged them open against the pots. I climbed down into the hold.

The boat was now listing horribly. Everything seemed as we'd left it down there. Still, I began shifting the bags of frozen tails to the high side of the boat.

A wave lifted the stern. A big one. In the steel bowels the rush of water as we raced down its face sounded like waterfalls. I braced myself for the heavy swerve the list would cause at the wave's bottom.

This one was sharp. We seemed to go over, and over, and I heard the pots grind on the steel deck above my head. There was a clang and a crash, and a thud from my heart as I realised what had happened: the pots had moved, the plug had fallen awkwardly at an angle into the hatchway, and the hatch cover had snapped closed, wedging it in.

I knew it was jammed because no amount of heaving and cursing made the slightest bit of difference: I was well and truly trapped with the ghosts of ten thousand crayfish.

I realised something else: I was stuck in a freezer which was still working perfectly. Now I was sitting still and growing colder by the second. I was starting to freeze like the crayfish beside me, and they'd have the last laugh: dead, they were worth considerably more than I was. I sat there shivering, as much in fear as from the cold, for not only was my position hopeless, but I am irretrievably claustrophobic.

At last I heard Ian shouting for me. He was convinced I'd fallen overboard. I shouted back. He couldn't hear. I shouted louder. Nothing. I screamed. He must have heard something, for he came back. I saw a chink of light as the hatch cover lifted a few centimetres.

'Bruce?'

'Yeah.'

'What are you doing down there?'

'I'm stuck.'

'Doesn't matter. The boat's going to sink anyway.'

His footsteps retreated, then returned. I heard him force the hatch cover back against the pots and lash it there as I should have done. He wrestled with the plug. It didn't move. 'It's stuck,' he announced, and went back to the wheelhouse. He returned and threw a big screwdriver down the gap.

'You'll have to get yourself out,' he said. 'I've got to look after the boat.'

I began levering at the plug. Nothing happened. Mustn't panic, I told myself. Oh what the hell, panic! Attacked the thing in a frenzy. Saw it move a fraction, calmed down, worked at that side. It lifted, and so did I, through the hatch without conscious movement, levitation of the kind that meditation never produced. I stood on the deck breathing proper air and taking no notice at all of what was going on in the wheelhouse. Another boat appeared in the murk to escort us. We turned around, very carefully because at one point we'd be side-on to the swell, and limped back to Endeavour Inlet.

I thought about Sally, and hoped she was thinking about me. I was completely isolated. I sent no messages and received none. I had no way of contacting her.

Our wedding was imminent. My chances of making it were not good. I didn't know much about marriage but I was sure all the best bridegrooms showed up for their weddings. My absence was bound to be noticed. I was, I thought, stuffed.

Much, much later, here I was deciding to live on the French canals and Sally was still saying, 'Let's do it.' Next day she went out and changed her mother's legacy into enough Euros to buy a boat and live on it for a year, perhaps two if we were careful, and it was done.

She seemed endlessly able to take my dreams and make something of them without flinching; for the trouble with dreams, with escape and adventure, is that the losses can be heavy. Sometimes lives might have been better left as they were. Changing ours removed us from family, friends, props, routines, and when things went wrong we were naked in the cold.

Chapter Four

A red sun seared the mist. Seven o'clock. We hadn't been up that early since we'd left home. We seemed quite alone in the world, not a common feeling in this tiny, crowded country. We unwrapped a New Zealand flag and hoisted it on the varnished wooden flagpole at the back of the boat. Perhaps we should have snapped to attention and saluted, but we did not.

Neither of us cared very much for flags. We'd found that when one was waved it was usually time to turn around and briskly head the other way. Besides, the New Zealand flag was at best ambiguous. Those who didn't think you were British believed you were Australian. You were expected either to order egg and chips or boast. Yet you were also required to fly your country's flag at your boat's stern.

This was a dilemma.

A few days before we left New Zealand, Glenn and Trish had presented us with a little black flag carrying a silver fern and underneath it, to make things perfectly clear, the inscription 'New Zealand.' It was the kind of flag you waved at an All Blacks' game and the daunting thing was that while the proper New Zealand stars and Union Jack puzzled almost everyone, the silver fern was instantly recognised right through Europe. In the world view we were a nation of fly-halves and loosies.

We stuck it on the front of the boat. No one ever got mixed messages from that one.

The water was still. Anyone could see the day was going to be hot (ignoring glum predictions from locals: 'You are very lucky. But it will rain tomorrow evening or the next day.').

The diesel's erratic rumble may have woken a few, but no one came to wave us off. We looked back over our home for the last three weeks. We'd liked it there. The yachthaven was eccentric, far from the clinical order of the marina in neighbouring Kerkdriel where ranks of spotless washing machines and driers stood outside pristine showers amid strict security. We knew about the security because we'd tried to sneak in with a load of washing. I preferred the anarchy of our own mooring.

We passed the pool where lay barges, the historic tug and a few houseboats, one of them accommodating a small boy who offered his little steel launch to marina sailors as a water taxi, shuttling them from boat to café all of one hundred metres away. He handled his boat as other kids rode bikes.

We reached the River Maas, turned left, and were on our way.

The sepia haze over the sun made us seem the centre of an old photograph. We were both nervous. The boat had sat on its mooring since the previous autumn, and it was asking a lot to kick it back into life at a moment's notice, the kind of life it had never known before; everything on it from boiler to fridge, bow-thruster to shower, about to be used not once or twice a month, but every day.

Sally, not quite knowing what a bow-thruster was, nor caring very much, was suffering from straightforward terror. Her job in the locks was to make the boat fast to one of the bollards set into the lock's side by looping a rope around it then hanging on. As the water in the lock rose, she had to unhitch the rope and put it around a higher bollard, and so on until we were at the top. It sounded easy enough, or might have, if she'd understood a word of it. I didn't really understand it either. You had to be there, I thought.

Huge barges passed us on both sides. I remembered a film I'd seen as a child called *Monolith Monsters*, featuring shiny black things which rose out of the ground and disposed of anything in their way by falling on it. I examined the waterborne behemoths fearfully.

We were content to take our time. In fact, we'd have been happy to go backwards, all the way to the Jachthaven de Maas, where there were no locks and still water.

Locks loomed in our minds.

We approached our first, about ten kilometres up the River Maas, with all the verve and joy the occupants of a tumbrel might have felt as they neared the blade.

How could a mere lock look so big and threatening?

Could it be because it *was* big and threatening?

What had happened to locks since we'd used the quaint little ones in an English canal thirty-odd years before?

Were the Dutch boasting or were they just mad?

This first lock, the Sluis Lith, looked rather like a cattle abattoir I'd once seen: a long concrete race leading to a huge gate behind which, we knew, the business was done. And bugger, the lights were green, summoning us in. Two ship-sized barges were inside already, along with a small cruising barge, and the lock-keeper was keeping the doors open for us. Escape was impossible.

I remembered Mr Benny's advice. 'Locks are not like life,' he'd told us. 'In locks you must never be first. You must always come second, or third.' All was going to Mr Benny's plan, so far. We swept into the pen, or chamber, and began mucking around with the ropes. This one? That bollard, the slimy thing on the wall there? OK? Wait, the rope was on the wrong side of the boat's rail. Fine — no, hang on, we were no longer attached. Oh damn, the ropes looked like a cat's cradle. Or mine did.

Sally organised her ropes and kept her fear to herself. She did her job perfectly; pointed out the bollard she wanted to tie onto so that I could stop the boat in the right place; dropped the loop over it; changed to the next bollard as the water level rose and carried the boat up. From the very first she handled her lines much better than I did. My ropes were always a mess, hers always ran smoothly.

Behind us, a man and woman lounged against the cabin of their boat, their ropes held loosely, extravagantly idly I thought, the couple looking as if they might just have a coffee during this pleasant interlude.

I ran hither and yon, my ropes went everywhere, and while I was still cursing them for being wayward, we were at the top. It had worked. Not quite according to plan, not within a long dog whistle of it actually, but here we were ready to leave the lock and head back onto the river.

We were delighted. We'd survived our first lock and we were still afloat and uninjured. Immensely relieved too. The stretch of the River Maas we'd left lay four metres below us.

'Sorry,' we shouted to the other boat. 'Our first lock.'

'Then you are making a good job,' she called back. 'Do not worry. Follow us now. You must let the professional boats go out first.'

Soon we could see why they waited. The barges set up tsunamis in the lock. The *River Queen* bucked against its lines.

Our new friends were on their way to France, too. She'd given up her job and he was on a sickness benefit. She told us this without self-consciousness. He was sick, they had to live, that was the contract. They'd built their boat themselves. They were going to cruise while there was time, and they wanted to help.

I loved the Dutch. We followed the woman. Stalked her, possibly. At the next lock, she signalled us to tie up and wait.

An awful lot of barges seemed to be waiting too, and they looked big even from this distance. Inside the lock they'd be monstrous. By now it was hot. We told her so. 'You are very lucky,' she said. Her husband appeared from the wheelhouse. 'They want us to follow in after the *Matilda,*' she called, pointing to a huge barge piloted by a young woman.

The *Matilda*? This gigantic chunk of iron was no jumbuck, and that oblong of water now being revealed to us by the opening gates certainly was no mere billabong. And how did they know to follow it? How would we work it out without them to tell us?

Still, we waltzed in after the *Matilda*.

Yup, she was big. Worse, she ran her engines, and propeller, and the wash and the inrushing water combined in an effect not unlike the rapids on the Buller River. But we did as we were told, and found ourselves squeezed under the barge's stern.

We clutched ropes as if our lives depended on it, and we were convinced they did. Then things went wrong. Sally got her rope around the bollard, but mine was hopelessly tangled. ('Bound to happen,' she said later. 'It's the messy way you do things.')

While I was sorting it out — all right, scratching away at the mess like a kitten with a ball of string — the lock doors swung shut behind us and we started to lift. We scrabbled, grabbed, cursed. Our friends politely looked away. Somehow we reached the top, the gates opened, the *Matilda* accelerated out, and the *Queen* wouldn't start.

Fuck.

Lots of beating the air and calling to the Almighty went on. Then I discovered the trouble: the boat was in gear. The engine wouldn't start in gear. I moved it into neutral. We started up and crept out shamefacedly. Not one of the barge skippers waiting to come in from the other side so much as wagged a finger.

We'd had enough for one day. We waved goodbye to our mates, who sailed serenely onwards. Instead, we tottered into a marina in a little village whose name we were quite sure was an omen: Grave. Yet friendly locals took our lines, told us we were welcome, gave us a map of their town which they insisted was very old and even more beautiful.

The harbourmaster appeared. He seemed nice. 'Where are you from?' he asked. 'New Zealand? Not very many New Zealand boats come here. I have been here thirty years.'

We were chatting to the harbourmaster, who was fascinated that a couple of people from the other side of the world had found their way to his tiny haven, when came the rustle of excitement that preceded a new arrival. Another boat was approaching.

Could it be? Yep, it was. The New Zealand flag.

A cruiser. With a Crusaders' flag at the front, and a New Zealand one at the back, and a name on the boat itself: *Crusader*, of course. They berthed, looked around them, spotted us, and for the first time in ages we heard that New Zealand greeting: 'How *are* you?' 'Sweet,' I said.

Rudolph and Louise from Templeton, Christchurch, not far from our own home in Sumner, en route to France. I could see the harbourmaster's astonishment. Who are these people? Why have they come here, all at once?

Louise came belting along the jetty. 'We can't find out,' she said. 'How are the Crusaders doing?' 'Back at the top,' I said, for I'd read my emails from home just the previous night.

Then we walked around the old town in the creamy evening, admiring houses going back to the thirteenth century and fortified walls even older, listening to the quiet chat of people in the cafés, crashing an opening in an art gallery (a glass or two of indifferent white wine, a polite smile, for these things are universal) revelling in this little village somewhere in Holland, and all was right with the world.

Some people like rivers because, after canals, they're like seas. The Maas becomes the Meuse when it cuts through Belgium and runs up into France, where it springs from somewhere in the hills near Pouilly on the Langres Plateau. In the meantime it was the Maas, wide and steady as befitted a proper Dutch river making its way to the North Sea near one of the world's biggest ports at Rotterdam. It flowed through meadows, and fields, and paddocks, and grassland, and whatever names the Dutch had for large areas of pasture, and cattle gazed at us in that goofy way cows do as we passed, and if ever they made a waterway large enough to carry boats across the Canterbury Plains, or the Hauraki Plains, it would be much like this, pleasant, flat, featureless, inhabited by contented animals.

So we left Grave and arrived at Wanssum some four and a half hours later in semi-comatose condition, jerked back to consciousness each time a barge appeared, closed with startling speed, and thundered by with its decks awash and the helmsman, or woman, sitting back in their chairs using their hands only to give us an idle wave.

The only lock assumed remarkable significance. You could not be bored around locks. We found later that as soon as you became complacent they bit you. In the meantime, we were much too scared to be bored.

This was a double lock. One of the two was already full when we reached it. Four huge barges were more than we wanted to mix with. We stooged around and soon the green light appeared on the other lock, and only one barge was waiting to go inside, so we nipped in after it and the day immediately seemed better. The countryside became more couth. Expensive-looking, rather grand houses began appearing along the riverbanks.

'Wanssum,' Mr Benny had told us, 'is a nice little place. You should stop there.'

He was partly right. Wanssum was little.

We reached the port by way of a canal leading off the river, lined with unpromising heavy industry sending up clouds of dust and making lots and lots of very knobbly noise. Perhaps we should have been warned. Instead of nice, Mr Benny might have described Wanssum as glum, or dour, or surly, any of which would have been closer to the mark.

The only mooring space available was very tight, involving some intricate manoeuvring which was watched by a posse of old men sitting in the shade of a tree in front of the marina's bar. They didn't look as if they liked what they saw.

By convention onlookers helped with mooring lines as you came into a berth, especially one as tricky as this. No one moved. Instead a man left his yacht on another pontoon, walked around and took our lines. Later he came over again, and asked politely if he could have a chat. His name was Martin and he was anxious for company, he said, when he was properly settled in the saloon with a glass of wine in his hand. He was forty, lonely, vulnerable. 'I do not like this place,' he said. 'It is dismal.'

Martin was travelling in a tiny plywood yacht his father had built forty years before. He was sailing it to the south of France. He was alone, and we thought that was only partly due to the size of his yacht, for Martin had an air of desperation that would not have been attractive to companions invited to share a space hardly larger than a shower cubicle, although of course his craft did not possess such a luxury.

His father was dead and his mother was in a wheelchair. Oh dear, we said.

'It is her own fault,' Martin said. 'She is too fat. You have seen how many people are on sticks or in wheelchairs here?'

We had. But hadn't we read that the Dutch were now the tallest people in the world? Well yes, Martin said. 'But all of Holland is sick. Holland is going to the dogs, unless you're an immigrant, or a woman, or disabled.'

By now we were getting some hints on why Martin was lonely, desperate etc.

How, we asked, would he live when he returned to Holland?

'I will get sick, or shoot someone. Either way they will look after me.'

And as the sun rose next morning we left beautiful Wanssum, just as soon as possible.

We had some fifty-three kilometres and two locks to travel through that day to reach Roermond, a large town on the base of the narrow tongue of Holland squeezed between Germany on one side and Belgium on the other. In one of them, the Belfield lock, our boat was the only occupant. We always felt guilty when this happened: first because all that complicated machinery, the hydraulics, the electronics, the great gates, were being operated by skilled lock-keepers shifting millions of litres of water only to lift one small boat a few metres in the air. And second, because we were so happy to be that one small boat.

Roermond was wide, spacious. A lake spread on one side and a fine port on the other. It also had designer outlet stores, which overshadowed its fifteenth-century cathedral in the town's list of attractions. I needed a hat. The temperature had risen into the thirties during the day, climbing into the forties inside the saloon. It was very hot. 'You are very lucky,' said the harbourmaster.

Also sunburned. Sally only had to be out in the sun for an hour or so to become deeply tanned. I only had to be in it for twenty minutes to become deeply pink. I slathered myself in sunblock until I peered fruitily from a white mask like strawberries and cream.

When you presented the kind of horizontal surface to the UVA which my dome did, you had to change the oil every half hour or so. Sally was always amazed that a surface of such high reflective quality could absorb any kind of rays at all.

The Dutch, fair as they were, did not like wearing hats, except for those butch little peaked caps affected by some sailors. Wide-brimmed sunhats of the kind common in Australia and New Zealand did not seem to exist here. Perhaps they weren't needed. Maybe we really were lucky.

Finally I bought the best hat I could find, a fey blue confection from the Hugo Boss outlet store. It cost 19 Euros, or some $38, and of course I immediately found a much better one in the Two Euro Shop.

New hat or not, I had no chance in the sartorial stakes within the marina. A strutting Dutchman inhabited the huge motor yacht beside us. He wore nothing but shorts so tight that any budgie smuggled therein wouldn't stand a chance. His wife, a tense-looking blonde, favoured bikinis of the kind that had fellow-boaties craning their necks, or at least those folds of flesh where their necks once had been. Now they expanded and contracted like bellows.

We were due to leave Roermond early next morning. The engine started with its usual reassuring purr. We idled past the rows of expensive craft and their serried ranks of German flags, for here we were close to the German border.

I pushed the throttle forward.

Nothing happened.

The engine maintained its quiet rumble.

Tried again.

Nothing.

I moved the engine nervously out of gear; the thought crossed my mind that perhaps the entire control was jammed, and we'd be doomed to travel in slow circles until we ran out of fuel. Then I remembered how much fuel we carried and cheered myself with the thought that we'd die of old age long before that happened.

But the engine slipped smoothly enough into neutral. I knew what had gone wrong. Two cables ran from the engine control and one, the throttle cable, had snapped.

We idled back into our berth. I went into the marina office. Did they know of a mechanic? Certainly, said the man behind the counter. He was a mechanic. He would replace my throttle cable. But not today. Today was Sunday.

Tuesday? I asked. For the next day, Monday, was Queen Beatrix's birthday. The queen had messed around with her birthday just as our own monarch did. She'd borrowed her mother Juliana's, which was just as well, because her own was in mid-winter. They'd moved the day to spring, and of course it was a public holiday.

Next week was very busy said the mechanic. But he could do it tomorrow, during the Queen's birthday holiday. I could see the sign flashing in his brain: penal rates.

So it was. The repair cost 200 Euro, or $400. Almost all of it labour, which for the hour it took him to change the cable would have run to a face-lift with a bit of liposuction thrown in. We did not mind, really. It meant an extra two days in this delightful city.

The work had an unexpected consequence, too. Many of the surrounding boats appeared rooted to the spot. They were beautifully built and equipped, capable of travelling long distances. Oceans would have been no trouble to lots of them. They could have turned on the radar, hitched the Global Positioning System to the automatic pilot, gone back to the margueritas on the sundeck and woken up in Brazil.

A few of them were making long journeys on canals, and they came by for a chat. The others scarcely stirred from their recliners.

The presence of an engineer moved them, however. He threw open the cabin door and lifted the living room floor, exposing the engine. It was boat-porn, like an aphrodisiac, exciting the blokes. They came over. They peered under the injectors, ogled the exhaust. They smirked among themselves.

The Belgian couple next door came over for the show too. They invited us back to their place, a leaf-shaped boat pointed at both ends, once a yacht with a lot of hull underneath the water. It looked unsuitable for canals, which most suited straight-sided boats sitting on top of the water. So much for prejudice; Europe had scarcely a waterway unseen by them and their craft. They bent a leery eye upon the Heineken beer we'd brought with us, then lectured us on how beer should really taste, with plenty on hand so they could demonstrate. Belgian beer was the world's best they said, and after a few of the thick glass bottles of malty brown beer I agreed that with the possible exception of Emerson's they were right. 'It's the one thing we do properly,' he said. We had a few more to prove it.

They asked me how they should spend the three weeks' holiday they planned in New Zealand that Christmas. In the South Island, I said. Maybe on the Taieri where Emerson's came from.

We were so busy drinking Belgian beer we missed the Queen's birthday celebrations. By the time we got into town there were only a lot of people wearing orange milling about in the main square and looking aimlessly happy as people do after a big occasion.

That evening a young couple lay above us on the harbour wall doing some serious bodily exploration. No one on the boats around took any interest. The couple simply didn't cut it against a naked DAF diesel.

And so we said goodbye to lovely Roermond. At a decent hour, for the Belgian beer was rather strong, we settled our bill at the marina office.

The woman there, so fresh she could have tutored daisies, wished us well.

We needed every good wish we could get. Faith defied logic, and our trust in the infallibility of our lovely boat had been shaken. Yes, it was only a cable, and the old one had operated properly for some twenty years before deciding to retire, but if one thing could go wrong, so could another, and as we set off for Maastricht we both prayed it would not happen that day.

'Whatever you do, don't break down on the Julianakanaal,' Mr Benny had warned us. The way to Maastricht lay along the Julianakanaal, and it did not take very long to get Mr Benny's drift. The canal was an ominously ordinary stretch of water, long and straight, boring as a drain, grim as a motorway. It was named after Queen Juliana. She must have taken a look at it and wondered what her subjects thought of her, truly.

Its function was to get canal traffic from one place to another as efficiently as possible and it did its job admirably. Great barges bore down, threatening to mince us against the steel canal-sides with sheer indifference. Each time one went by we were astonished; perhaps Londoners felt the same way when they heard the whistle of a bomb above their shelter and found themselves alive after the explosion.

The barges catching us up from behind were worse. They were like those nightmares when you can't get away no matter how hard you run. The *River Queen* began ignoring the speed limit entirely of her own volition. Breaking down on this canal would be like running out of petrol on the southern motorway during rush hour. You could expect minimum help and less sympathy.

We did not break down. Instead, we were confronted by the first of three locks, two of them lifting us thirteen metres. Horizontally you could take thirteen metres with a skip and a jump. Vertically, you prayed for Scotty to beam you up. Especially when the height was marked off in slimy concrete whose progress through life was measured in chips and scuffs and dashes of scraped paint.

We'd developed a new system for these locks. When we nuzzled up to the lock wall Sally would take her line from the post at the middle of the boat and loop it around a bollard on the lock wall. We could then hold the boat on just one rope, with me attaching a second as a back-up. She felt more secure there and we passed through all four locks without trouble, although always I remembered a bit of advice about public appearances from a seasoned after-dinner speaker: you should never lose your nervousness. It kept you on your toes.

We reached Maastricht a little after four p.m. We wanted to moor in the old port, the Bassin in the middle of the ancient city. The Bassin was guarded by its own lock, in a narrow entrance leading off the river. The lock was operated by a nautical gent in crisp whites topped by a perfectly-trimmed beard. My, he said eyeing the silver fern, another New Zealand boat. 'We've had two of them in here. One stayed all winter.'

We were to meet those people much later. Had it been cold, we asked? Not a bit, they said. They'd loved living in the old city. The others, we supposed, had been the Templeton two, who had been rushing to get down to the south of France. We'd seen them on the river, shepherding a cruiser whose engine had broken down. They'd looked disconsolate. They must have passed us while we were in Wanssum.

Our guide told us to take any berth we wanted and left with a farewell proving he'd even taken the time to learn our language: 'See yous.'

We tied up next to a Dutch boat named, ominously, *My Way*. A young, fit-looking woman emerged to take our lines then went back to join her husband. He was in a wheelchair, with a lift to take him up and down the companionway steps.

Their boat was not big, and for a while we wondered whether they were completely happy in it, for we'd hear whimpering from somewhere in its bowels. Then one day out sprang a couple of bull terriers big enough to need a boat of their own: preferably, given their rather evil disposition, towed well behind.

We were to see a lot of them over the next few months, once sharing locks for a day. He'd steer the boat into the lock, she'd take a line from the bow back to a bollard, he'd keep the engine running and the propeller turning, and the boat would lie neatly against the lock wall, no hands. She'd return to the after-deck and light a cigarette, darting a quick, pleased look at us messing around with two ropes and lifting them from bollard to bollard. The dogs slavered.

Commercial barges used the same trick. Why didn't we all? The convention was that you turned off your engine in locks, especially French ones. The practice, however, was much honoured in the breach.

Safely tied up in Maastricht, we looked around. A lot of money had been spent around the Bassin. Old warehouses had been converted to cafés, restaurants, apartments and galleries, with a promenade running its length.

Yet the port accommodated only a dozen boats. Most voyagers went on to a modern marina a few kilometres up the river, easier to get into and much cheaper, for the Bassin charged almost $40 a night.

We didn't worry about the money. We were in the middle of Maastricht, which vies with Nijmegen as oldest city in the Netherlands and lies at the bottom of the tongue. The entire ancient splendour of it lay a moment's walk from our mooring.

Maastricht had survived the centuries but not the age. Some of its fine old churches had been converted into a bookshop, a café, even a hotel, whose clientele enjoyed far more privacy than the congregation of the neighbouring Basilica of St Servatious, which as the oldest church in the Netherlands was flooded with tourists.

Outside the Basilica, an old lady getting along with the help of a walking frame smiled in the sun, admiring the warmth of the stones and the elegant forms they'd made ten centuries before.

Then her walking frame went over a kerb. She fell backwards trying to save herself, first on her bottom then, in very slow motion, her head hitting the cobbles with an awful soft thunk.

We were right beside her but already she was trying to struggle upright. She was dazed, but not too much to know we were speaking to her in English. 'I'm sorry, I'm so sorry,' she said to us. A small man came out of the crowd, and two women. They seemed to know her and took charge. At least, they offered her more comfort than we could. She scrabbled behind her in a panic: her pills. Sally handed them to her. 'Thank you, she said, 'oh thank you.' She wanted to vanish into the crowd.

We walked away, both of us near tears. Both our mothers would have said the same: so sorry to have caused you trouble, for being a nuisance, for creating a spectacle. The humility of another generation, the self-effacement of the old.

Maastricht soon swallowed us all, bustling, lively, alive. We stayed four days, and felt as those other New Zealanders must have, that four months would not have been enough.

Slowly we began coming to terms with another fact of canal travel: you lived a life, you lived it often in small villages and rural areas where tourists were unknown, by necessity you lived part of the life of its inhabitants, shopping in the same markets, finding your way around, working out the best way of doing the many things that needed to be done. You travelled at not much more than a walking pace, but you were still a bystander, part of the passing parade, not quite a tourist but not all that far removed from one either.

Sally was unhappy. The locks scared her. She keyed herself up for each of them. She dealt with routine locks and near disasters alike. But each of them seemed to sap a little bit of her soul. I could see her steeling herself for each new hurdle, determined not to make a mistake. Yet only one thing was constant about locks: there was always another.

Escapes had been hard on Sally.

Not long after we'd married we went to London. I got a job in Fleet Street and Sally headed a drug addiction unit until we discovered she was pregnant. As the months went by, something seemed odd. 'I think there are too many bumps,' said her cousin, a doctor. He gave her a scan, not then a common procedure, at least in the part of London we lived in. He looked at the screen for a moment and announced, 'Twins!' Our sons Sam and Simon were born a few days later, three weeks prematurely, their tiny chests heaving as they fought for air in their incubators. One of them struggled for his life, too. Solemn nurses advised us to have him christened immediately so that he could flee his brief, innocent time on earth in a proper state of grace. We declined, but prayed for him anyway, and called him Sam because the nurses said every Sam survived there. We thought them so beautiful we could scarcely bear looking at them. Alone, far from home, Sally cried, and hoped, and one wonderful morning the nurses told us the tide had turned.

Of course, our lives changed forever. Children strip away dross, and the imminent loss of one of our babies seemed to fuse us into a single entity.

We began thinking of the clean air and the freedom and the good state schools back home. So when they were eighteen months old we loaded our VW motor caravan, Sally and the boys onto an Italian cruise ship in Genoa and they sailed to Auckland while I flew to Christchurch and got a job. When they arrived we sold the van at a handsome profit and used the money for a deposit on a beautiful Hurst Seager house looking over the sea at Sumner, where the magic mountain on the end of the Kaikouras showed its white tip on clear nor'west days.

Sally was completely happy there. We thought life could be no better than this and we were probably right. Even in the grabbing scrabbling culture of the thirty-somethings we knew these were halcyon days.

We restored the house. I went back to university and completed a degree, wrote a newspaper column and laboured over scripts for David McPhail's TV comedy *A Week of It.* The kids started school, Sally slowly went back to work, first at high school, then at polytechnics.

The house was all Sally wanted and we both vowed not to leave. Then I became restless and joined the *Listener* and we moved to Wellington until I persuaded the editor that the magazine needed a South Island office and we drove past Tapuaenuku down the Kaikoura coast, past the rock with the hole where my dad and I used to fish, all the way back to our house on the hill, our souls full of freedom, the huge skies of the south, the sense of coming home.

But soon I was lusting after another old white house on the vestiges of an ancient farm in Port Levy on Banks Peninsula.

I wanted change. I couldn't go and work for anyone else. Television was too flaky. Besides, there wasn't much space for short, fat, balding guys. Paul Holmes had already grabbed the short spot and it was only OK to be bald if you could talk about rugby, although television being what it is the fat spot was still vacant. But all three in one? You'd do better applying for a seat in Cabinet, where short, fat and balding were job qualifications.

Radio? If I'd wanted to sum up my world in two sentences I would have become an All Black. That left newspapers, and I'd already left them.

I began casting around for other ways to make a living. Lots of money in advertising, but I couldn't stand the suits. Public relations paid well too, and offered refugee status to runaway hacks, but having to be so unrelentingly nice to everyone, particularly those hacks who hadn't had the good sense to run away; well, let's say I'd rather live on rolled oats.

Sally was by now head of a department at the polytechnic. Her job demanded every bit of time and attention she could give it. She had other things on her mind than her partner's mid-life crisis. Yet she took me seriously.

On long walks on the beach we thought, we reasoned, we envisaged, we explored. In the end *The Darling Buds of May* appeared on television and David Jason looked so happy in his country idyll we made an entirely rational decision. We'd go farming.

Of course I had all sorts of fears and reservations. Sally said, 'Let's just do it.' So we did, and Sam and Simon sobbed when we sold the house we said we'd never sell with its huge bay windows and vast rooms and all the ornate mouldings and skirtings and panelling we'd stripped and varnished and the work and hopes and dreams and peace and satisfaction.

Sally didn't cry. She just clutched our hands hard as we left, and never looked back at the place she'd loved more than any of us had.

That winter's day we drove through snow over the high pass to Port Levy.

The new house was full of people I didn't know. A log fire warmed the kitchen. People carried beds up stairs, filled bookshelves. One new neighbour brought pikelets, another pork bones. As a beginning I could scarcely have scripted it better, but the first act was tougher, filled with loss for Sally.

Port Levy was too remote for two young men at university. 'We're supposed to leave home,' they said. 'Home isn't supposed to leave us.' They stayed longer and longer in the city each week, and finally moved into a flat. The farm cost Sally the companionship of her sons, and it almost cost her life too.

Each morning I drove her over the pass separating Port Levy from the world, and she took the ferry from Diamond Harbour across Lyttelton Harbour and caught the bus on the other side. And one day an out-of-control port tug hit the badly-driven ferry and almost sank it.

That morning I was scarcely back at my desk in the old farmhouse when the telephone rang. Chris Moore, who made the journey with Sally each morning, said, 'Don't worry.' Are there more worrying words in the English language? I panicked immediately. 'There's been a rather nasty collision between the ferry and a tug,' said Chris, 'and Sally is ... don't worry, she's all right.'

Lurking chaos had caught up with me and overtaken Sally. I'd spent decades shoring up the palisades but here it was. Education, possessions, the solid keepsakes of middle New Zealand, were all swept into the chasm I saw before me. Chris had survived the crash, coped with his own fear, but it meant nothing to me at that moment. I cared only about Sally, and the entity that had surpassed anything I could have been alone: she and I.

The ferries had been running for at least one lifetime. As Wolf Cubs we used to catch them to Diamond Harbour, a sparkling little bay encircled by volcanic cliffs. They were no more than old wooden launches really. One had carried a framed placard boasting of an ocean rescue long before: ''Twas the *Onawe* that braved the stormy seas…'

Sally had caught the *Ngatiki* on her way to work that morning. The boat had almost reached its berth in Lyttelton port when one of the harbour tugs came pounding out from the wharf, rode up onto the ferry's cabin and all but crushed it in half, 'like', said Chris, 'a bomb going off.'

The passengers had seen it coming. They'd lined up in the stern mesmerised by approaching disaster. Sally dove over the side and struck out in the icy green water. The tug's black hull swept past her, crashed into the ferry, slid back. Sally felt herself being sucked under. Exhausted by fright and cold she fought to the surface, certain she was going to die until she looked up into the face of an Asian seaman leaning over the rail of a freighter. He dropped a lifebuoy beside her, the two of them alone in their universe. She swam for its light, kicked back towards the ferry, still afloat amid the wreckage. A woman grabbed her hand and hauled her onto the boarding platform at the back of the boat.

I found her in the port's medical centre, wrapped in blankets and little silver heat pads to fend off hypothermia. She had blood in her hair. It was someone else's.

She smiled at me. I felt dizzy with love and relief.

She was elated, alive. I was distraught.

The young English doctor came in. He had sailed his boat to New Zealand, liked it, stayed. He said Sally would be fine, and could leave soon, and there was a camera crew outside. Sally didn't want to talk to anyone. The doctor volunteered and I cravenly ducked out the back way, with Sally.

We watched the television news that night. Sally was shown being carried away on a stretcher and the sight of her still body terrified me again. She was the only casualty. The media likes heroes and one or two of the passengers volunteered but no one mentioned the Asian sailor.

Someone from the port company telephoned and said he supposed Sally was angry and anxious to know whose fault it was but she didn't. She was just happy to be alive. *I* was angry and anxious. Next day we both went over to the port to thank the sailor who'd saved her life but we weren't allowed aboard the ship and no one seemed to know who he was.

We never really settled down after that.

I'd loved the farm, she'd loved the house on the hill. She'd lost her family home and all the growing up the four of us had done there. I was only losing a dream.

One of the myriad media legends insists that if a marriage features in the women's magazines, it is doomed. I'd boasted in the *Listener* that my relationship with Sally had lasted into its third decade and was beginning to settle down. I offered useful tips on how to do it. Fate immediately took an oblique shot.

None of the reasons for escaping from the city to the country seemed important any more. We just wanted to live our lives as well as we could.

I sat on a friend's verandah beside the bay one night, surrounded by life and ghosts, watching the gold light fade from the hills and the warm nor'wester caressing the darkening sea and thinking how lucky I was to have lived on our farm in that tiny, close community. They'd made me a better person.

Sally understood change better than I did, though. She knew that journeys may not be the start of something new; they may be the end of something old, and dear. But she came along anyway.

Chapter Five

Borders have become virtual within the EU. The striped gates blocking the road, the squitty-eyed customs officers in little grey boxes have long gone, of course. But now there's not so much as a bureaucrat with a ticket punch. Even EU citizens still had officials in their minds, however.

Our Belgian friends in Roermond had told us that before entering their country we must first visit the Belgian customs house. In the EU? Yes. We shrugged. They knew best. After all, they were Belgian, and there it was marked on our chart: *douanes*, customs.

If we reached the Lanaye lock, they said, we'd gone too far. We reached the lock. We'd gone too far. We looked for the customs house. We could not find it. We turned back from the lock and found a space between barges beside the canal.

I walked back. Nothing. Only a broken-down clutch of buildings on the outskirts of the last town before the border. I walked into the town. Its inhabitants seemed mystified. I put it down to my bad French. Yet even when they spoke English they knew nothing of customs. They were interested to know what I was doing there. 'All this way?' inquired a woman cutting narcissus in her garden. 'In a boat? Perhaps you are not so lucky. It will rain. It rains a lot in Belgium. Sometimes it rains for weeks.'

I walked back, past the abandoned buildings. Wait a minute. What was that faded sign on one? *Douanes,* it said. Bugger. Customs were here once but it looked as if only carbon-dating would tell when.

Back at the boat I heard shouting. A Russian barge wanted our space, demanded it. The woman crew was shrieking at the top of her voice. Sally was trying to explain that she was on her own and could not move. The crew of the neighbouring Dutch barge joined in. Her man is not here, they shouted. Leave her alone. The bargee screamed at them instead. They yelled back. Gestures flew. I arrived at the crescendo, started up, fled. Behind us the fight went on.

So we left Holland and entered Belgium, at the Lanaye locks.The Lanaye locks lifted boats fourteen metres. The canal boat legend was, the bigger the lock, the easier it was, because the big ones offered easier moorings and less fuss. The story seemed to have been suspended for the Lanaye locks, which were famous. Or notorious.

They were huge. Passing New Zealanders had fretted over the locks in their weblogs. Canal travellers discussed them and looked glum. Some people said one of the locks wasn't so bad, because it had floating bollards and you could lie alongside one of them, tie up and sit tight while it rose along with the water level.

Others said another lock still had fixed bollards, vertically spaced so awfully that only a basketball star crossed with a gymnast and standing on tiptoe on the boat's roof could free a rope from one bollard and heave it over the next one above. There was a fifty-fifty chance of getting a good lock or the bad one, they said, and we who had never won a raffle in our lives knew just which one we'd finish up with.

Our voyage through Holland had taken us through big locks, but there were comparatively few of them. The Lanaye locks would be the biggest and meanest we'd been through yet. We were not looking forward to it. Now they loomed ahead. From where we cowered on deck they looked like New York streets, chasms between skyscrapers. We drifted warily into one of them. The lock had floating bollards. Oh relief, oh joy.

A truly enormous barge and three canal cruisers snuggled alongside them.

We hitched up to one of the bollards gratefully. We could tie tightly to it, for as the water level rose, you simply ignored the feeling of abyss, and up you went.

On the other side of the lock beside us lay a German vessel which seemed to have been built from a child's picture book. The boat was pure fantasy, bright blue, with little steps and varnished decks and bits and pieces everywhere, and very high and narrow like a plank on edge, so it seemed a miracle that it could remain upright.

Instead of tying onto a bollard the woman crew on the German boat fixed her rope to a ladder. The skipper then held onto his bollard with a boat-hook, a recipe for the disaster which followed.

I heard a scream; as the water rose the woman's rope had faithfully stayed where it was, tied to the ladder, and was pulling the little boat under. The man lashed out with a knife; the boat popped up like a cork. I fancied its crew was flung into the air, but it may have been an illusion; arms, legs and whole bodies seemed to fly everywhere.

The man had now lost his precarious hold on the bollard, of course. Free of any restraint, the boat spun like a ballet dancer while its crew did what any sensible crew would do in the circumstances: he froze and she screamed. As they pirouetted past she frantically proffered a rope; I grabbed it, and tied them on to our boat, which meant poor Sally was now holding two vessels on her own. But she was much better with ropes than I; if it was capable of being tangled, I tangled it, then scrabbled while she spoke sternly. Now she simply tightened up and hung on.

Safe, and with nothing to do, the German couple found someone in the same fortunate situation to chat to: me. They told me they were going through France then back through Germany, and I wished them luck with even more sincerity than I had prayed for it myself. We met them often over the next month. She always greeted us warmly. He all but ignored us. We reminded him of his ignoble moment.

The Lanaye lock-keepers glanced through our documents and gave us the papers we needed to travel through their country's waterways to France. Welcome to Belgium, they said. But the weather, you are not so lucky.

It started to rain. It rained almost non-stop for two weeks.

Describing a nation in a few words is stupid, of course, but fun, and that's why so many do it, like me. We met the Dutch at random: in supermarkets, in towns and villages (we were usually asking the way), as neighbours, sellers, passers-by, functionaries, advisors. Without exception they were a kindly, gentle lot who often went out of their way to help, like the man who actually took us where we wanted to go. They lived by some unspoken social contract: everyone obeyed the rules, written and unwritten, because they believed the rules were good for them all.

We learned to trust them: not easily, for New Zealanders believe the rest of the world is intent on robbery. We found that when they said they'd do something, they did it, so after a while we simply took them at their word. And so organised! Every kilometre of their canals was marked, every direction, depth, height.

Belgium seemed so much less prosperous, despite accommodating the world's biggest bureaucracy in Brussels. Its income from the manufacture of grey suits alone should have spread largesse upon the land.

At first we travelled through heavy industrial scenery. Factories groaned and clanked, poured dusty substances into barges moored alongside. Others lay abandoned in a mess of girders, ironworks; peeling buildings showing their innards. Deserted coalmines lay all about.

Liege looked unpromising, but was not. The city was bright, and lively, and its narrow streets, some closed to traffic, enticed us. But after only a night we had to go.

Why? I'm not sure, now. Belgium simply did not figure in our plans. We'd thought of it as a nondescript nation so uncertain of itself its people scarcely knew which language to speak — a choice piece of arrogance, for most chose to speak English to us.

We were foolish, of course. Any nation which produced Georges Simenon, not to mention The Singing Nun and Tintin deserved much more respect. But to us, then, Belgium was simply a corridor between Holland and France, to be traversed as quickly as possible, and the sheer momentum of that stupid notion had us on the move first thing next morning.

We steamed to Huy, where prejudices could put on their slippers, stretch and sigh contentedly. Perhaps Huy had been named by travellers who had passed through the grotesque and derelict landscape, for it was pronounced like a good spit. We tied up in the shade of a nuclear power station.

I sat on the deck that night, looking at the view, aka steam belching from the cooling towers and turned boiling red by its lights, rather as I imagined hell might look, although I thought I knew how hell felt.

We'd stayed in Endeavour Inlet, Fiordland, in that past age, fixing the trouble that had caused our return then waiting for the weather to clear, for it was awful again. Puysegur Point, the southwest corner of New Zealand, was the

Winston Peters of weather; if there was a storm to be had, the point found it, and we were anchored right under the lighthouse.

Days went by, then weeks. Sally had no idea where I was, except that I wasn't where I was supposed to be, getting ready for our wedding. I became alarmed, then desperate, then frantic.

Just as I'd given up hope of getting married, the weather broke. We shot off through Foveaux Strait, towing my only pair of jeans behind the boat to clean them, until — as the second night at sea approached — we could see Otago Peninsula rising from the twilight ahead. We passed under Taiaroa Head with great Pacific waves beating against the basalt. Unloaded the crayfish at Port Chalmers in the dark, went on to Dunedin Harbour, tied up, went to bed.

I awoke next morning to a cold clear autumn day, too anxious for breakfast. My jeans had set to the consistency of concrete. I mounted them and walked stiffly into town with no real idea where I was going.

I hadn't known Sally very long or very well before we left. She'd moved, but I didn't know where to. I hadn't spoken to her for months, hadn't received so much as a letter in that lonely place, for the postie didn't call in Fiordland and the radio wasn't up to it.

It never occurred to me that she might have been sensible and called it off.

Automatically I headed for George Street and the first person I met that day was her sister Donna. She said, 'Sally has found a flat for you. Here's the address. Don't forget the wedding. It's on Saturday.' My jeans crackled as I tore up to Union Street and knocked on the door. Sally answered. I'd never seen anyone so lovely. She had never seen anyone so …

She was more beautiful than I remembered. And immaculate. And, I thought, a little puzzled.

'It's me,' I said helpfully. She hugged me, perhaps a little awkwardly.

'What's that smell?' she asked. 'And who made your jeans? A blacksmith? And what have you done to your face?'

Grown a beard was what I'd done, and I thought the sun had done a nice job of bleaching it and my hair too. But I was ready for compromise. I shaved off the beard. Then a strip of white skin stretched from one ear, around my chin to the other. She screamed. 'You look like a peppermint stick,' she said.

So there I stood, reeking of fish, which of course I couldn't smell, dressed like a bag-man and coloured like a carousel.

But we were married in the little stone church in Sumner, Christchurch, with our friends and family, and Sally's hair black against her white dress, and me like a sunset in a rented suit.

When we awoke the first morning back in Dunedin and Sally was getting dressed for her post-graduate teaching course she asked, 'What are you going to do now?'

I'd like to say I thought for a moment, but I didn't. Instead: 'The boat's down at the wharf. It's all ready to go. We've fitted a toilet specially for you. We'll get it tidied up a bit and we'll be off.'

Now there was a pause. She seemed surprised. 'You mean,' she began, 'you think I'm going to live on that boat for months on end? Drop teaching for fishing? Live in the most faraway place in New Zealand, if not the world?'

'Yup, it's a great life all right isn't it?' I said.

'No,' she said.

She picked up her bag and left the house, and that was that, really. I went back to work at the *Otago Daily Times* for a few months then helped start Radio Otago. We leased the boat, and it sank, and the insurance left nothing over, and we began our marriage flat broke, and scarcely knowing each other, except that we each believed the other could be a little unreasonable at times.

The remarkable thing was that through all of those months Sally never wondered whether I'd turn up; nor, when I did, did she wish that I hadn't. We'd stayed in love since.

Now we had been married for thirty-seven years. Henry had lived until he was seventeen. He was so old the dog ranger declared an amnesty. Our two sons had finished four university degrees between them and were starting their first business.

I'd become smug. I'd begun dispensing anodyne advice.

I felt that somehow we'd discovered the secret, even if we had not a clue what it was. I wrote about the ingredients of a happy marriage: love, labour, luck, lust, laughter. Yet love, I'd found, took many forms. Most lit my life. As for the rest, I just ducked.

Huy was home to an armada of high-powered rigid inflatable boats (RIBs), those overpowered inner tubes you saw dashing after America's Cup yachts in great clouds of spray. Which they did on the River Meuse too before entering the little port and disgorging their passengers, crowds of excited children. This, the harbourmaster told us, was the annual outing for disadvantaged children.

I asked how you qualified as disadvantaged in Belgium.

'You know,' he said. 'Disadvantaged.'

How nice to live in a country, I thought, where you could put things right with an Evinrude.

Rain was falling in great, wet drops when we set off for Namur in the morning. The first of the two locks was all right. We went through on our own. The second was named L'Ecluse des Grandes-Malades, or lock of the very sick. We should have been warned, even if the lock was named for a nearby cliff rather than the terminally ill. It was horrible.

We went in but the doors did not close behind us. In his control room high above, the keeper was invisible. We waited in the rain, growing colder and more depressed by the minute. A barge finally hove into view. It came into the lock. The doors closed. Then opened again. Another barge. Now we had to move to make way for it. We could scarcely hold the boat against the wind funnelling through the chamber. Our hands were sore from rope burns. The gates closed again and finally we were through, to face the port.

In Namur the Sambre river branched off the Meuse and headed straight for Paris the quick way. A procession of barges turned off the Meuse to make the point.

But we were going the slow way. We could always turn off for Paris later, if we wanted to.

In the meantime we stuck to the Meuse and passed the little blue German boat tied up under a bridge. Her crew waved to us rather forlornly, as streams of water poured onto her from the railings above. It was wet, cold, windy.

Namur was lovely, even in the rain. The river took us past grand old houses and under a bridge and ahead lay the little port nestling below trees on one side and a huge fortress on the other.

First the wind caught as we came alongside, angling us so awkwardly I backed into the stream for another try. Then, when we lay beside the pontoon at last, I made a mess of the stern rope and the back of the boat drifted rapidly away.

Sally, caught as she was disembarking, had to long-jump across the widening stretch of water between wharf and boat, landing on a pontoon which wobbled so dangerously we both thought she'd be pitched in. It would not have mattered much, for we were both drenched. But if you've travelled all day cold and wet, and within grasp of sanctuary you were threatened with ignominy too … well, I crossed my fingers and hoped for the best.

The most insensitive bloke would have sensed disaffection in Sally that day, although it was difficult to wrench frozen facial muscles into an expression of sympathy. She was fed up with the canals. Where were the ones she'd seen in pictures, with all the flowers and colourful boats which had never been belted against concrete walls, and jolly crews who lazed in the sun with little umbrellas in their drinks, rather than being drenched to the marrow and all but chucked into a cold brown river?

She wanted to stay in Namur two nights, at least, to rest, look around, drink some wine, eat some good food. After all, that was the whole idea of a canal cruise.

Before we left New Zealand I'd talked to Kathryn Ryan on her morning show *Nine to Noon* on National Radio. Surely, she'd asked, this was just another way of tripping around, another form of tourism?

I'd hoped not. Sally and I had spent a lot of time on the subject. We'd already been around Europe three times in a van, once on our own, once when our sons were babies, the third time when they were twelve. In vans you zipped through some towns, stopped at others, took in a cathedral here, a castle there, found some semblance of community with other van travellers amid deep discussions about the best places to park, where to get cheap petrol, how to score a free breakfast. You'd stop for a while, perhaps even for a couple of days, but soon you'd want to move on to the next town because there was so much to see, although every place along the way somehow lost a bit of its lustre in the rush.

We'd talked about that a lot before we decided to live on the canals. We'd decided that the important word was 'live'. Both of us abhorred tourism, the vacant business of wandering from place to place picking up tiny snatches of misinformation, bereft of experience and knowledge, collecting items as currency for retailing back home. Tourists always looked as if their pulse rate were nearing zero, like people watching TV, the only difference being that they were passing the picture instead of the other way round. An awful lot of trouble would have been saved if the world had been made inside out so tourists could sit in the middle and watch it revolve around them rather than vice versa.

The Japanese were the world's best tourists, because they recognised the truly stupid nature of what they were doing and had refined their techniques accordingly: they spent their days asleep in buses, waking only to take the photographs of the next attraction for the folks back home, or to shop, or to file into their hotels for the night and go to sleep again.

No, we wouldn't be tourists. Nor would we trip about from place to place. We would live on the canals, move at a walking pace, know where we were, live the way of life. Yep.

So I should have been warned when we reached Namur. Yes, we were anxious to get to France, but we'd cracked through Holland, and now we'd nipped over Belgium at such a pace we'd allowed five days and four nights for an entire nation. How indifferent was that?

Constantly being on the go made Sally cold, miserable, exhausted. I was simply cold and miserable. Why were we moving? Why were we moving so *fast*? In the rain? It was spring; the weather might be better tomorrow. We had a whole year, possibly two.

Looking back now, the answer is clear: I don't know.

We should have stopped right there, talked about the trip and how it was going, gone back to the basics, re-evaluated, but it was all so new to us, living so long on the boat, confronting fresh challenges each day.

Ahead of us lay France and literally hundreds of locks rather than the handful we'd been through so far. Our plans lay in front of us. We were confronting the truth of modern travel: we were concerned with the future, not the present.

Yet here we were in a very fine part of Belgium. From here the country changed, the river carving through the deep valleys of the Ardennes. Huge trees shaded our mooring in Namur. Flowers bloomed in brilliant bands of colour, waiting to be smelled. People idled by and stopped to chat. A little town lay on our side of the river and a much bigger town on the other, both of them so steeped in history it leaked from every street and alleyway. Cafés beckoned. Not 200 metres from the boat was a bar full of welcoming eccentrics. We could get wi-fi, a wireless computer hook-up, from the boat. What more did we want?

We decided to stay three nights in Namur instead of the one we'd planned. Sure enough, the sun came out. We put the sun umbrella on the after-deck, set up the chairs and the table, sat in the warm and drank red wine.

We studied the ancient fortress rising above us on the V formed by the Meuse and the Sambre. It looked impregnable. Part of it was designed by the famous strategist Vauban. He'd made a nice solid job of it. Its vast ramparts stretched for hectares. Whole armies had hidden there in chambers and tunnels now open to tourists.

Yet it had been overrun so often its stone stairs were worn down with all the dashing hither and thither. The Belgian army made a stand there in World War One, probably feeling as safe as their forbears had. The Germans took the place in a couple of days. We climbed its steps, peered over its walls and into mysterious tunnels, marvelled, then went back to our current conflict with a contemporary adversary, just as mighty: American Express.

We'd opened a Euros account in New Zealand then discovered there were only two ways of carrying Euros to Europe without the bank account we didn't have there: cash or travellers' cheques. We didn't like the thought of carrying a year's cash. We'd have to divide it between us. Sally was safe as a vault. My own worry wasn't theft. I'd forget where I'd put it, or I'd lose it.

Yet travellers' cheques were obsolete, weren't they? The bank assured us they were not. In fact, in these days of card theft and electronic mishap, they were regaining their old popularity. So they said. They outfitted us with lots of American Express travellers' cheques.

When we reached Holland I checked the internet. American Express said I could cash them at such and such a bank. The bank said I could not. I rang American Express in Amsterdam. Sorry, said an American voice. All right, I said, I'll come to your office and cash them there. Sorry, he said again. The office was no longer open to the public. But, but, but, I said, this was ridiculous. Go to a money changer in the Damstrak, he said. But they charged like angry heifers, I said. Go to Potsbank, he said, they would do it for 1.75 per cent.

So they did. I gritted my teeth as I took the money. Although 1.75 per cent wasn't much, it piled up over the thousands of Euros we needed to outfit the boat and stake the first weeks of our journey.

The American Express website had better news for Belgium. We could cash our cheques free at a couple of named banks. We went to the first. Go away, they said. On to the second. Bugger off, they said.

Sally and I joined forces and advanced on the bank's main branch in Namur. Sorry, said the teller. Try somewhere else. New York perhaps.

I demanded to see the manager.

Amazingly, he arrived. He spoke English too. I explained the problem. 'Of course we will cash them,' he said. 'We are obliged to. The other places? They are just small branch offices. They did not know.'

We exchanged the maximum amount we could that day, went back the next and did it again. The day after that the bank was closed for the weekend.

The next town, Dinant, was smaller. I anticipated trouble. Obviously, so had the bank manager in Namur. 'Tell them,' he'd said, 'that they must cash your cheques. It is compulsory. Threaten to ring this number.' He wrote it down, on his bank's letterhead, and attached his card for good measure.

When we sailed off to Dinant, I went to the bank, presented the cheques. 'We cannot,' said the teller. 'You can,' I said. She fetched the manager. A pleasant, placatory man arrived. He studied the cheques with a puzzled look. I told him what the Namur manager had said. He shrugged. He telephoned. He cashed the cheques. 'I am sorry,' he said. 'This is the first time for us.'

In France, American Express promised that every post office would cash their cheques, free. I approached the first post office with trepidation and very little anticipation of success. I'd rehearsed my line. '*Je voudrais*,' I said, '*à changer les cheques des voyages Américain Express*.' The teller looked at them. She cashed them. And that was that.

As we left Namur Sally told me she thought she was married to a good man, a better man than I thought I was, and that she'd lived a sweet life. I left the town in high spirits. A little praise beat boring analysis every time.

The final lock of the six we tackled that day had a Tunisian operator. He was the first Belgian lock-keeper we'd seen. Always before they had been invisible behind tinted glass windows high in their control towers above the locks. This one descended from the skies and held the gates while he told us his story. He was effectively a refugee, he said. He hated Moslems and Tunisia wouldn't let him back. He'd taught himself English. He was proud of his command of the language. He was Belgian now. Tunisia could get stuffed.

We moored in Dinant, admired the fine town as we sat on the deck in another warm evening. Next day we rose on the last of Belgium's locks and crossed a border marked only by a long hose snaking down to the water from the back door of a grocery shop. This was the last place we could buy Belgium's cheap fuel. In fact, it was the first place, because the era of cheap fuel in Belgium was over. The news did not seem to have reached the border, however.

We paid 55 Euros for eighty-one litres, all we could cram into our tanks. That worked out at 68 cents, or $NZ1.38 a litre, by far the cheapest we found in Europe, and less than half the price charged by many places in France that year. Then we started the engine and crossed into France.

Chapter Six

Givet was a border town once known for the suspicion of its customs officers and its lack of gaiety. The reputation didn't worry us. We were from Christchurch, whose customs officers may once have been the most baleful in the country — although it was a close-run thing — and ten o'clock in the same era was bedtime. If Christchurch could turn itself around, so could Givet.

As it happened, formalities in the French town were slight. The EU had delivered the coup de grâce to *les douaniers*, suspicious or not. The paperwork now centred upon the *vignette*, the ticket which, hung in our front window, gave access to canals, waterways and locks. We filled out forms for a year's use of the locks and got a remote control to work them. '*C'est tout*?' I asked *l'éclusier* at the end of it all. 'Isn't it *enough*?' the lock-keeper replied in English. Thank God for the EU. The *vignette* was delivered smartly. Welcome to France, the lock-keepers said gaily.

The *vignette* cost 377 Euros, around $750, best value of any piece of paper we've acquired from any bureaucracy anywhere.

The canals in France were slowly being abandoned by commercial traffic, and sustained by a surge in pleasure boating. Some 8,500 kilometres of waterways were now being maintained largely for people like us.

Every lock was a masterpiece of ingenuity, some more than others; each one was different. Some were operated by remote controls like a television set, others by hidden cameras, others by long handles hanging over the canals which you turned, or pulled. Some were opened by hand, by crank handles, or by spoked wheels and chains. Some had easy-to-reach bollards close to the edge, designed so the ropes slipped off easily, some had bollards a long way back from the edge so you became acrobat and contortionist all at once, some had bollards resembling a bullock's head — but harder to lassoo.

Lock-keepers still flourished on parts of the route. In places we had our own lock-keeper for the day. He or she travelled alongside us, opening and closing the locks as we went, and at the end of the day handed us on to another lock-keeper for the next stretch.

Most asked where we wanted to go next day, and at what time we intended to leave, so they could have the first lock ready for us. Some even lived in beautifully-kept, flower bedecked lock-keepers' cottages, just like the ones in the tourist posters. More often, now, the cottages were lived in by people with no connection to the locks, who sometimes put up signs asking you not to bother them; or the cottages were abandoned and slowly falling into disrepair, usually in fully automated sections of canal where you saw an *éclusier* only if something went wrong.

All of this you got for your $750, depending on the size of your boat. Some grizzled at the cost. To us, it was a bargain.

We didn't know any of this in Givet. We were beginners. Besides, it was hard to discuss the intricacies with your mouth full. It was Sunday afternoon, but unusually a shop was still open. We fell upon the baguettes, the Roquefort, *lapin* pâté and the $5 Bordeaux as if we'd been in training for this moment since we'd left home. In a way we had, for we'd found the food so far sustained life without necessarily encouraging it. Besides, everyone told us we'd soon lose weight on the canals, and it was true. All the springing about, chasing ropes, squeezing up and down steps inside and outside the boat and getting around either on foot or on bicycles was paring us down. A few extra calories could make no difference; after all, look at what they did for the French, who scoffed fat as we did green-top milk and stayed irritatingly half our size.

Why did two nations of bakers, the Dutch and Belgians, produce not a decent loaf of bread between them? Apple turnovers and eggy rice tarts were all very well, but quite hard to fit into the toaster.

We were moored in a mysterious kind of marina (we later found others like it here and there as we went through the Ardennes): a port whose floating pontoons, with power and water laid on — presumably partly paid for with EU and government subsidies encouraging small-town enterprise — were falling apart. With about eighty berths, this one was largely barred by the kind of tapes used around accident sites. We ignored them, tied up, and became one of two boats staying free in the port overnight, for ashore the *capitainerie* housing the harbourmaster was deserted.

As for lack of gaiety, how could anyone say such a thing when there was a concert to be held in the town auditorium that very evening?

The concert would celebrate the arrival of spring. Rain dripped on us as we went along to the theatre, where the municipal choir was performing under the direction of a lady whose modest walk spoke of much local acclaim.

'*Bonsoir*,' Sally greeted the woman in the caisse, in her best French. The single word alerted the woman immediately.

'Where are you from?' she asked.

'*Nouvelle-Zélande*.'

We could see her counting the kilometres in her head.

Then: 'You are music-lovers?'

More starved for community actually, although we did not say so. The Mayor read a speech which was easy to follow, as it merely thanked a very long list of people in the international mayoral tradition. Then the choir struck up with 'Sweet Adeline Rose'. Altogether you might have been in Waipukurau but for one big difference: the theatre was packed.

The audience put on the real performance. The concert started thirty minutes late, as people came in, greeted everyone in their row, all of them standing up for the occasion no matter how often it happened, kissed each cheek two, three, four times, discussed sons (a resigned shrug), daughters (what can you do?) and grandchildren (*absolument charmants*), then brought up to date the auditorium at large.

They were an appreciative audience. *Madame la Conductrice* got a standing ovation and a huge bunch of flowers and we got our $20 worth and went off home amid a laughing crowd.

Next morning off we went, past the huge citadel that guards the Meuse over Givet and into the deep river valley. The great press of people, the tombstones of doomed enterprise and the scars of those still working, gave way to the quiet peace of forests, the clear birdsong that follows rain, the grebes and swans on still water no longer brown, but green. Yellow irises sparked its edges, water lilies yet to flower. Cattle — creamy Charolais, of course, what else would fit the picture? — watched us idle by. Fishermen waved — although later in the canals they were sometimes to become surly — from tiny cribs on the water's edge.

We stopped at Revin and tied up to a little Dutch cruiser accommodating an obliging man, a charming woman and a Jack Russell whose mission was to nip at our heels every time we crossed their deck to get ashore.

Flowers covered the quay. They flowed from baskets, beds, anything that would hold enough soil to plant a begonia or petunia. The mass of colour stayed in our retinas when we closed our eyes, like looking at the sun.

Even the commonplaces of living were romantic, in their own way.

Revin's crowded port accommodated a one-size-fits-all shower block.

Everything was more or less in the same room. To get to the men's and women's showers you had to pass the men's open urinal; or from my side of the porcelain, to have a pee you had to be prepared to go public. Men and women dressed and undressed in a common space outside the shower cubicles. The squeamish might have found it difficult yet it all worked out well enough; that is, no one was so hideously embarrassed by the amenities they refused to use them.

We needed gas. But the EU had yet to sweep everything into the same basket, and gas had so far escaped the broom.

'*Non, non, non, non*,' said the woman at the gas depot when I hove into view with my Dutch gas bottle.

'*Pourquoi non*?' I asked. Why not?

'*Non*,' she repeated firmly.

I could see no difference. Both bottles held the same gas. But I bought a new bottle anyway, and lugged it back to the boat, where it proved to be five millimetres greater in diameter than the old bottle. Five millimetres was a tiny amount but enough to stop it going down the hole in my deck, built to fit Dutch bottles exactly. Serious steelwork would be needed to accommodate the French bottle and I wanted to avoid that at all costs, for I suspected all costs would certainly be the outcome. I took the bottle back. Earnest negotiations followed, for I had broken the seal. But my money was refunded and, joy, I spotted a new lightweight plastic bottle, much smaller, which would fit, but held the wrong sort of gas. When would the right sort arrive?

'*Mercredi,*' she said. Wednesday. It was Monday.

'OK, *Mercredi*,' I said. '*Certainement*?'

'*Peut-être Vendredi*.' Perhaps Friday.

'*Certainement ou peut-être*?'

She shrugged. Not Thursday anyway, she said.

What was wrong with Thursday?

'*Nous ne travaillons pas*.' No work Thursday. One of the mysterious public holidays.

Of course, this transcription leaves out the ums, ahs, and false starts.

I studied French at school for three years and learned to read and write it. Before I left for the canals I took Alliance Française courses in speaking the language.

Understanding the French on their home ground was a different matter, however. The French ran their words together. Picking out individual words in a spoken sentence was like being presented with a Brittany *ragoût* and asked to identify the ingredients.

Speaking the language was as fraught. You might know the right words. Pronouncing them properly was another kettle of *poisson*. If you got the emphasis wrong, you got a blank look. You might as well be speaking English, which, however universal elsewhere, was not so in France.

Sally had never taken any French courses, yet she understood the language better than I did. When someone was speaking to us in French they usually turned to her. I would be trying to understand the words; she'd be listening to what they were saying.

Both of us, eventually, could work our way through a conversation in context such as buying groceries, or cashing travellers' cheques, or talking to lock-keepers or a port captain, or even discussing the weather. Once you knew the subject the words followed.

A wider conversation remained difficult. For me it was like a movie when the soundtrack didn't match the pictures. They'd be on their third sentence while I'd just worked out the first and was framing up my reply.

So in Revin the port captain was watching me attaching a hose to fill our water tanks. A simple task, usually. But she had something urgent to say. I didn't understand. She made desperate shushing noises. I looked around for the approaching typhoon. She described great circles with her hands. I wondered if we should take cover.

At last, it dawned. She was saying that I should let the water run around the hose for a while, to clear out any stagnant remains of the last fill. The relief in her face as I understood this simple instruction might have greeted the liberation of Paris.

In Revin we were confronted by one scourge of the Ardennes. This was a very small town. A war memorial rose in its centre, very much like those in small towns all over New Zealand. The difference was that all four sides of this memorial were covered in names. Four boys were from the same family. No Private Ryan here.

World War One had ripped the heart out of this village, stripped it of young men. World War Two had taken another generation. The pattern was the same throughout much of rural France.

Some German boats took down their flags in this part of France, from tact perhaps, or respect, or even guilt.

Herman never did. Herman parked his boat and sat in a deckchair with a look of beatific happiness. He was red-faced, and rotund, and laughing. He was everyone's jolly German. He should have worn leather shorts and braces, although he preferred baggy shorts and T-shirts. He had a thin, nervous, nice wife and a fat red boat. Their dog was the friendliest Rottweiler we ever met. It could have smothered burglars with dribble. Herman wanted his dog to toughen up. I'd walk past his boat and say, 'Here boy!' and the dog would leap over the side and Herman would scream, 'Halt!' The dog would sit there with a grin full of goobs until Herman decided he'd made his point. 'OK,' he'd say, satisfied I'd got his message: his dog was not at just anyone's beck and call. The dog came on at full speed, drooling like a steam locomotive, and I'd need a crack at the unisex showers.

Herman's brother usually tied up next to him. The brother had a little white boat and a big red-haired wife. She talked a lot but I never heard him say a word.

They left Revin one wet morning with the *River Queen* close behind. The heavy rain made the wooded canyons in which we were sailing even greener and deeper.

We travelled to Bogny-sur-Meuse, where the four giant stone warrior sons of Ayman and their equally huge stone horse glowered down on us from a cliff top. Who could be craven under that lowering gaze? I went into the local store and rejoined battle.

Yes, they had the right kind of gas cylinder, with the right kind of gas.

I bought it promptly. Then found my regulator wouldn't fit.

Le Boss called for help. The *bouchier* took off his cap and apron, left his meat counter and together we tackled the problem, brought it to the ground, kicked it around and finally called it quits.

I left it for another day, although whether we'd get another day soon seemed entirely uncertain, for calamity awaited in the first lock of the morrow.

The day was bright. White swans swam among yellow irises. Blue and yellow dragonflies flitted about the boat, landing on sleeves, sitting on knees.

We were travelling with the couple who'd welcomed us alongside in Revin, she outgoing and garrulous, he mild and largely silent.

They were Dutch, however, so they went through the automatic and remote-controlled lock with smooth efficiency. We followed them in. 'Always,' Mr Benny had said, 'come second.'

This time it was a very poor second. The lock filled, the other boat left, we were held up by a rope which refused to flick off a bollard. When it did, a bell began to ring, warning that the lock doors were about to close. I could see us trapped inside until the next boat came along, perhaps from the same direction, when we'd have to go back down, then up again.

Never!

I pushed the throttle hard forward. The idling engine belched a great cloud of smoke.

Now the yellow lights on the lock door were flashing, and the doors began to close. Century-old slabs of wood and iron covered in slime and gashes made me think of that old film about a commando raid on France, when the survivors were paddling their kayak grimly ahead while the harbour gates closed on them. As a boy it had brought me to the edge of my seat. As a man I kicked the seat right out of the way and wished I'd never had the price of admission to the real thing.

We were going to make it, weren't we? A door hit the back of the boat with a bong unmatched by any bell tolling doom in my darkest hours. And stopped, immediately.

We were through! Didn't matter that in leaning over the side to see the damage only a scream from Sally saved us from ramming a bank full tilt instead of in hard reverse amid another great cloud of smoke. Behind us the lock doors stayed where they were, closed to the exact width of my boat's backside.

My first thought was, thank god for safety mechanisms.

My second was, what will I do about the lock?

My third was, let's get out of here. What did they pay lock-keepers for, after all?

So we tied up thankfully in Charleville-Mézières, and awoke next morning to the much more pleasant bells from the nearby church, soft as organ notes, while Charles le Gonzague, Duke of Nevers, who founded the town in the seventeenth century, leant cockily on his bronze sword below. I knew what he was saying: 'I made this.'

Charleville-Mézières was a big town: 60,000 people. The town had been turned over to the Germans so often — four times since 1814 — its citizens were giddy. In 2008 it became famous for the 'Ogre of the Ardennes', a serial killer who went hunting virgins with his wife. Press reports described poor Charleville-Mézières as a bleak north-eastern town whose only previous claim to fame was as the birthplace of the nineteenth-century poet Arthur Rimbaud.

Yet the cafés were full, young people promenaded, tourists wandered. Its brochures featured a woman standing on a bridge looking at the town beside a dog with its paws on the top rail doing the same thing. She was showing it the town's attractions, notably the Place Ducale whose excellent arcades echoed the Place des Vosges in Paris. The dog wore an expression of polite interest.

The Duke had been a smart businessman. One of his industries still flourished in the town. Perhaps his successors did not quite cut *la moutarde*.

They'd built a new marina and camping ground, with sports track, kayaking centre and indoor swimming pool surrounded by parkland. The new marina was a fine amenity. It was also deserted, spaces for more than eighty boats empty while the pontoon on the riverbank outside was crowded.

The reason was this: the functionaries of Charleville-Mézières (for this was a municipal project) built a footbridge over the entrance to their new marina, a splendid bridge, beautifully curved, a joy to walk over. It was also just three metres above the water at its highest point. A large sign said so.

The standard height of bridges and tunnels above the water on French waterways averaged about three-point-six metres, allowing most boats to pass underneath with no trouble. If the height were to be lowered, the canals would become impassable for some vessels and for others, such as the *River Queen*, canopies would have to be taken down, masts lowered, and windscreens folded flat. All of this could be done; but it was bothersome, and when there was an alternative outside the marina, well, let's put laziness aside and just say most chose to moor on the river.

'Where is your boat?,' asked the woman in the *capitainerie*, which doubled as the camping ground office.

'On the pontoon,' I answered, and seeking to make a point, I added: 'because we cannot get into your marina.'

'*D'accord*,' she said, as if there was nothing to be done, "*C'est trop petit*.' I thought I detected a note of resignation, and nodded apologetically. The bridge, as she said, was too small.

But the bridge proved not to be three metres high. A fellow-voyager measured it by the simple expedient of driving under it, and found it to be at least three and a half metres high, which was the height of his bimini, or sun-roof. A height of three and a half metres would allow most vessels to pass underneath, into the grand, new, deserted marina.

A new sign would make the millions they spent on the marina a good investment. It would also be much cheaper than a new footbridge.

Why did the sign remain unchanged? Well, why were shops closed apparently randomly, gas cylinders just a tiny bit different, internet cafés as rare as Toyotas, computer keyboards so different from the world's standard they turned any sentence into code, bureaucrats as whimsical as Sarkozy's politics? Because that was France and that, of course, was the very reason we all were there.

We needed another telephone because the global roaming we'd organised on our New Zealand cellphone was stupidly expensive. We never could access the messages Vodafone assured us would be so easy to retrieve, so we left the phone turned on, when it would always ring in the small hours of the morning. That morning it had rung and a man invited us over to his new house for a drink. Where? I asked. In Titirangi, he said, and was this Ben?

We decided to buy a French pre-pay card for our mobile in Charleville-Mézières. The business was complicated … still, first a pre-pay card, next the world. I was feeling cocky about my French. I got my come-uppance: I asked a young woman in a boulangerie whether they were open the next day, which

I knew was one of France's many holidays. She looked at me as if I were mad. I asked again. She looked scared. I cut out the chat and reduced it to two words: '*Ouvert demain*?' Open tomorrow? She looked around for help in case this maniac was also *dangereux*. Defeated, I retreated. And yes, next day the boulangerie was open.

We set off from Charleville-Mézières one bright morning in mid-May. We had to make a decision here. We could stay on the river heading south towards the Mediterranean. Or we could turn off, head for champagne country, perhaps stop in Reims for the famous cathedral, then tootle a mere couple of hundred kilometres on to Paris. But the first part of that journey promised forty-six locks in only 106 kilometres, almost a lock every couple of kilometres. We knew that if we stuck to our southward route we'd be facing much worse than that, lock-wise. That was later, however. This was now. We had been through comparatively few locks by then. They still worried us.

Ahead of us the Meuse shone in sunlight. Water lilies sprouted flashes of yellow. Irises laid gold along the banks. Fiery poppies grew thick in the fields. Clouds of soft white fluff billowed gently down the river. Iridescent blue butterflies danced in the warm air with huge dragonflies, now black and yellow.

We chose the river.

Polite grey herons stood to attention as we passed, immaculate in pin-stripes. Water-fowl roosted in floating nests, fish rose to the surface, greatly agitating the fishermen so evenly spaced along the riverbank, and here was Ratty, his coat a rich brown in the morning light, diving for his hole in the bank with a stroke of his strong tail. Perhaps he was thinking of lunch, although in a different way from the fictional Ratty: the French made water rats into pâté, *pâté de ragondin*.

The old towpath vanished and reappeared; on the opposite side, trees dipped their boughs into the water.

A lock-keeper took off his hat and bowed deeply when we thanked him for his efforts. He pointed at our little back flag with the silver fern.

'All Blacks!' he said, and gave us a thumbs-up. '*Bonne chance*!' Then: 'Where will you go today?'

'Dun.'

'And tomorrow?'

'Verdun.'

'What time will you start?'

'Eight o'clock.'

A pause, a *moue*. 'Non. Eight-thirty'.

'*D'accord*,' we said.

We weren't in France to muck around with the French way of life. We were there because of it. Early starts were a stupid New Zealand habit best left behind.

Bells rang the hour from village churches along the way, sometimes the same hour; who cared if ten o'clock came a little later in some places than others? Certainly not the man who ran a stop on the way, grandly titled Meuse Nautic on the chart which declared it to offer all sorts of services to the cavalcade of *voyageurs*.

We stopped there for fuel alongside a German couple taking their yacht through France to the Mediterranean; he plump and genial, she lean and muscular and looking as if she'd like nothing more than a romp in the mountains.

Two tired-looking pumps reclined by the bank, as if they'd last passed fuel around 1996. Nothing else equipped the Meuse Nautic. No buildings, not so much as a hut. A sign invited us to press a button on a concrete wall. We did. A crackly recording told us that if we really wanted fuel, and the owners weren't there, we should use our credit card. We checked. The owners weren't there. No one was. The countryside seemed entirely uninhabited.

The credit card slot was marked with a huge cross, and in case we were unsure of the message, it had been blocked off with a couple of kilometres of black tape.

Time passed. We talked. Then chatted in a desultory manner. Then lapsed into long silences. We watched a coot bobbing in its nest on the river, fanned gently by a shading branch.

A Weimaraner, sleek and brown and bred for hunting, bounded up with a stick the size of a log in its mouth. The dog galloped through our small group like Boadicea and her chariot, the stick gouging limbs on all sides, then turned to mop up the walking wounded. Its owner, a woman, appeared, we hoped with bandages. But she offered something far better: hope. She tried the button too. She appeared cross with the response. This was a slight upon her country. She dug in for the long haul. She borrowed a mobile and began telephoning. A dozen calls later and she was on track. The man who owned the pumps was working at a camping ground on a lake not far distant.

She kept going. The Germans, whose phone it was, began looking uncomfortable. The fuel was getting very expensive. At last, she looked triumphant. She had reached him. He would come. In twenty minutes, thirty at most, and just in case, she waited with us, while her dog galloped back and forth with its wooden sword, sparing only its owner.

Just as we were about to call for blood transfusions, the man who owned the pumps appeared in his tiny white van. Perhaps the vehicle was small only by comparison, for he was huge. The French gene had passed him by. Everything a Frenchman was supposed to be — handsome, elegant, charming — he was not. He was short, fat, exceedingly ugly and as it turned out, greedy.

First he pulled a large stick out of an underground tank, read it with much frowning and shaking of head, wiped it on the grass and replaced it complete with dirt and weeds. He filled first the German boat, then our own, then he grew fins and bit us all for $2.80 a litre.

So the scene was set for the next stretch of river.

The day, bright as hope itself, turned sullen as we entered the war zone.

All through the Ardennes little villages, even the smallest, heralded the tragedy with memorials of stones packed tight with names: *Mort pour France,* 1914–1918. So many dead, a countryside robbed of youth.

Consenvoye did badly in both wars and was much damaged in the last one although its eighteenth-century church, well-placed beside a bar, survived.

A little down the road was a German cemetery. Beneath its black iron crosses lay 11,148 German soldiers killed in World War One. Some were unknown, and some were Jews, for in that war they were allowed to die for their country rather than because of it. But most were named on the crosses and in a list left in a little locker at the gates alongside a visitor's book. There'd been a few visitors that year, not many; some from the United States who'd left messages in German.

The cemetery and the books were pristine, which spoke volumes about tolerance in the nearby town which had suffered so much. The cemeteries of the French, and the Americans, carried white crosses in the traditional way of good versus the evil black, although it didn't matter; the sadness was overwhelming no matter what the colour. All those laughing young men.

In Verdun the Great War had become an industry, for this was a depressed region whose economy had taken another blow from the competition of newly-industrialised nations. Villages were full of abandoned factories and empty shops. Death had filled the gap, at least partly.

A French military cemetery accommodated ranks of Moslem soldiers' graves, as well as a Canadian bomber crew whose headstones were poignant with the grief of parents, sons, daughters.

A stone sculpture buried in a corner near the cemetery's entrance carried an especially bitter tableau: a man in working clothes, bloodied and bound, hanging Christ-like from a post carrying the inscription: 'To the victims in both wars of the barbarian Nazis tortured and shot.' Underneath were the graves of a local doctor and an unknown Frenchman executed by the Germans in 1944.

The road outside carried busloads of tourists to old trenches, an ossuary containing the bones of 130,000 unknown soldiers, remnants of the Maginot line (there was a statue of its designer striking a pose, despite his creation's famous failure), the ruins of the fort of Souville which was said to have saved Verdun, although as that town was largely razed it was a Vietnam-like rescue.

The village of Fleury-devant-Douamont survived the invasions of 1792, 1814 and 1870 but met its end on February 21, 1916. Then it was taken and retaken sixteen times, completely destroyed and along with eight others never rebuilt. Now its streets and houses were marked with posts: here the Rue St Nicolas, where there was a wash-house and a farmer's house, there the Rue Mathelin where lived the baker, the plumber and the wine-grower. The townsfolk never gave up: the collection of shell craters and old stones still had a legal entity and a mayor.

Maurice and Denise from Waikanae first appeared in Verdun.

They'd bought their little black and cream boat from its boat-builder owner in Holland sight unseen. The boat was deserted when we arrived. Its neatness was intimidating. I coiled our ropes defensively and fixed them to the rail. When Denise arrived, she said, 'Look at the ropes on that boat Maurice, we'll have to tidy up our act.'

Their boat had suffered from the weed choking the waterways that spring; it clogged their engine cooling water, and the engine overheated. They'd stopped it then ran aground, and had spent hours waiting for a mechanic, who worked far into the night dismantling their engine and replacing its ruined impellor.

Maurice was feeling ill. They'd been to the local hospital, where tests showed his heart to be in good sound condition. The doctor gave him a prescription for some strong heart medication. 'I think it's the stress,' said Maurice. 'I know what would cure it,' said Denise who I thought had had enough of canals for a while. 'A For Sale sign.'

But we were leaving next day, with Carla and Paul, a Dutch couple we'd met on and off along the way with their small white terrier Chica. Carla had wanted to swap books. Sally was about to give her an Anita Brookner when she remembered she'd hidden 500 Euros in it. Sally had stashed a lot of cash around the boat: in crockery, books, pots, a packet containing a bottle of Optrex. She kept a list of hiding places written in a notebook, in code. If she lost her mind, we were broke. 'Oh,' she said, 'I had it in Virginia Woolf then I moved it to Anita Brookner.'

Was Brookner a safer bet than Woolf? Carla was noncommittal. She gave us one of Colin Dexter's Inspector Morse mysteries in return.

We were booked into the first lock at 8.30 a.m; the two Frieslanders who'd tied their boat to ours for the night had booked for 9.30. Next morning we set off in company with Carla and Paul — to find the Frieslanders, and another large, expensive Dutch boat waiting at the lock ahead of us.

Paul was outraged. That his countrymen could behave so! 'It is our time,' he declared, thumping his watch. 'No,' said the other boat, 'it is ours!' The Frieslanders remained silent. They were from the far north of Holland and even in the Netherlands extremities were mysterious, like Southland.

We said nothing either, for we were transfixed. The Dutch, so good at peaceful co-existence, were on a collision course. Everyone was angry.

Suddenly Paul rammed his boat into gear. 'Come on,' Carla shouted to us. We followed them, bumper to bumper, weaving through the other two boats, dodging bellows. 'Sorry,' I said, 'I don't speak Dutch,' although the opposing skipper was outlining his grievances in rather too fluent English.

The manoeuvre was illegal, of course; overtaking in the lock chute was forbidden. We had right on our side, we believed. We were fighting over perhaps twenty minutes only, but the port of St Mihiel where we were going was small; second place meant we'd be doubling up.

Trouble, such as it was — for there was very little of it — usually seemed to involve the larger, richer boats whose crews seldom joined the community of kindred spirits gathering at any stop. They paid for their own space. Naturally they were seen as wankers.

The Kiwi way was not to let ourselves be pushed around. But it was not the Dutch way. When we arrived I said to Paul: 'You have the killer instinct.' He looked crestfallen. It was not his style.

The second Dutch boat went by with their noses in the air, but the Frieslanders stayed. They tied up beside Paul and Carla, who invited them over for drinks. Before the afternoon was gone they were exchanging advice and good wishes. The Frieslanders proved to be father and son although Paul said of the son, 'I don't think he has things all in a row.'

We watched them exchanging advice and good wishes as the soft light fell around us. Unemployment here was high. Youths were learning to juggle so they could become buskers. I remembered New Zealand in the nineties.

One young man came over to talk as we watched fish plopping in the still river. He was full of eagerness and energy and hope. He warned of a coming thunderstorm, told us of the limestone cliffs around the town and asked wistfully where we were going, and it was only later, when thunder rolled around our heads and lightning lit the white cliffs that I realised that we'd been talking in French but had found a common language.

That evening we went to the church of St Etienne, which housed the best-known work of the sculptor Ligier Richier. Thirteen life-sized marble figures depicted the entombment of Christ but we were there for the Roman centurions, who gambled slyly on the side. I thought I recognised the two of them.

Sally wandered through the market hall, one of the very finest. Stone cornucopia of fruit and vegetables and swathes of flowers sculpted in tiles decorated the ornate exterior. The inside was bare; no market that day.

I cycled through a forest pocked with craters, criss-crossed with old trenches. Evening was closing in. A fox crept onto the road, watched me for a moment then fled into a field of young wheat, leaping through the rows so his head and tail popped out of the green stalks every few seconds then vanished into a copse on the far side.

Clouds gathered. Huge drops of rain began falling. In a moment I was in the midst of another thunderstorm. I saw what seemed to be a stone shelter beside the road and ducked into it. The rain fell quiet as I looked around.

I was in a concrete cavern, its roof strengthened with heavy steel beams, slits in the walls letting in grey light. I took a torch from my bag for comfort; the place was dank, sinister.

A dirty blanket and an empty bottle hinted at its most recent inhabitant and I thought I heard the sound of footsteps running away through a tunnel. Perhaps it was the ghostly sound of boots, for clearly I was in an old German bunker from the first World War.

One steel and concrete-lined room led to another, and another; tunnels led off under the hill, shafts went down into the bowels, stone steps rose to stone-lined trenches so perfect they seemed ready for another war, should anyone care to emulate the wartime generals in stupidity, or to believe their grandiose claims. How the French, in trenches shored up with wood and bundles of branches, fighting with inferior weapons, must have quailed. Instead, town statues depicted them in heroic stances, grimly repelling the invader or saving women and babies.

French troops died of thirst while the Germans drank running water pumped from springs, and lit their dugouts with electric lights. Their officers furnished their messes with wall-hangings and even a grand piano. Their trenches still commanded the heights, often adorned with elaborate arched entrances and inscriptions.

Down on the River Meuse Herman the German and his wife had donned large blue swimming togs and were splashing around near their barge. The French waterways were often polluted and the river here became an open sewer at busy times like this. A few French townspeople watched curiously as the pair frolicked in the water.

I thought I heard le coq crow.

A lone black kite soared above us searching for prey as we left St Mihiel next morning, Dutch crews holding our stern as we turned about in our own length to double around the sandbank lying beside our mooring.

We were bound for Commercy, where lay a hunting lodge built by Stanislas, the voluptuous gent whose sensual lips adorned many statues in this part of France. Stanislas had been king of Poland, twice. That ended in tears, but he had the good fortune, or good sense, to marry his daughter Maria to Louis XV, and the French king handed over the Duchy of Lorraine in exchange.

Later we caught the bus from Toul to Nancy to walk in the Place Stanislas, where the duke had been at his most elegant, creating a plaza so elliptical it was Parisian.

His hunting lodge proved to be a vast, elegant palace whose grounds once ran through avenues of trees across the river and away into the middle distance. We tried to trace them as we stood on the palace's first floor surrounded by the work of local artists who'd collected it together for an exhibition but seemed preoccupied with the bizarre.

The interior was a disappointment. The lodge had been burned out by a negligent incendiary bomb dropped by Americans in 1944. It was restored, at least in utilitarian fashion, in the 1950s. On the riverside under its walls lay a huge *lavoir*, one of the places where women until the sixties and even the seventies beat their washing against stones worn flat and smooth over the centuries, rinsing them in an ingenious series of pools. The *lavoirs* ran from industrial, no more than a row of worn stones beside a river, to picturesque, housed in heavily-timbered buildings, many of them now restored and preserved. A palace full of courtesans must have generated a lot of dirty washing, especially if they were all as rotund as the fine duke. Against such splendour the village lay modestly.

The next day we set off for Pagny-sur-Meuse. 'Good luck,' cried a Dutch traveller. 'We'll need it,' Sally called back, and we did.

We had five locks that day, every one of them devilishly crafty, with bollards nicely out of reach and their operating mechanisms all set a good distance from any likely mooring point, so we had to do what we'd vowed not to do and climb slimy ladders.

The Pagny Post Office said it was open, but lied. Everything else was closed too, for this was Monday; except, fortunately, the boulangerie, where Madame sold us a quiche Lorraine on its home turf, a delicious custard tart, a bottle of limoncello and a fine bottle of lemon juice.

Visitors were so rare that in the evening when I went for a walk on a long, straight road I passed houses whose curtains seemed to twitch. Within ten minutes a police car cruised slowly past, did a U-turn and came back for another look. Not from round here, they concluded, but harmless, even if he was walking. They left me alone. Then we set out for Toul.

Before we reached the town we had to negotiate the 866 metre Foug tunnel, our first long tunnel. That day it was unlit and as dark as, well, an 866 metre tunnel through solid rock.

Sally sat on the foredeck and focussed our powerful spotlight first on one side then the other. It gave me the creeps. Sharp lumps of hewn rock burst from the darkness, ready to hack their initials in the side of the boat. Sally would call, too far this side, or too far that. When her voice rose to a scream I knew she was serious.

The 866 metres crept by metre by metre. The light at the end of the tunnel seemed no closer. Sally shone the beam on the middle of the arched roof above; all I had to do then was keep the silver fern on its little flagstaff at the front of the boat directly under the beam. It worked. We came through without a scratch.

Then we went downhill in the locks for the first time. It was much easier than going up, despite horror stories. People sat around in the evenings nattering about ropes catching and threatening to capsize the boat as the water level in the lock fell.

We all carried sharp knives to cut the ropes if this happened. Mine was a fish-filleting knife I'd found on the boat. Sally's was a vicious-looking blade like a small machete, sharp as a razor.

'You must be careful,' Paul said. 'Do not stand in the middle of your boat. We know of someone who was standing there when his rope jammed around a bollard on the way down. He grabbed his knife and cut it. The boat fell back into the water, but then it bounced up again, and as it did the cabin top rolled over and crunched him against the side of the lock. He was very badly hurt.'

We entered the first of the staircase of locks running down to Toul as nervously as I remembered once walking into a cave full of wetas. The water fell gently. So did we.

The next one too. We swapped places with Paul and went first, ignoring Mr Benny's rule. We seemed to be on the brink of a long drop, the valley spreading below us, Toul majestic in the distance. Down the hill we went, lock by lock, as if on broad, easy stairs descending to a magnificent garden.

We tied up in a large marina within sight of the city walls and walked through an ancient gate in the fortifications to the Hôtel de Ville, or town hall, usually the grandest building in any town for French councillors and bureaucrats had something in common with their New Zealand counterparts: they liked living plumply at the ratepayers' expense.

We were eating white goat's cheese and black prunes and planning French hot dogs for dinner (*saucisse à cuire non fumée de Meuse* in a fresh baguette with caramelised onions, tomato paste, French mustard, with Camembert for me and Roquefort for Sally) when Denise appeared.

They had travelled from Verdun to Toul, where Maurice had collapsed on the street. She had hailed a passing motorist, a young Frenchwoman who immediately bundled them both into her car and rushed them to hospital. Maurice was promptly surrounded by specialists. The cardiologist could find nothing wrong with his heart, the haematologist and the other doctors giving him a clean slate also.

The cardiologist looked at the pills Maurice had been prescribed in Verdun. 'Throw them in the rubbish tin,' he advised. The French loved drugs, and the Verdun doctor had worked on the principle that if one drug is good, a much stronger one must be better. All of this attention cost Maurice nothing in Verdun, $100 in Toul. Still, they were worried. What was wrong?

They came over for a drink. They'd decided to leave their boat in Toul. Maurice made plans for what would be done to it while they returned to New Zealand until next year. Denise looked thoughtful. She told Sally, always a sympathetic audience in such matters, of her fears, the sleepless nights, her inability to eat breakfast on departure days. The locks. Maurice was dismissive. 'Nothing has happened. We've got through everything.'

True, but I could hear the chords responding deep within Sally. The two women began chorusing like pipe organs.

Sally was grieving over her lily. Its delicate blooms had delighted her for weeks. Now one lay on the cabinet like yesterday's wedding dress. 'It's what they do,' she said. 'Slowly disappear.' But it was more than that. 'My lily has got me through,' she said sadly.

Maurice was feeling better, but still was not well. 'Perhaps I have a virus,' he said. 'Perhaps it's the water,' said Denise.

Duncan arrived from the hire boat yard which Maurice had asked to look after his boat. Duncan was English but his accent had a strange tang. 'I've been in France for twenty-five years,' he said. 'A lot of people think I'm South African.'

Maurice was cheerful. Duncan would make a few changes to his boat, get rid of its faults, make it better. Denise looked as if she wished Duncan could make Maurice better too, although Duncan had definitely lifted his mood.

Next morning Maurice looked better still, despite he and I emptying a bottle of Medoc the night before.

So, they were staying, we were leaving. I was sad to lose them. They were kindred spirits. We talked to each other as people could only do when they knew the nuances of Waimate and Waipu. They gave us an All Black pen as a parting gift. It was nice and fat and easy to hold.

I wished I'd had it yesterday, to give to an *éclusier* entranced by our silver fern.

'The French are…' his hand had flicked like a snake. 'But the All Blacks are…'; he'd crouched like a weightlifter in a cling and jerk. He'd looked glum, and later I learned that the All Blacks had beaten a lack-lustre French side the night before. I'd tried to cheer him up in a patronising kind of way: 'But you beat us in a World Cup game once.'

I'd looked up the right word in French. '*Ecrasés*,' I said. Flattened.

Not for the last time.

Chapter Seven

At seven it had already been light for a couple of hours, and a delicious smell of newly-baked baguettes hung over Richardmenil.

Madame la Boulangère was fresh as her bread. In boulangeries across France Monsieur le Boulanger was kneading and moulding and baking out the back while Madame greeted customers with a smile as wide as a celebrity presenter's.

For this was a show of strict conventions.

You entered. Madame wished you *bonjour*. You urged her to have a very good day in return. Madame passed some pleasantries about the weather. You agreed merrily, especially if you had not understood a word. You asked for a baguette, or a croissant *ordinaire*, or if you were feeling expansive, a croissant *au beurre*, for in France butter was not to be regarded as the enemy within. It was compulsory, like wine. You counted out the change into a little dish on the counter. Madame then counted it too. '*Parfait*,' she'd say. '*Au revoir. Bonne journée, m'sieur*.' '*Au revoir*,' you'd agree. Not a single step was to be missed under pain of the polite silence that, loud as a fire alarm, told you that you'd made a gaffe,

One of my delights in France was getting up early and going into the village for the morning's baguettes and croissants. The fragrance, the Thai-silk touch of the long, golden sticks and the joy of the new day.

We'd left Toul through vast locks, big enough for ships, but we were alone in their slimy depths. The countryside bored Sally; it lacked New Zealand's drama, and the locks both scared and upset her, the last because they were so dirty. Constantly filling and emptying with dirty brown water, the waste of boats and countryside, the oil and grease of passing machinery, they were bound to be a little untidy. Sally hated mess. She looked at the grimy, dripping lock sides as if they would be much the better for a good wipe and a bottle of Jif. She wondered whether the locks would get better. Of course they would, I said, but she didn't believe me.

Sally's eyes were beginning to darken. One night she said, 'I just don't like the canals, especially the locks. They're dank and claustrophobic. And boring.'

How could it be?

I'd read the books, and the weblogs, and we'd seen Rick Stein's television odyssey through the Canal du Midi and thrilled over the romance of it, and we'd watched our close friends Trish and Glenn grow to love the canals as a way of life, and listened to their friends regarding their lives in New Zealand as mere gaps in the real thing on the French waterways. No one had mentioned this.

The locks certainly didn't bore me; I was still too much on edge. The countryside, forests, the wide, still Moselle in its wooded valley, soothed me. I knew Sally's mind was made up. Only sheer magic would change it now. I watched her spirits slowly sink in French valleys beaten up by wars and world markets. She longed for the Pacific's light.

The second to last lock of the day had been back down to intimate proportions. Its cranks and handles were wound by a slatternly woman who obligingly let me do most of the work while she berated Sally for putting her line around a ladder, which you're not supposed to do but everybody does. In her spare time she argued with her ugly daughter, who looked much older than her mum. We tied to the riverbank, where the last light of the day caught a heron, lighting it like a statue. Tomorrow would be another day and sure enough, it was.

Next morning I heard my first '*Achtung*!' outside a war comic.

It came from a boat called *Chérie*, and *la chérie* was a stern woman watching our approaching bow with the stare of an Alsatian observing a postie coming through the front gate.

We were doing sixteen locks together. This was number one. The day had started badly.

We had arranged with *l'éclusier* to be at the first lock at eight-thirty a.m., with the *Chérie.* Both boats were there on the dot. So were two Dutch boats, both of them barges. They were in front of us.

The *Chérie*'s skipper emerged from the high captain's chair on his aft deck. He wore a pair of very tight shorts and nothing else. His hair lay as perfectly as a bowling green. His bronzed torso had the shape and colour of a glass of Pilsner. He was tiny. He bounded around his deck haranguing the Dutch boats like a bantam rooster sorting out his chooks.

One of the Dutch boats shouted back. They were booked, yelled the skipper. For eight-thirty. Impossible, shouted the German, eight-thirty was ours. He opened his throttle, passed one of his antagonists and headed for the lock.

The second Dutch boat was too smart for him. It moved into the lock and stopped, half in, half out.

Its crew regarded the Germans implacably. They weren't going to move. The Germans could bugger off. It promised to be a very long day.

For fifteen minutes the two sides glowered at each other. Then the Germans retreated.

The skipper climbed off his boat and strutted off to have it out with the lock-keepers. His back was full of muscles, every one of which twitched indignantly.

We saw him stalking back. They hadn't just booked in four boats for eight-thirty, when the lock could only take two at a time, he said. They had booked in six! But he looked relieved. Honour was satisfied. This wasn't personal. This was just the French doing what they did so well. The French! He was almost smiling.

He and his partner went through the locks like robots. He would bring his boat to a smart halt at the front of the lock, she'd handle the ropes and catch the bollards and she was taking no nonsense from them. Then we fitted in behind.

The locks were mechanical; the gates were wound open and closed with cranks. The convention was to get off your boat and help. The lock-keepers liked it, and New Zealanders liked helping; besides, it was faster.

But the German wasn't going to help. He had paid for his *vignette*. Let them do it.

He watched me impassively each time I marched past him to do my stint on the crank. After six locks I was growing tired. After ten I was cranky myself. I tried to hide my irritation behind a bit of passing conversation.

'Nice boat,' I said. 'Is it an Altena?' My boat was an Altena. I thought them excellent. The German looked at me contemptuously. 'This,' he said, 'is a Linssen.' The BMW of boats. I gave up, and we kept to ourselves until we arrived in the town of Epinal.

The town had had a bad press in the cruising guides. It was said to be a dull city, with an ugly yacht basin and nothing except a cartoon museum to commend it.

We were not surprised by the museum. Rural France had lots of museums. Embroidery museums, and museums of felt, weapons, bricks, tiles, foundries, mines; the French government and EU subsidies promoted small town tourism. They scored a fifty per cent success rate on our boat; Sally went to a few, and loved them. I preferred the cafés.

But the short canal leading to Epinal was beautiful. It travelled over a little aqueduct, then wound through trees and fine houses to a yacht harbour we liked at first sight. The city rose behind it as prettily as any guidebook photographer could hope for.

The Germans were already there, in the last remaining spot on the stone quay. I spotted an empty pontoon on the less-favoured side and headed for it. 'Is better?' the German shouted across the water. I shrugged. How the hell would I know?

He cast off his lines in a trice and sped after me, taking another vacant pontoon directly behind. We both tied up. A man appeared at the cabin door almost immediately. He was wearing his badge of office, a leather satchel. Quick off the mark, I thought, reaching for the Euros jar, then I realised he had a problem.

'Your boat,' he said, 'was travelling far too fast.'

'*Mon bateau*?'

I was amazed. I'd idled across the harbour.

'*Oui*,' he said. 'The harbour is very shallow, and not only that, the wake bounced off the stone walls, and that makes it worse. You were going too fast,' he said again.

'*Non*,' I said.

'*Oui*,' he said.

'*Non, non, non.*'

'*Oui, oui, oui.*'

'*Je ne le croix pas.*' For I didn't believe it.

'*Moi, je le croix!*'

A treacherous thought occurred to me. I pointed to the German boat behind.

'He,' I declared, 'was going faster than I was.' Which indeed he had been. The Frenchman was undeterred by this crafty attempt to shift the blame, even to a nation so blameworthy.

'*Non*,' he said. 'You.'

I apologised. Placated, he took the money and went on to the Germans. I watched. Boy, were they going to get it!

The two chatted for a while. The Frenchman gestured in my direction. They both laughed. The Frenchman left. There was no justice, I thought. I went inside and closed the door. Well, said Sally, you probably *were* going too fast. I sulked. Sally doesn't sulk, but I do.

A tap on the door interrupted. The German stood outside. He extended his hand. 'Hello,' he said. 'I am Herbert. That is Liana on the boat.' She waved. 'We would like to invite you aboard our boat for a drink.'

We climbed onto his immaculate *bateau*, sat in padded teak chairs on the teak deck.

'Picon?' Herbert asked.

We had no idea what Picon was. But it sounded good. 'Certainly.'

He fetched two more long glasses. He poured beer into each. Then he added the bright orange liqueur.

'Santé!' he said, although we were not so certain of good health. But I thought of what we mixed with beer back in New Zealand — lemonade, raspberry, wine. Couldn't be worse. In fact, it was better.

'To Liana,' said Herbert. 'It is her birthday.'

'Herbert has a Plan,' said Liana. She produced it. The plan was written like a graph. The towns along the way were carefully plotted. Each had a date alongside it. The dates were much closer together than the towns. Herbert was covering a lot of water in not a lot of time.

'I am going to Lyon,' he said, 'and I only have three weeks' holiday.'

He was planning to go to Fontenoy-le-Château next day. To get there he had to go through forty-eight locks. Most canal travellers agree that ten locks and thirty kilometres makes a good day. We drank to Herbert's adventure.

'I am not his wife,' Liana announced. Perhaps she thought we looked all too formidably married. 'We have been together eighteen months only. But I love my Herbert.'

Herbert laughed. We drank to love.

'Now we go to the restaurant,' said Herbert, pointing to the brasserie on the quay. We could see them across the water, Liana towering over little Herbert even at the table, Herbert firmly in command.

Next morning Liana and I walked to the boulangerie. She told me that her life had been difficult, that she'd been married to an alcoholic for thirty years until she could stand it no longer and left him four years ago, that her husband had since stopped drinking and wanted to come back but she would not have it, no, never, that their son would have nothing to do with his father because of the way he'd treated her, that she did, really, love Herbert now.

I suggested her husband must be very sad, too. She looked at me. 'Nuh!'

In the course of buying two baguettes she had become entirely human. So had Herbert.

Back at the boat, something had happened. Herbert came over, his face grave. 'I have a problem,' he announced. 'A big problem.'

He had water in his diesel. He stood there with his water hose in his hand. I drew the obvious conclusion. The fuel and water fillers were often close together on boats, and easy to confuse. 'Ah,' I said, 'so easy to do, to put it in the wrong hole.'

'No, never!' Herbert was so indignant he refused to let me into his engine room to help, showing he was a shrewd judge of diesel mechanics, not to mention girth.

'You go on,' he said. 'We will catch up.'

Yeah, right, I thought, imagining the long, long line of locks ahead, and confident we would never see Herbert or Liana again. We waved goodbye to Liana. Herbert was down in his engine room. We could hear clanking as we passed.

We went up a long flight of locks with our personal lock-keeper. He was a handsome man with lots of curly dark hair and graceful gestures and Sally voted him cutest lock-keeper in all France.

He saw the silver fern. He loved *le rugby*. He loved the All Blacks. What did I think of the Wallabies? Mugs? He bounced around the lock with glee. Mugs! he called. Mugs! passers-by called back. Sally loved him.

At last we reached a long, peaceful stretch on the summit. Our lock-keeper went off with arms full of wine.

We were on the second highest canal in France. Graceful trees brushed our cabin-top, villages snoozed in the sun.

We stopped for the night beside the little village of Chamousey, where we bought delicious *charlottes*: mousse encased in sponge with red and white currants and raspberries on top. They came in little gold boxes. We ate them on the boat, watching three women and a little girl playing statues on a green lawn surrounded by red roses. Their grace delighted us, the warm evening lulled.

Three little boys came to fish. They caught four, the size of herrings, and put them in a bucket of water. They asked politely for a drink of water. Sally poured them some juice. They could speak a little English, which they were learning in school.

How old were they? she asked. They told her: two were eleven and one twelve. '*Et vous*?' one asked. Sally told them. They looked at each other. 'Wow,' they said in French. 'They are a hundred and sixty years old.' They offered me a fishing line. We talked about France. We talked about New Zealand. They asked about kangaroos, which they pronounced *kung*-aroos.

'Do you like the Vosges?' one asked. I was startled. The Vosges? I remembered a sign, several locks back. Of course. That was where we were. The Vosges. I'd fallen into the lassitude of tourism, not even certain where I was. But:

'Yes,' I said. 'It is very beautiful.'

Sally gave them two Florentines each. They looked at each other.

'Perhaps you'd like fish for dinner,' one said. He offered the bucket. Sally was touched. 'Thank you,' she said, 'but we have dinner already.' She gestured at the kitchen, where vegetables for a salad lay on the table.

The boys looked relieved. They gripped the bucket and set off for home. '*Au revoir*.'

By now it was past seven o'clock. There'd been no anxious calls from home, across the canal. France always seemed safe to us, and the boys' parents evidently agreed.

The evening fell into slumberous dark. We were alone, for the town had only a single mooring.

New Zealand seemed light-years away, and just as remote when we reached Forges d'Uzemain.

The village had all but disappeared. No matter how small the place, it could usually boast four essentials: a boulangerie, a café/bar, a beauty parlour and a chemist.

Only the green neon cross of a pharmacy shone from what had been the main street of Forges d'Uzemain; the village had been honed down to its bones and in a nation notorious for over-prescribing (although the French thought it was just right), and an ageing rural population, the chemist could always count on repeat business.

It was a hot day, and a long one, and one lock had not been working, or rather had worked too well: its gates would open, the lights would turn green; but before we could enter, the gates would close and the lights turn red. The lock would empty without us, and repeat the performance on the other side: the gates would open, the lights turn green, then red, etc.

A Swedish yacht on one side of the lock, and the *River Queen* on the other, circled for an hour, cursing the thing as it filled and emptied, until an *éclusier* showed up, pressed a button and fixed it in a trice.

The wide, shady pool at Forges was as welcome as the bottle of cool Mâcon white which we lost no time in opening. A couple of fishermen dipped their lines. The village was so quiet it might have been uninhabited. Even the bread came by van.

A voice called in the silence. 'Ah, you start without me.' It was Klaus.

Klaus was a huge, tanned German who looked twenty years younger than his age, sixty-seven. He was jockeying a speedboat barely disguised as a cabin cruiser, taking it from Germany to Spain, where he had a house.

His boat, *Anne*, was named after his wife. The boat was fibreglass. It was only seven metres long. Every slicked-back line of its hull, each flame-shaped window, all the soft tucks in its white upholstery and both of its powerful rumbling petrol engines suggested a boat not really suited to the canals.

He was travelling so slowly that his twin engines kept fouling their spark plugs, a condition I imagined extended to Klaus himself. Klaus longed for the Saône River and a stretch of water where he could hit sixty kilometres per hour instead of six, and feel the wind in his long, golden hair.

He seemed designed for the Costa Brava too.

But Klaus was configured for anything. He enjoyed his life. The heat, the frustrations of that day; they were all part of it. He threw his head back and roared, 'I have had a *wonderful* day.'

His crew was his son-in-law Mick, an Australian who wore surf shorts with Billabong inscribed in large letters over the backside. Mick had been a fitter and turner in Melbourne and of course had been made redundant in the early nineties. He had retrained as a mechanical engineer but could not find a job. His German wife, whom he'd met and married in Australia, had suggested they go and live in Germany for a while. So they had; Australia, as New Zealand had done so often, lost a well-trained young man, probably forever, since he now had a good job and was embedded in his new country. He lived in a house next door to his father-in-law, Klaus.

I asked if he wanted go back home. He looked wistful.

But Klaus looked happy with the arrangement. He telephoned a local farm restaurant. Madame arrived promptly in a van and whisked them off, sat them outside and cooked them a dinner of home-cured ham and fried potatoes. I got the feeling Klaus was used to getting what he wanted.

He'd headed a motorcycle company and still rode a huge Harley-Davidson. When his only daughter had announced she was marrying an Australian, Klaus had sent a friend to check out her intended. The report had come back positive; luckily for Mick, I thought.

Family and friends were taking turns to join him along the way to Spain, a week or so at a time. Not his wife Anne, however. 'She does not like being so far from a beauty parlour,' said Klaus.

'Ah,' said Sally. 'This is a bloke's pastime.'

Klaus's hand flapped, as if swatting away the kiss of death.

Klaus had a problem too. Just as he was leaving he had seen the boat of his dreams in an advertisement, and had bought it sight unseen. He had put his own boat up for sale, and to his surprise he had sold it immediately.

Klaus had meticulously planned his trip to Spain through France. But the boat's new owner wanted it back in Germany; Klaus's new boat was already in Spain. What to do? Simple, he reasoned.

'Klaus is a great planner,' said Mick. 'He loves it.' He'd take the old boat on the trip he'd planned, all the way to Spain, fly back to Germany, collect his car and the boat's trailer, drive to Spain and haul the boat back home again. No problem. 'A *wonderful* journey,' and Klaus's laughter boomed over the quiet water.

We'd met him a few days earlier, when the lock-keeper, for his own esoteric reasons, had signalled both of us past two waiting Dutch boats. 'I'm really sorry,' I called to them as we passed. 'Who cares?' cried Klaus. 'They are only Dutch.' It was a joke, I hoped. But Klaus was so full of life he could be forgiven anything.

We were talking, and laughing, and pouring champagne to celebrate Klaus's splendid day on the water when twin horns echoed around the anchorage. It was the *Chérie*. Herbert and Liana waved happily from their deck. 'Hello again,' said Liana. 'Ho,' said Herbert. They tied up beside us. How could they have caught us up, so soon? 'We have done many, many locks,' said Liana.

'*C'est impossible*,' I said.

'No it isn't,' said Liana. 'The engine problem messed up Herbert's Plan. We must catch up.'

Herbert brandished his Plan. 'Tomorrow we come with you. Tomorrow I will catch up.'

What had been wrong with his fuel? Sally asked.

Herbert's face grew very grave. 'We had to drain the tank,' he said. 'It had a lot of water.'

'But how did it get in there?'

Herbert looked even darker. 'There could only be one way,' he said. 'Someone must have done it.'

'Sabotage? While you slept?'

Herbert nodded sagely.

'But who would do that?'

'The Dutch do not like us,' he said obliquely, then used a description we were to hear often — usually from Dutch people talking about Germans. 'They are polite in their own country, but outside it …'

Outside, Dutch voyagers moved gently around their boats, checking their lines, and ours, asking if we wanted them to buy our baguettes from the van that came by from the baker's in the morning and save ourselves the walk. They seemed unlikely saboteurs.

Next morning we were shaken by Herbert's stentorian roar. 'The lock lights!' he cried. 'They are on. We go, now!' We were off, a full half-hour before we expected. Herbert threw off his lines and was already speeding down the river.

We raced through the automated locks. Herbert went in first, fixed his lines as Liana ran to the operating cord and yanked it while we frantically sorted ourselves out ahead of the closing gates.

It still wasn't fast enough for Herbert. After four locks he put Liana ashore on her bike. She was to pedal down the river and use her remote control to open the locks for us.

'No waiting,' Herbert shouted triumphantly.

'I have changed my canal trip,' Liana whispered, on one of the few occasions we saw her again. 'Now it is a cycle trip.'

We had done double the number of locks we usually aimed for when we pulled into our own anchorage for the night at Fontenoy-le-Château.

Herbert sped by, honking. Liana stopped on her bike. 'Bye!' she cried. 'We must go on. Herbert has his Plan!'

Mick climbed off Klaus's boat and set up a barbecue beside the water.

His easy manner suggested an Australian doing what he did best. He produced a couple of steaks. The Danish owner of the boat next door looked on sourly. 'It is not necessary to do that here,' he said, in German. Mick pretended not to understand such an un Australian sentiment.

Fontenoy-le-Château was full of past glories. The castle it was named after sat atop a hill. A circular tower, a few stone stairs and a shape marked on the ground by the stumps of walls were all that remained, the rest quarried by townspeople over the centuries for building stones.

An embroidery museum lay below the ancient church. Sally went in and was seized by the curator, who seemed short of customers. The curator had hit a lode. Sally was fascinated by what had once been the most important embroidery centre in all Europe. Some 700 skilled embroiderers had once worked here. They'd produced trousseaux for Princess Margaret and Grace Kelly. In the 1950s and sixties their work graced Europe's top fashion houses. A single survivor silently embroidered in a corner of the museum.

Changing fashions and the new order had done for the lot of them, as it had for the town's other big industry, cutlery. The town once accommodated thousands. We imagined them thronging the narrow streets. Now it was down to 700 inhabitants.

Houses sported hand-written For Sale signs. My hammer hand twitched.

Doer-uppers! Shops lay empty. Signs over abandoned cafés, charcuteries, drogueries dotted the streets. One of them sported a dead three-legged horse in its window. We wiped a hole in the dusty windows and discovered that it had been stuffed as part of the set for a French film. All of it — shop, fittings, film posters, horse — was for sale.

A short ride rising steeply through forest countryside, past a huge, abandoned factory, lay Bains-les-Bains, whose hot pools once added lustre to local attractions.

We took our togs, for it was a fine Sunday afternoon. The town was full of people strolling its streets, and we should not have been surprised that the hot pools in their fine new building were closed. Instead we sat in a café and ate purple cassis ice-cream, the best we'd ever tasted.

Yet we loved Fontenoy. Its intimate streets invited us to stroll, do nothing other than revel in the strength of the old stones, the simplicity of the architecture. Faded pink and cream houses lined the bottom of the cliff above the river. The town's only statue was of Gilbert, a poet. Perhaps there had not been enough bronze for its other famous son, Arsène Remonal, the *colosse Jurassien*, locally famous for tipping the scales at 314.5 kilograms (not, despite local belief, a world record).

In the mornings I'd wait with half a dozen townspeople for the boulangerie to open its doors. Then we'd file inside where Madame stood behind the counter, bright as the rising sun. '*Bonjour*!', she say. '*Bonjour*, Madame,' we'd chorus, like a class of schoolchildren.

Each would then talk to her in turn, about the weather, their plans for the day, who had done what only yesterday, what a fuss there had been when … We stayed for a bit.

We ate eggs from a lock-keeper whose chooks roamed around his lock alongside five barking dogs and two dispirited magpies in a cage. Then we lay under leafy trees and gasped in their shade. The heat!

And a head came into view.

It belonged to Beni, a Welshman.

'I have someone from New Zealand aboard,' he said, and we sat up to view the émigré. Gillian was from Waiheke Island. When Beni's crew defaulted, she'd stepped into the breach, a position she seemed to be regretting.

Beni had spent six days crossing the Andes on horseback with a taciturn guide, riding through gullies and mud by day, terrified by night, then being apprehended by the army at the end of it all for not telling the police in advance. Instead of being thrown in irons they'd sat him down to a dinner of wild boar.

Beni clearly thought the pig the highlight of his trip, which made me think he'd have been better just going to a good restaurant. Then it turned out he'd owned one of those, with a bed and breakfast, in Spain, where he'd also done up haciendas for sale, and restored an old olive mill.

He'd built a twelve metre racing yacht in steel. In another boat he'd sailed across the Pacific, whisked by the trade winds, visited the Galapagos, the Marquesas, all the way to New Zealand.

He seemed to me a prize bull-shitter, although we later learned it was all true, and that he'd done much more. Yet he seemed not a happy man. He drank a lot of Calvados, although anything would do. He'd fill a glass with the instruction, 'Get that down your neck,' and he said such things as, 'You've got lot of class. Trouble is it's all third class.'

We talked to each other through a red and yellow thong hanging triumphantly from his lamp. Not Gillian's, she said. He claimed to be an adroit boatman constantly let down by his crew, and he shouted at Gillian often. 'For fuck's sake catch the rope,' he yelled as he berthed behind us. 'You can do that can't you?'

'Trouble is,' he said to me, 'it's so hard on my tod.' She said nothing. I marvelled at her forbearance and was not surprised to hear she'd quit a few days later.

By then, we'd sailed on to Corre. The days had turned hot. We sweated in forty degrees. Trees made a tunnel of the canal. Even the herons were too languorous to fly away at our approach. A dog barked at us, but made no noise except a faint huff, as if its voice had evaporated.

Corre looked dusty and tired, but to us it was celebratory. It was the end of the long, long run of locks, so numerous and whimsical that the most dedicated canal travellers were relieved to arrive at its rather desolate waterfront.

We'd wondered whether we'd ever get this far. We were 773 kilometres and more than 200 locks from Alem.

A group of young people picnicking on the bank spotted the silver fern at our bow and took up a chant: All Blacks! All Blacks! Some held their thumbs up. Some held them down. Either way, we didn't care. We thought, my god! Wasn't there anything else we were known for?

Not for our boat-handling skills, despite the America's Cup

I'd started taking our silver fern flag in at night. After all, it had become a valuable souvenir. The All Blacks were currency. We set off next morning in a perfectly-executed manoeuvre — for the sea.

In Corre's shallow port, it just kicked up a fuss.

Mud roiled to the surface. The wake bobbed boats up and down where they had no depth of water to bob up and down in. It brought the Dutch onto their decks in an instant. 'Nay nay nay,' they said.

Hire boaties had a chance to get their own back for some of the indignities heaped on them by proper boat people, for bad habits such as scaring them in locks and passing at speed and never, ever helping with lines in a port. They presented stony faces.

We did not much care. At last we were on the wide and welcoming Saône River, where locks were to become rare. Water lilies composed themselves into delicate patterns at the water's edge. Charolais looked clean as schoolchildren in the morning light. Fields of green wheat rose to wooded hills. The roofs of churches were patterned in richly-coloured Burgundy tiles, zigzagged like the jerseys our mums used to knit for us. They rose above houses that might have been forever readying themselves for postcards. Fish plopped in the still water, lightning flashed and thunder grumbled and only a few fat drops of rain fell on us. Four old university friends from Switzerland in their rental boat lazed along the river on their annual get together.

In Port-sur-Saône we bought cheese cut from huge rounds. A keeper came out of her rose-covered house at the first lock with a rich red cherry tart whose crisp pastry, smelling like honey, was still warm from her oven; and fresh eggs, and she cut a plump lettuce from her garden and passed that across too.

We went through the long Savoyeux tunnel in eerie mist and emerged into bright sunlight and at the next lock we bought a bottle of rosé and a jar of pale golden honey, smooth as oil. Bottles of pinot noir and *vin de pays* lined lock-keepers' sheds, their cottages now beautifully-kept, their gardens ornate, roses red as a royal riband.

Lizards sunbathed on the warm stones, church bells rang out, the Saône stretched before us soft as silk. Hawk-like black kites hunting for prey drifted over fields filled with yellow and mauve wildflowers dotted with scarlet poppies.

In lovely, old Seveux we bought cakes from the pâtisserie, one of them light sponge filled with chantilly with a dribble of red and yellow liqueur and topped with strawberries, the other chocolate mousse crowned with chocolate liqueur and nuts. The cakes sat on lace doilies in boxes decorated with idyllic summer scenes and tied with gold ribbons. We looked away from the empty factories, deserted houses, the charcuterie and boucherie now open mornings only, although the port was brand-new. It offered eighty berths and its signs boasted of local government initiative.

We travelled with the four Swiss whose shared youth seemed to have served them well, all of them sleek and prosperous and now in their late fifties. They were personable souls, taking turns at steering their boat, laughing at each other's efforts, calling to us over the water. As boys do they bought lots of wine from lock-keepers and decided it was best drunk while still fresh. The boat took to wobbling but all ran smoothly, oiled as they were, until the last lock before the town of Gray.

We went first, stopped and were busy with our lines when we heard a crash behind us, the sort of crunching noise that echoes merrily around the boardrooms of repair firms.

Three good old boys were hanging over the bow. There was a lot less to look at than there had been formerly. Where much of the bow had been, a large hole now featured. The lock gate had a smug look, as if it had lunched on rental boats before and this one wasn't bad, as an hors d'oeuvre.

The helmsman was doing his best to look indignant; he'd done his job all right, why hadn't the other three done theirs? And what was the lock gate doing there anyway?

The crew looked at the damage, discussed it with serious faces, then they shrugged and went on, water lapping gently into the hole. We wished them bon voyage, although we thought it might be a short one.

I told the story to a group of canal boaties later. Each one of them topped it with one of their own, the best being the crew of drunken Australians who'd steered their boat full tilt into a bridge buttress. The boat had not faltered. It went straight to the bottom, all standing.

We found ourselves in a big town again, full of bustle and traffic and people with work to do. We ate salmon steaks seared in a little oil and balsamic vinegar with sliced tomatoes and Madame's cherry tart for dessert. Sally bought cheese from a market. A small piece cost $25. It was delicious. We ate it reverently.

A couple from Havelock North came aboard for drinks. The man told us they were lucky to be alive, for on their second day out their rental boat had been on the very brink of bursting into flame from an electrical fault. Was he upset? Was he suing the rental boat company for nearly killing both of them? Was he asking for extra time to make up for the company spoiling part of a very expensive holiday?

Not a bit of it. In true New Zealand fashion he was pleased he'd been able to stop the fire and save the boat, grateful to the company for putting things right with only one lost day.

The woman asked Sally, 'How can you spend all that time aboard a boat, with a man?' Sally took to her immediately. The temperature reached forty-four degrees in the cabin.

In the mornings we breakfasted on *ficelles*, baguettes so thin you could pick your teeth with them.

We admired a British narrowboat scarcely wider than the baguette but we were getting used to British eccentricity on the canals. In Toul we'd seen a huge British-owned French *peniche*, or barge, pushed along by a Yamaha outboard clamped to its rudder while its crew picked their way around decks cluttered as a scrapyard. In Mouzon we'd met an English couple who lived, permanently, in a craft which looked as if it had started out as a packing case on a dinghy. It was painted with ornate reeds and wildflowers, so now it looked like a chocolate box instead. A yacht in Charmes was hung with so much impedimenta it was scarcely possible to believe it could float, much less cross the Mediterranean where it was bound for. Vegetables, herbs and flowers grew in boxes on its deck. The more ridiculous the boats, the more grandiose their names. *Catherine of St Arnaud* and *Bullivant of Arvin* were as cranky as *Ditherer of Doncaster.*

You could stop anywhere on the French canals, as long as it was not in a lock approach, or in spots likely to endanger others. Most boats carried long steel spikes they walloped into the canal or riverbank, for mooring to trees was forbidden; the ropes would booby-trap the towpaths, popular with walkers and cyclists.

Our spikes merely used up space in a cupboard. We liked the convenience and company of the little ports, not to mention the electricity, water and shower blocks they usually offered. More often than not they charged for these services although it was never very much, usually around $20 a night.

Perhaps because of the cost, love of solitude, or because they just wanted to rough it in that peculiar way of theirs, many of the British would not only sail in strange boats, they'd moor them in odd places: in tiny creeks, or against forbidding walls, or in the case of the packing case boat, on a wrecked pontoon abandoned next to a car park while on the other side of the river we tied to sound pontoons, plugged in our power cords, and used the showers, this time free.

I had to catch up with our emails in Gray. Off I went on the eternal quest for an internet connection. This large town boasted only one public facility, so slow it took half an hour to send a single email. I gave up and went across to the Office de Tourisme for help. Its director loved canal boats. She talked about them endlessly. She offered me her computer while she talked to Sally.

I wrote emails on her French keyboard, full of misspellings, exclamation marks and asterisks, like comic-book swearing. Meanwhile she talked for almost two hours scarcely pausing for breath. She told us she often travelled in passing canal boats, once for several weeks.

Weeks? She was nice, but I would have been looking speculatively at the river after mere hours. She asked where we were berthed, and could she come by? For the rest of our stay we peered furtively from our cabin, ready to duck. She turned up again months later. She'd hitched a ride.

In Pontailler an Englishman in a rental boat boasted of his exploits in Hong Kong where by his account he'd been the sole bulwark against the evil Chinese, and deeply resented being forced to hand over the colony. But he'd made up for it back home, where lifeboat services up and down the country had succeeded in daring rescues through their good fortune in securing his services.

Now he was employed as a delivery skipper and was in great demand because of his courage and skill in bringing his customers' boats home undamaged, usually through hurricanes.

Muffled as it may have been elsewhere, he could still hear the British lion roar. He said, 'If we've made so many mistakes, how come so many people want to come and live here?' We'd found the subject of immigration usually woke the dogs. His quiet wife retreated below.

Four Americans in the boat on the other side of him had been listening intently. The two boats fell to discussing politics. The Americans complained that the war in Iraq had become a fiasco. 'No one likes us,' one complained.

'Especially not in Europe.' The Englishman was unrepentant about his country's role in the war. He said, 'It would have been cheaper to nuke 'em.'

Sally asked what he thought of Tony Blair. 'Our politics are different,' he said. 'I'm a conservative, and he's a bull-shitter.'

The Americans were now discussing French cuisine. 'I'm an offal eater,' said one. 'You're an awful eater?' asked another. 'An operator?' chimed a third. 'But tripe!' continued the first. 'My god.'

And in St Jean de Losne, meeting-place of canals and rivers, we stopped for a few weeks. It was mid-summer. This was the place where we had to decide which way to go. One path led to the south of France and the Mediterranean, the other to Paris.

As we drew close, we saw a familiar shape.

The *Chérie*.

'So, at last you stopped,' I called.

'No, no,' yelled Herbert. 'We have been to Lyon.' Lyon was 200 kilometres further down the river. 'Now we are on our way back.'

Liana blew us a kiss. She waved a piece of paper triumphantly. The Plan.

We were not so well organised. We tossed a coin. Tails South of France, heads Paris? A hell of a choice. The coin glittered on the blue carpet. Heads. Paris.

Chapter Eight

Life moved quickly for us in the otherwise slow-moving village of St Jean de Losne.

St Jean was a barge town. Barges, or *peniches*, lined the banks of the Saône River skirting it. Some were still working. A growing number were not. Sometimes they had been abandoned altogether. More often they had been converted, or were in the process of being made into mobile homes. They were ideal for the job, thirty-eight metres long and five wide and blunt at both ends. They were square-bottomed and with a little added height on deck above the holds they made an easy two storeys.

I went into a converted *peniche* in the River Seine town of Melun several months later. A double, curved staircase like a Georgian mansion's led into its depths. Everything was on one floor and the roof was as high as a cathedral's. Two families lived in the *peniche* and there was plenty of room, although I'd been living on a boat for most of the year by then and perhaps my frame of reference had shrunk.

Not far above St Jean de Losne a canal branched off the Saône and led up to the Marne River, and eventually to Paris.

The canal leading towards the Swiss border and eventually into Germany led off the Saône at St Symphorien, only a few kilometres above St Jean. The Burgundy canal turned off in the middle of St Jean and led into the famed wine district. Below St Jean, at Chalon, the Canal du Centre headed south, then changed its mind and curved back into the depths of Burgundy;

it joined the Seine River in the run to Paris and offered an alternative route, the Canal du Nivernais, for those who wanted something more rustic. The Saône itself became the mighty Rhône below Lyon and rushed off in no-nonsense fashion all the way to the Mediterranean.

St Jean lay square in the middle of this great cobweb of waterways. All roads led to it although, like the previous subject of that saying, the town had had its disappointments. It was once the most important barge centre in all France. Perhaps it still was, although much of the commercial barge traffic had retreated to the north.

St Jean itself hadn't changed much. Lorries squeezed through a main street designed for horse traffic. A maze of little streets wound through the old part of town. The new part was still a work in progress.

The main harbour, a big sheltered basin divided in two by an island and filled with hundreds of boats, lay behind the old town. On the other side of the first lock into the Burgundy canal converted barges lay four deep. Not all of them were completed homes for the wayward. Many were still dreams. Yes, you could bark your shin on these fantasies, but there was nowhere to lay your head, or make your tea.

They were still rusting shells with a few holes for windows.

Some would be finished; some bore obvious signs of their owners' dreams turning to nightmares ending one dark night in them sitting upright in bed, mopping the sweat from their brows and thinking my god, what am I doing?

One boat, a fine British-made barge, nearly new, had been sailed to the south of France by its proud new owner. There it had caught fire. Now it was for sale in St Jean de Losne, its blackened insides with their struts and walls and unidentifiable organs exposed like an accident victim's autopsy which had discovered a broken heart.

A rusting hull, bare of superstructure or any fitting at all, lay upside down in a yard. Only the marks where engineers were measuring the thickness of its plating showed this was someone's dream. Months later the amount of progress was invisible to the naked eye. I hoped its owners were young, for they'd certainly be finishing it on their pension.

I watched a woman working on a huge iron wheel. Possibly it was her ship's steering wheel, for it was imposing enough. She had a length of chain, and she was running it up and down each section of the wheel in turn. A pile of rust lay below the wheel, although her rich red colour said that she'd managed to intercept quite a bit on its way down.

At the back of the boat, out of cursing range I noted, her partner was welding chunks of steel which one day, that day which undoubtedly sparkled in their minds as they crept exhausted into bed each night, would be a nice little saloon, the pretty curtains in its windows left undrawn so passersby could look inside, see the pools of soft light thrown by the brass lamps, sense the air of contentment pervading the ship, and be smothered in envy.

In the meantime she was tired and dirty, he was irritable and half-blinded by welding flashes, this was a lovely Sunday afternoon when people, those lucky souls who were not doing up boats, were strolling around, doing nothing but enjoying the sun and admiring the view which included, of course, the toiling couple.

When you saw a finished conversion, oh joy! This was the vision that drove them on, the pot of gold.

I was admiring the beautiful lines and clever design of a fine Luxemotor, a Dutch barge, on the waterfront when its Australian owners appeared on deck and invited me aboard. We chatted under a white canopy on an after-deck the size of a Pakuranga patio, reclining on plush chairs which might once have graced the *Queen Elizabeth II*. Then we walked on polished floors through two big bedrooms, two bathrooms, one household-sized shower, a kitchen relegating the term 'galley' to real estate agents' jargon, and a laundry complete with full-sized washing machine and drier. The whole thing would have put a Vaucluse apartment to flight. The Australians had once been part of a syndicate of eight who'd shared the boat in a three-year contract. At the end of it two couples had bought out the others and here they were, strolling their floating estate like graziers.

We parked first on the quay on the Saône itself, below the Café National under an avenue of trees shading seats where townspeople met to chat. And watch.

Eyes that had seen thousands of boats and barges come and go were not to be messed with. We berthed very carefully. Scarcely had we tied up when, to our joy, Glenn and Trish came bounding down the broad steps towards the boat. Their barge, the *Johanna Grietje*, was in dry dock, being painted shiny deep-sea green and black.

Friends! From home! Much as we'd enjoyed reconstructing ourselves and our lives for the passing parade we'd met on the journey, we longed for these two, who'd shared much of those lives. For an hour we gabbled pure Kiwi, a language distinct from any other. We yarned, boasted, lied, confessed, had lunch, got drunk and repeated all of the above.

Yet in an odd way the conversation was constrained. There seemed to be holes in it, no-go areas, an unease we'd never felt in New Zealand. Sally felt she was letting people down. 'You're so lucky,' everyone said. When the whole world wanted to cruise the canals, live in Paris, revel in *la vie Française*, what was *wrong* with her? You must be extraordinarily brave to question the mythology of romance. I wanted to spend that year, and the next, on the canals. I knew Sally no longer did. She longed for the light, the freedom of the South Pacific, but she didn't want to tarnish our friends' dream. So both of us felt fraudulent in the face of their enthusiasm, their love of canal life. We'd been cooped up in a boat for months, often in the rain. We hoped we'd feel better within their aura.

Our introduction to the expatriate community came the following day.

Expats formed a tight community in St Jean de Losne. They organised evening lectures. Two elegant women ran the most unusual library we'd ever been in. There were no cards, no records, no lending routines. You took as many books as you liked. If you wanted to bring some back, that was fine, but it didn't matter if you did not. The system, or lack of it, seemed to work. The shelves were full, overflowing into stacks on the floor.

Books in the library were often aging gracefully, rather as their borrowers imagined themselves. Sally picked one out and flicked through it. 'Look,' she said, 'it's by P.G. Wodehouse.' A nearby Englishman leapt on this colonial gaffe. 'Actually,' he said, with a kindly look, 'it's pronounced 'Woodhouse.' Sally, who knew that, said 'I know.' The Kiwi translation was fuck off. But I could foretell his anecdote at dull dinner parties.

Next morning Sally set forth with the walking group. I would have gone too, but I had other things to do, such as lying on the settee reading.

I watched them walking along the opposite riverbank, quite a lot of them, engrossed in conversation: Americans, English, Australians, New Zealanders, some of them canal boaties, some expats; but no French.

That very afternoon I was introduced to the inner circle, the British expat community. It was our first real encounter, and I was staggered: not by how curious they were, but how incurious. Not only did the British live in a group that had been portrayed and satirised in books and plays everywhere, and knew little about the people they lived among, the French, but they didn't *want* to know.

I found many expat Poms to be, well, not attractive. They loved the French way of life, and although they weren't prepared to live it completely, they all agreed on one thing: it was better than home.

France was full of English people disappointed in home. Their views ranged from critical to apocalyptic, the last from an apoplectic gent in his seventies who echoed Enoch Powell's elderly 'rivers of blood' speech from a neighbouring boat: 'The bricklayer, the man on the shop floor, they've had enough, it'll only be a year or two before they rise up and there'll be blood everywhere.'

Only if there was nothing on TV, I thought, although as the BBC at that moment was once more being eviscerated, that seemed likely. But enough of what? Immigration, mainly.

The French, on the other hand, seemed unlikely to rise up and leave blood on anything, at least nothing edible. They were content with their way of life, indifferent to any faint criticism, in love with their country and polite to visitors, as opposed to beating and robbing them. They were poor tourists themselves; they saw no need to go somewhere else. Everything they wanted was right here, or if needs must, in some other part of *la belle France*.

My neighbour had had his boat custom-built in England, although getting it finished had involved much time, many threats of court action and promises of physical violence. He was very proud of it in a conquering sort of way, the same sort of way William must have looked upon dead Saxons; he'd beaten the hordes to get where he was today.

I could hear arteries throbbing when he discovered I was cooking dinner.

'I thought New Zealanders were supposed to be he-men. He-men don't cook.'

'Yes they do,' said Sally, 'and you should see what he's like in an apron, naked.' Our neighbour clearly felt he should not see any such thing. He retreated below decks to his sports channel in a rush of limp-wristed gesturing, perhaps to watch the All Blacks from a whole new perspective.

We hadn't been in St Jean very long before there was a tap at the door.

The Major. He had a clipped way of talking and a one-sided conversational style: you were there as the audience, not as a participant. For all that, I liked something about him, although it took some time to realise that it was his vulnerability.

The Major sat to attention in the wicker chair and told us precisely why he'd abandoned England eleven years ago for his little village near St Jean de Losne, deep in France. 'Too much of the ay-u,' he said.

The ay-u? The British way of addressing him, he said: ''ey, you!' He didn't like being spoken to like that. French manners were perfect. They treated him as an individual. France was a country of order. He liked order.

Perhaps he wasn't a major. He didn't use the title, but he fitted it perfectly. His manner was upright. His legs were smooth as a boy's below his shorts, although he was at least seventy. Perhaps he shaved them. His moustache ('in French, it's feminine, *la moustache*', he said with great satisfaction) curled and twirled in a thicket above his upper lip. If a ferret had stuck its head out of it and looked around, I would not have been surprised.

He would never return now. His wife? He watched the postie go by on her bright yellow Vespa scooter. Here even the rubbish collectors wore designer uniforms. 'If something happened to me,' he said, 'my guess is that she would stay.'

Perhaps. In Corre we'd met a Belgian woman who'd married a Frenchman. She'd lived in the village for thirty years. 'I'm still an outsider,' she said. 'I have made no real friends here. If Jean died I'd go back home tomorrow.'

You heard people saying the same thing about Waipawa or Waimate: twenty years and still not a local. Rural France was like that: tight. Polite, but closed to strangers.

The couple were caught in the expat Brits' dilemma. We were to see it more often from then on. They'd sold their homes, perhaps under the influence of the dozens of television programmes waxing on the delights of buying real estate abroad: *A Place in France, No Turning Back, Home or Away* and many others. They'd bought houses in France, or poured their money into a home-sized barge.

Back home the houses they'd sold were worth far more now. In some cases their value had doubled.

Their homes in France had not. The French did not treat their houses as commodities. Houses were to be lived in, often by generations of the same family. They tolerated the British buying into their towns and villages, but with a wariness that went beyond the traditional aloofness between the two nations.

Meanwhile the British had fallen out of their market back home. They'd literally made their beds in France, and now they had to lie in them. Perhaps the Major's widow would have no option: their house, he told us sadly, had not increased very much in price, while houses in their home county had gone through the roof.

In the walking group that morning he'd promised Sally cherries and true to his word, arrived with a brown paper bagful. They were so bright and sharp they had to be eaten by morning or they'd go bad. So we ate them, and thought of the Major and his wife, and we felt sad, and lucky.

Visitors arrived. Jude, an old friend from Christchurch and her mate Jackie, whom we'd met once or twice. Their train pulled into the station at thirty-three minutes past the hour exactly. Trains ran to the minute in France. I watched a man in a peaked cap flag the train away and asked him to call us a taxi. '*D'accord*,' he said, and did. Don't try this at home, I thought.

I saw Jude's and Jackie's faces fall as they inspected the boat. Let's face it, boats were small, unless you wanted to hump a load of steel the size of a steam locomotive around the canals. Our alleged double bed was, well, chummy. Canal cruisers were like messing around in playhouses. You had to get used to living on them and even then they got no bigger.

Men loved it.

Women did not.

Sally and I had lived on a boat in Westhaven in Auckland for a while, after our children had moved to the queen city. The boat seemed big at first, although it was not as large as the *River Queen*. The way it shrank was amazing, like a woollen jersey someone had left too long in water. In the rain it shrivelled even faster, and rain is not unknown in Auckland.

You needed to be neat in your habits on boats.

I was not neat. I was messy. What's more, I was clumsy. If there was something to trip over, I'd trip, and if something was available to drop, then *crash*, down it would go.

These peccadilloes went unnoticed when you were on a boat with other blokes. They regarded mess as wildebeest treat mud, something to wallow in rather than worry about.

Sally cleaned up after me, although no man would be surprised that I was surprised I'd left anything that needed cleaning up. Little things, the odd puddle of soup, the occasional pungent grundies, the tea-towel put to good use on the oil dipstick — heavens, I'd only used a corner of it — seemed to assume unusual significance on a boat.

Boats had remarkable numbers of sharp objects: sills, stairs, controls, latches, rails, doors which were always shut when you wanted them open, and open when you expected them to be shut, and lots and lots of edges.

I bashed and crashed around them. Sally merely stumbled occasionally but there was a difference: I did not bruise, but she did.

She bruised badly. She'd brush against something and next day a great purply bruise would mark the spot. She whacked her arm and the bruise was still visible when we returned to New Zealand. After a particularly hard day on the canals she'd be the colour of grapes and was not mollified when I said she had the tint of exceedingly fine pinot noir. I was relieved we weren't at home. Someone would have called the police.

We'd bought our boat with guests in mind. The accepted formula for visitors on boats was six for drinks, four for lunch and two overnight but everyone wanted friends aboard, and we longed for them.

Still, I could see Jude and Jackie thought three nights would be quite enough. As they inspected the bathroom the estimate broadened: the three nights would be long ones.

The boat's bathroom was airily described as *en suite*. In fact it was en our faces, for it was separated from our bed in the aft cabin by a narrow alley.

That space would by entirely occupied by a night-time user who would then have to perform various convoluted acts behind a door with all the soundproofing of a Japanese paper wall.

This was clearly exercising their minds. I saw them deciding a prolonged bout of constipation might be no bad thing.

We hung a curtain beside the bunk to give at least an illusion of privacy. No one risked it. In the mornings the two shot out the door towards the port toilets like unplugged balloons. A trip on the river was called for, if only to divert attention.

Auxonne lay up the river just a couple of hours away. On our way down we'd passed it without stopping.

So we took them there, affecting nonchalance. Oh dear. Nonchalance was fatal on the waterways.

In the only lock on the journey I talked idly to Jackie, holding the ropes with what I thought was easy grace, pointing out the ineptness of the boat behind and describing the proper way of doing things.

Sally yelled a warning. Her end of the boat was neatly secured to the lock.

Mine, however, was swinging wildly while I nattered on. As the back careered to one side of the lock the front headed determinedly for the other. There came a dull thud, as of steel on concrete, the kind that foretells several hours with a paintbrush and the services of a blacksmith's hammer.

With *le capitaine* chastened, not to mention chastised, we arrived in Auxonne, an ancient town linked to Napoleon Bonaparte. Although we passed on the chance to see his bath we intended a good look at the very old church, Napoleon's barracks, the fine houses.

Then something happened which demonstrated the truly fickle nature of tourism even if you were not, strictly speaking, tourists.

Three elephants strolled out from the church. You did not expect elephants in church, nor in a French village, any more than you'd look at a French menu and imagine the village ducks living happily ever after.

But these were indubitably elephants, wandering along tail to trunk as elephants did.

The fine old church, the barracks, houses, market, bath and all were instantly forgotten. An elephant hunt was the go.

They were not difficult to track. Small town, big elephants. Besides, the middle one, the littlest, had a large appetite for the begonias and geraniums which grew so profusely from flower boxes along the way. Its delicate trunk reached for them as a child's hand sought sweets, grabbing a bunch and stuffing them quickly into its mouth.

Pandemonium broke out.

Shopkeepers rushed to their doors: '*Non, non*!' Small children squealed: '*Le petit éléphant* steals *les fleurs*!'

The keeper beat the offender with his stick and loosed a tirade which the elephant might have understood but chose to ignore. A few steps farther on the trunk nipped out again and a bunch of cyclamen-coloured begonias made the supreme sacrifice. Shouts, yells, oaths faded as the procession shambled back towards a circus on the edge of town.

We'd quite lost our appetite for antiquity. Elephants carried the day. Jude had sponsored an elephant, along with bears and other endangered species.

I felt I should check her suitcase, which I thought quite big enough to hide one of the animals inside.

So we returned to St Jean de Losne, and cracked a few bottles of Burgundy, since we were in the area and felt under an obligation to pillage the cellars. But this was the thing about drinking French wine in France: you could drink vast quantities of it, and very often did, without falling overboard nor feeling the slightest tap in the cerebral region next morning. (Do try that at home. Expect the hammer blows of remorse.)

It was odd.

Lots of things do not travel out of France very well. Pastis does not taste the same in the high latitudes of the South Pacific. Baguettes look the same, should taste the same — after all, they can't be all that difficult to make, can they? — but they do not. French style is chic in Paris, fussy at home.

Some still tsk sadly, yet New Zealand has developed its own style, in wine, in food, in clothes. This view of the world divided New Zealanders in France.

The Francophiles were by far the majority. They loved France, and everything about it. Most had only a rudimentary grasp of the language and the sad fact was that they did not know much about the inner workings of the country. So they loved what they saw and France to them was romantic, chic, a people who had unlocked the secret of life. Good luck to them all, I thought, for a little knowledge here was not so much a dangerous thing as the whole secret of romance. Nothing kills magic like analysis.

New Zealand usually fared badly in these comparisons; a curl of the lip, a dismissive laugh about the way things were done back home. The old cultural cringe never went away; it just morphed into a more sophisticated form. Yet from here, our way of life seemed to me bright, open, free.

St Jean de Losne, meeting place of waterways, housed many nationalities. Americans lived on huge barges converted for living; or, like Toby and George, on ex-hire boats. Toby was blue-eyed and direct, George ruggedly handsome in a marine hero sort of way. In 1991 Toby had found she had breast cancer. She said, 'It was such a huge shock. I stopped everything next day.' They left their business and sold it a few years later. They built a house in Hartford, Connecticut, which they still owned although now they spent their year living aboard either a houseboat in the Bahamas or their canal boat in France.

'We love it,' said Toby.

'Wow,' said George.

Others lived on service pensions, or by undisclosed means, although all by New Zealand standards seemed flush.

Murray spent four years in the Israeli Army, was an expert in martial arts, and a jeweller. Ian was a Canadian architect, now ninety, and spent much of his time piloting his big converted barge. The Dutch were usually retired, although many of them seemed too young: fifty-five was a good age to stop work. Germans too; but canal cruisers of those two nationalities were in France for a few weeks, or a few months, and usually voyaged with determination, so weren't really members of the club.

New Zealanders and Australians were members by right of birth; we were the perennial travellers. And Brazilians, South Africans, Norwegians and a dozen other nationalities. But seldom the French.

A few years ago, the story went, you seldom found the French cruising their own canals. I could believe it. The international urge to live near water — any kind of water with the possible exception of sewage farms, although they do quite well in Christchurch — seemed to have eluded the French. Except for fishermen and women — mainly men, lots of them — the French turned their backyards on the canals, no matter how picturesque those quiet stretches of water. Now more French were cruising canals; French flags were not common, but no longer rare either, although as few spoke anything but French they generally didn't join the club either.

Jude and Jackie went home. I set about some maintenance on the *River Queen*. I changed the engine oil, cleared the filters, cleaned the water tank, scraped and painted bilges, greased everything that needed greasing. Everything was running perfectly, as it had since we left Alem in Holland. We both touched wood, just in case.

There was plenty of wood in the boat to touch. The cabins were lined in teak. The furniture was built of it. Evidently no one had given a thought to the rainforests in 1987, when it was built. But a bloke always needs more wood. There were a couple of things I needed to make and I went off to the timber yard.

Timber yards were the same the world over. You went in, you were ignored for a decent interval. At last you attracted someone's attention. They appeared to be deaf, stupid, and have no command of any known language. You explained what you wanted. You got a blank look. You ran through it again. The blank look changed to one suggesting that you might just be the dumbest fellow the yardworker had met this week and boy, that was really saying something. To save further humiliation you settled for the closest thing you could find to what you actually wanted, went home, tried to make it fit, threw it away and went to another timber yard fully expecting the same to happen, as it did.

Except in St Jean de Losne.

The French seemed to be great do-it-yourselfers. They had New Zealanders beaten hands-down, although Kiwis believed they were DIY world champions. Their *bricolage* supermarkets sold everything you might need to build a house, and most of the French shopping there on Saturday mornings seemed intent on doing just that.

They loaded giant supermarket carts with doors, electrical cable, spouting and downpipes, heaters, sinks, hot water cylinders, four-by-twos and cheap power tools, and pushed them into long queues at the checkouts, where they chatted to someone on one side about rewiring a house and to someone else on the other about the best way of installing a swimming pool, then discussed the pros and cons of a sabre saw with the woman at the till. You could spend an hour in those queues, and I sometimes did.

I needed only a single piece of timber in St Jean de Losne. I braced myself for the ordeal. I was the only customer in the yard and sure enough, everyone had urgent business elsewhere.

I finally pinned one down. He beamed, as if I was the one he'd been waiting for all day and, moreover, this was the most delightful task he'd had to perform in his entire timber yard career. I told him what I wanted, in French. He caught on so quickly I thought I might try French back home in New Zealand too, since English never seemed to work. He fetched my piece of wood.

I went into the office to pay for it. Again I was the only customer. Six clerks filled every seat behind the counter. Every one of them was engaged in work of national importance. They peered into their computer screens anxiously. Finally I caught an eye and held on to it. I was charged $8, which bought a knot-hole in a bit of boxing-grade pine in New Zealand.

Naturally, I'd miscalculated. I needed another piece to finish the work. I went back. Found the same man who saw me instantly this time, for we were now friends. We shook hands. We chatted a bit. The weather was fine. Would it hold? Until the end of the week perhaps.

I told him what I needed. The same as this morning. He fetched it. We shook hands again. I went into the office. Caught the same eye, without delay. Now, I was known. Charged $16.

What should I do? I could complain that I'd paid half that amount in the morning. But as an experienced shopper I knew he was as likely to add an extra $8 to this afternoon's bill as halve it. And $16 was still cheap. I paid up. We wished each other *merci* and *au revoir* and *bon journée.*

The next day was the blessing of the barges, an annual ceremony in St Jean.

We were turned out of our mooring on the waterfront for the occasion, and moved into the big marina behind the town.

The greetings changed. We heard 'hello' more often than '*bonjour.*'

I went down pier B, full of permanent boat-dwellers rather than mere passers-by such as the *River Queen*, and on my way back met a woman at the top of the access ramp. She was staring meaningfully into the distance. I realised she was demonstrating immense patience and polite restraint as she waited for the interloper to clear out of her way. And her dog's way too, for an overfed beast sniffed asthmatically around her feet.

'*Bonjour*,' I said.

'Hello', she said. Then, to her dog, 'Oh come along, do.' The animal drooped off behind her.

In the nearby square housing the supermarket, the Office de Tourisme and the library, a troop of schoolchildren appeared, marching in twos. They appeared to be demonstrating against something, for several held banners. They seemed very young to be protesting, we thought. They *were* very young. Their placards insisted upon tidiness. What did they want? They demanded that rubbish be cleaned up. When did they want it? Now!

They stacked their placards and banners neatly against a wall, then set to picking up all the rubbish in the square, supervised by their teacher in designer work gear, tight camo pants and fitted yellow roadworker's jacket.

The French took an enlightened attitude towards rubbish. They didn't want it spoiling their streets and countryside. They recycled everything. They put out huge bins for glass, paper, plastic, even run-of-the-mill garbage. The bins were everywhere within easy reach. They were collected by men wearing bright green overalls with white stripes.

At my brother's house in Brittany, in a tiny hamlet as remote and rural as anywhere in France, they'd arrive in the early hours of the morning and empty the rubbish bin so the sun rose once more on a litter-free landscape.

Roadsides, beaches, parks, streets were kept spic, span and rubbish free.

France was as clean as Britain was not. Over the channel England had begun experimenting with once-fortnightly rubbish collections. The level of garbage in the streets, already alarming, rose to dangerous levels. So did the wails of the British expat community in France. 'The country's going to the dogs,' they cried of their former home. In this case literally.

Meanwhile, France — the nation that abhorred Thatcherism, refused to live according to the current economic ideology, and broke all the rules — like the bumblebee flew on regardless.

The French lived by their own code.

Rob and Jo were New Zealanders from Nelson. They'd been away from home for several years, living part of the time in England earning enough money to spend the rest of it in France on their little steel boat.

Rob had the ultimate French lunchtime experience.

Despite everything, lunchtimes often took us by surprise. To the French they were more sacred than Sundays, and they bent their knees just as reverently as they sat down to eat. Lunchtime as much as anything defined the French: doing things their own way, living their lives they way they wanted in defiance of modern economic demands and most of all, of course, both loving and respecting eating.

We'd gnash our teeth as we arrived at supermarkets or gas stations a few minutes late and find ourselves confronted with a two-hour wait. But lunchtime was an essential part of the French way of life. It was an easy habit to fall into. On the *River Queen* a long lunch followed by a siesta became ingrained. I feared it would lead to serious culture clash back home.

Rob needed a mobile telephone to use in France.

He went along to the telephone shop in plenty of time, he thought, to emerge fully fitted out for the modern age of communications by lunchtime. He bought a prepay SIM card for the new phone. He could not get it to work. The shopkeeper couldn't get it to work either. The man became agitated, not so much because he was selling Rob a dud as because of the time. Lunchtime approached. He wanted to close the shop. He had better things to do. He wanted Rob to leave, taking his new phone with him.

Amid splendid villages and smooth water: *River Queen* canalside.

Bruce, *in vino veritas*

… and Sally in the *River Queen's* dinette.

Coming up to the Savoyeux tunnel in eerie mist.

Montargis, eccentric canals lit by flowers.

Tying up in a lock: Sally organised, Bruce not.

Left inset: lunch, courtesy of lock-keepers.

Lock-keeper's cottage, Canal du Centre

... and the flowery lockie himself.

Blessing the barges, St Jean de Losne.

Three generations and still no fish.

Bumblebee jousting, St Mammes.

Even the bikes grow flowers.

Montceau's drawbridges, like rainbows opening.

Entertaining locals, deep in le Guetin lock.

Above: cold and wet but the sensible keep smiling.

Main picture: Briare, most beautiful aqueduct in all France.

Verdun-sur-le-Doubs: strong currents, great Danes.

Bon appetit: dinner canalside.

Of all the gin joints, in all the towns, Trish and Sally walk into this one.

Look, no boat: Buschy in the River Loire.

Above: that flag.

Main picture: under the golden girl, the Arsenal, Place de Bastille, Paris.

Canal boat romance: *Johanna Grietje.*

Rob wouldn't go. Quite reasonably, if you weren't French and this wasn't lunchtime, he argued that he had bought a telephone whose prime object was to talk to other people, in which area it was a complete failure. The discussion grew heated on one side and impatient on the other.

Finally the shopkeeper could stand the sacrilege no longer. He marched to the door. He went out. He closed the door behind him and turned the key.

Rob was locked in. He thought of various emergency numbers but his phone wouldn't work. He yelled. No one came for, of course, this was lunchtime.

An hour and a half went by before the shopkeeper reappeared. Perhaps he'd made a special concession for Rob, and had knocked half an hour off his lunchtime.

He was not alone. The gendarmes came with him. They listened to both points of view. They deliberated. They had no Consumer Guarantees Act to guide them in the matter, but they had the ties of nationhood which were almost as good, at least if you were the shopkeeper. Rob was elected loser. The shopkeeper looked gratified. Oh well. Rob went back to his boat, found his old mobile and fitted the new SIM card. It worked.

In the evening I went along to the meeting called to sort out details of the ceremony for blessing the barges. It was held at the Café National, on the waterfront, where people sat decorously under parasols on the riverbank and ate cheap, good, food. The café degenerated as you penetrated its inner recesses; by the time you reached the bar you were among drinkers as dedicated as West Coast regulars, and glimpses of the rooms behind showed the kind of confusion which made newspaper headlines when someone died and trucks were needed to cart away the rubbish.

Murray told me that of course my name was Bruce, coming from New Zealand. I laughed politely at the warty old joke. Expat Poms turned up.

The one who tried to seize control of the meeting and like a deputy head prefect get everyone in order was called Caroline, of course. She was dressed all in mauve except for a cream pashmina.

The café owner appeared, smoking a pipe the size of a tuba. The head of the bargees' association arrived. He was dressed in a cape of emerald green with cobalt linings and he wore a gold chain around his neck. The Bishop accompanied him, and the Master of Ceremonies. They talked rapidly in French. Surprisingly, we all understood: the big boys and girls were to go first and everyone else was to keep out of the way.

The blessing of the boats went perfectly.

The Mayor made a speech, the Bishop conducted a long, long service.

With one thing and another it took all day. The MC blasted away for eight hours, the Miss Jean de Losne pageant chose a modestly-dressed winner who said nothing about world peace. Coloured lights flashed on the merry-go-round.

The boats were covered in flags and bunting. The barges were blessed. They went down the river in convoys, followed by a flotilla of lesser craft. We watched from Ian's barge. Someone said it was all a little boring. 'This is a village of two thousand people,' Ian said sharply, 'and they're enjoying themselves.'

And so they were, lining the streets and the bridge, gasping at the fireworks. The Miss Losne contestants entwined themselves around their boyfriends, the grown-ups filled the cafés, the bogans screeched around on little motorbikes, and everyone had a jolly good time until around midnight when, the air still warm as a bath, they began drifting home.

In the port the Germans parked on their expensive boat next door asked politely if I would look after their space while they went down the river for the evening. They were drinking cocktails, and after a few more they gunned their engine and went off with great dash. Towards midnight they returned.

The captain backed his boat into its space with panache. There came a huge crash. The entire jetty shook like jelly. People rushed from their boats, at first in alarm, then with the piety unique to boaties everywhere when they see someone else mucking it up.

The stainless steel ladder on the back of the Germans' boat was horribly twisted. The jetty was damaged. Eight-year-old Oscar from a neighbouring Kiwi boat itemised everything for anyone who might have missed the details. 'Look at that! And look underneath! It's all broken! And that bit over there!'

We all pretended to be deeply concerned but really, it was the end of a perfect weekend.

Chapter Nine

Sally and I had travelled quite a lot. We started young, for travel was compulsory, like sport. You needed a note from your parents to avoid it. If you had not gone overseas in your twenties you could go along to social welfare and get a disability grant.

Going overseas was a huge adventure then. You had to save, and sacrifice; the air fare would have bought quarter of a house, or a Holden.

You could still have gone by sea, but voyages to the other side of the world were already becoming whiskery and you were required to spend endless boring weeks on the ocean wave, for this was long before shipping companies took those same endless boring weeks and repackaged them as cruises.

Besides, we loved the idea of flying. Women dreamed of becoming hosties on international flights but hardly ever got there, because they needed the looks of Sophia Loren and the ambitions of a nun, pregnancy being a certain way to crash and burn.

Men were not so lucky. Male hosties were unusual. The real male job was pilot, but you might as well aspire to be that other ruler of the heavens. If you wanted to fly it was much easier to scrimp, starve and save for five years or so and buy a one-way ticket — to England of course, where else? England was the start line to the world, where you could get a job, scrimp, starve and save enough to buy an old van and go around Europe, or if you were truly adventurous, down the Kathmandu trail. The British welcomed you, if not with open arms then at least with a separate queue at the immigration desk befitting your superior skill in being born into the British Commonwealth. Even the Americans gave you a visitor's visa without requiring a strip-search by a marine with hair like a shearer's comb.

Flying was luxury beyond earthly dreams. The food! Three courses from a menu the size and style of a Mills and Boon novel. With wine, like meals in the movies! And service from angels who waited on you hand and foot.

Flights were not just a way of getting there. They were an end in themselves, a season of luxury only dreamed of back home in the flat. To travel hopefully was a better thing than to arrive, said Robert Louis Stevenson, and nothing was more hopeful than Flight TE 471 to London. Men practised the smooth confidence of Sean Connery, women the style of Diana Rigg. I remember asking the startled hostie for a Manhattan, which after a moment she fetched; at least, I think that is what she mixed, for I had no idea what a Manhattan was.

So, on Sally's and my very first trip to London in 1972, my second trip overseas and her first, we settled back into our roomy seats in our Air New Zealand jet, talked, read (for there were no movies), ate so many meals we could scarcely believe we'd once got by on a meagre three a day, drank and hoped, and it was huge fun.

Now flying was simply awful. Even before you climbed on a plane you volunteered to be treated like a criminal, waited endless hours on seats any decent park drunk would despise, wandered aimlessly around shops that sold junk at allegedly cheap prices, and brooded over the metaphysics of messages declaring your flight had been delayed due to operational requirements.

You were marshalled first into pens then races and finally into seats so small that considerable effort was spent advising you how to reach the other end alive.

The hosties had morphed into cabin attendants whose anonymous title scarcely disguised their real function, which was to poke plastic packets of various substances at their charges and prevent them from rioting.

If you were foolish you ended your trip at Heathrow; if downright stupid, you finished at Los Angeles. The Americans forced you to wait for hours in subservient silence, for otherwise you risked being shot, or imprisoned, or both. The British merely subjected you to lengthy suspicion from persons who looked like fish, then they lost your luggage.

On our first trip to Britain Sally became pregnant, not just with child, but with two of them.

She gave up her work in drug rehabilitation. I quit my job as an ice-cream packer, where I'd dressed in Arctic gear to spend thirty minutes loading refrigerated trucks from freezers followed by thirty minutes thawing out and eating the evidence, ice-cream from cartons dropped by numbed if sticky fingers. The job had been better than its predecessor, however. Then, I'd worked for a famous cosmetics company whose television commercials showed men in white coats measuring out rare and precious essences by the dram. In reality they became scruffy individuals such as myself wearing dirty overalls, dumping sacks of chemicals into huge vats according to a handwritten recipe pinned to the wall, and staying one step ahead of the dole.

We were both only too happy to chuck the work and use our remaining free time ahead of parenthood to climb into our VW van and head for Europe on the assumption (wrong, as it proved) that once the twins were born our travelling days would be over.

The van's hold on life was precarious. I bought it cheap, from a man who professed to be selling it reluctantly only because he was going overseas. That was probably the only truth he told, for as the true character of the vehicle was revealed, I had no doubt he left just as soon as he cashed the cheque.

We fitted it out extravagantly with a double mattress and a gas cooker but the engine went from whimsical to cantankerous. I took it out and presented it to a man who claimed he could recondition it extraordinarily cheaply and when I found out neither claim was true he had evidently joined his countryman in urgent business overseas.

The engine haemorrhaged oil in a particularly dodgy way. Underway, it was well-behaved, but when I switched off the engine a solid stream of black stuff would pour onto the tarmac until the engine cooled.

Oil was not as expensive then as it is now, but it still took a chunk out of our budget. We couldn't afford to have our progress through Holland, Germany, Greece, France and so on charted by a series of oil puddles, so I devised a cunning plan.

Whenever we stopped, Sally would take a container, crawl under the van and place it beneath the leak. When all was ready, she'd call out, or at least give a strangled cry, and I would switch off the motor. The oil would pour into the container. When the engine had cooled, I would pour the oil back into it. Simple in conception, efficient in effect, but like all brilliant strategies this one had its drawbacks.

First of all, Sally did not like her side of it one bit. Crawling around under a dirty car was not her idea of having a good time *en France*, especially when the oil leak was not quite where she thought it would be, so that instead of pouring into the container it gushed over her. This was not strictly my fault but as every bloke knows, when the belle tolls, she tolls for thee.

Second, as her pregnancy advanced, it became harder for her to fit under the car.

And third, as a result of the above we stopped as little as possible, so that Marseille might pass in a whiff of exhaust or whoops, was that Venice?

You might think that all of these problems might have been resolved simply by me climbing underneath the car and Sally manning the key. But Sally was not at one with anything mechanical. In her hands a toaster endangered the staff of life, a remote control was capable of launching a nuclear weapon several oceans away. She chose not to turn the key on the grounds that it might blow us up.

The consequences were lasting. We never bought another dunger, I never again was party to any indignity on her part, and our twins were born with flat spots.

All right, none of that was true. But we developed a lifelong abhorrence for tripping, the kind of thing where you cover long distances stopping for only a day or two, the two-week tiki tour of Europe, the 'It's Tuesday, this must be Paris' school of travel. Air travel also, for us, became a means to an end and was otherwise to be avoided at all costs, barring business class.

From the sale of the van onwards we would never again hop from place to place, we decided. Instead, we would stop, live, sniff the begonias, join the library, quaff local wine, befriend villagers and know the names of their children, vote for mayor, live in a farmhouse with a local woman to dust the heavy oak furniture and chat merrily about villagey doings, graciously receive the townspeople's thanks for adding so much to their life and culture, and never, ever crawl under a car again.

By and large we stuck to it, although as in all of life's ambitions certain areas remained unfulfilled; perhaps the letter of thanks was in the mail.

Wouldn't a canal boat be just another form of van? asked Sally. Wasn't travelling by boat just another way of tripping from place to place? asked Kathryn Ryan.

Good gracious no, I replied grandly to both. Life on the canals would be slow. We would stop often, for very long periods. We would find congenial towns and villages and live in them, possibly for months at a time. We would discover the best place to buy wine, patronise the finest boulangeries, stroll around in the evenings amid surroundings we knew intimately. Our boat would be as a snail's shell, a handy place to duck into when the day's slow doings had been done.

At least one of the above was true. We knew how the snail felt: at home but a little constrained if it wanted to swing a cat.

Otherwise, well, mistakes have a way of creeping up, and when at last you hear their slither they are waiting with a four-by-two.

So far we had been rather hurried. We had spent our time in rural France, which seldom heard the whine of a Nikon. Canal travellers might not know much about the big picture, but they were on intimate terms with the little one.

We had seen a lot of towns and villages and decided most of them were closed. Actually, many were. The thirty-five hour week, which we'd admired from a distance, meant that opening hours were quixotic at best, especially in small businesses with few staff. When business was already slow, the short working week seemed to sap energy from a town, choking whatever industry was left after foreign competition, a grudging economy and an inexorable drift to bigger towns and cities had taken their toll.

Many houses looked as if they had not been inhabited for a very long time. The rest kept their shutters closed.

They were romantic, of course. They'd huddled amid their streets for centuries. The great stones and those lollipop shades of blue and pink and yellow spoke of generations of lives lived. Their silent mystery seemed more comforter than shroud. Still, sometimes when we wanted to chat we could not find anyone to chat to outside the lock-keepers and Madame in the boulangerie.

As with all canal travellers, our community tended to move along with us in boats. When we'd explained our philosophy of canal travel to Glenn and Trish, they'd smiled; being good people, they were still smiling when we joined them, although by then smirks would have been quite in order.

For we'd dashed right along. We'd nipped through three countries, Holland, Belgium and France, and we still had no idea where Mademoiselle was, much less Armentières. *Parlez-vous? Mais non.*

Now we were making a sprint for Paris.

Glenn and Trish had limited time for the trip. If we wanted to go with them we had to keep up. And we did want to go with them. Oh well. In Paris, we promised ourselves, we'd stop.

We set out one morning with the Saône River lumpy as our throats, for a cold wind was blowing and we'd liked staying in St Jean de Losne, and meeting our friends there. Now, though, we were heading for adventure with our mates.

It was late June, and the cuckoos had stopped their clocks. We pulled in beside the big fuel barge moored on the river near the entrance to the Canal de Bourgogne and filled our tanks with diesel, cheap at around $2.20 a litre. Madame topped us up smartly then summoned us into the barge's wheelhouse to watch her write what seemed to be a book, which she then handed over to us in the form of a receipt. '*Au revoir*,' she said, and '*Bonne journée m'sieur.*'

We would certainly have a good day, we thought, for what could be nicer than embarking for Paris via the famous wine villages and vineyards of Burgundy in the company of friends?

We had three possible routes to choose from.

The Canal de Bourgogne ran through Dijon, whose churches, cathedrals and palaces nodded above narrow streets thronged with people, possibly including those same citizens whose closed houses hunched amid rank grass in the more rural villages. It led through the Pouilly Tunnel, running four kilometres below a rocky ceiling so low it would scarcely let our boat pass, and promising a kind of diversion we had not so far met.

The Burgundy canal was not the most popular route. Lots of people didn't like it. Carla and Paul had gone that way. They texted us. Unusually for them, for they delighted in wherever they went, they seemed a little disappointed. It was beautiful, they said, but not as fine as the Canal du Centre.

The Canal du Bourgogne was also strong on locks. Its 242 kilometres had 189 locks, or 1.3 locks a kilometre. We'd have at least fifty more of them than we would through the Canal du Centre.

Locks were part of canal cruising. Locks and canals went together like, well, love and marriage, although not even death did them part.

Some enthusiasts loved locks. Glenn did. Others did not.

We were more or less neutral on the subject; that is, I rather liked them, Sally rather did not, so one balanced the other. Still, they said ten locks a day were enough for anybody, and our route already called for more than that; why tempt fate?

The Canal du Centre was shorthand for several canals. It became the Canal Lateral à la Loire, then the Canal de Briare, then the Canal du Loing before it finally poured its contents into the Seine. First it looped down until it was about level with Lyon, and at its lowest point dribbled off on a false start to the Mediterranean before ending abruptly at Roanne.

On the way up it passed the Canal du Nivernais, which was our third way of getting to Paris. The Nivernais was narrow, shallow and eccentric, but cute. Some people said it was the most beautiful canal in all France and worth the risk of grounding, or banging into something. Glenn did not agree. The people who said that, Glenn said, had never lived in New Zealand. The Nivernais was countryside. You might as well go to Te Kuiti.

Glenn's opinion regarding the Nivernais had to be respected, because usually he loathed countryside. He made an exception for the French countryside. The French countryside, he said, was beautiful in a way the New Zealand one could never be, if it lived to be a thousand. He loved the French countryside. So if Glenn reckoned the Nivernais was boring, his was the kind of scientific assessment that had to be taken note of.

On the other had, Glenn and Trish had already travelled up, and down, the various Canals du Centre. They reckoned them to be beautiful beyond compare, the towns delightful, the croissants the most delicious in all France, served up by delectable Mesdames so stunning of visage it would be all we could do to stagger from their boulangeries and brace ourselves for the day's voyaging. One in particular, he insisted, would serve her customers only if she was properly dressed in a negligée. And the wine! We'd never find finer Burgundy in a supermarket anywhere.

The last argument swung us completely. Almost as many epicures back home had visited the vineyards and wineries of Burgundy as had hired boats on the canals. They desired us to visit this vineyard or that winery. Their earnest expressions would grow an overlay of nostalgia as they urged us to visit the wonderful little place at St Léger-des-Vignes, or their favourite vintner near Santenay.

As our average price for a bottle was somewhere between $5 and $6, I wanted to be in a position to match these connoisseurs palate to palate: you simply must visit this little supermarket just out of St Thibault, I'd say, you'd find it quite delightful.

So the Canal du Centre it was.

The Saône was sullen that spring morning when we set out. The *Johanna Grietje* had gone ahead while we filled up and we were alone on a brown river. Herons hunched like private soldiers forced on barracks drill. Swans swam out to us and hissed. Fishermen stared moodily at floats which stayed still as a dead carp.

We went through a lock and the bow-thruster gave a sad croak and died.

Luxuries on New Zealand boats, bow-thrusters were standard on Dutch cruisers. They were little motors turning a propeller set in a tunnel running across the bow of the boat below the waterline. When you worked a lever like a PlayStation's, it would push the front of the boat to one side or the other.

At first the *River Queen*'s had remained idle, for I decided they were props for people who could not properly handle boats. Oh well, perhaps just a tweak here, because it was a tight space to squeeze into after all. And, might as well try a burst there, just to get the front of the boat lined up properly without mucking around. Then, wouldn't a decent blast of the bow-thruster with the helm over unglue us nicely from the side of the lock? Well, yes.

After a while I could no longer imagine a world without bow-thrusters. I pitied New Zealand boaties. They knew not what they did not have. I used ours all the time. When it expired I grieved, giving dismal tweaks of the lever every now and then as if trying to resuscitate a pet I could not quite believe had dropped off the perch.

Ahead of us the *Johanna Grietje*'s tall wheelhouse appeared suddenly around a bend.

I'd boasted that we'd catch her up in a couple of kilometres in our fine powerful cruiser. She after all, was an old barge with an old engine. Now we weren't far from Verdun-sur-le-Doubs, some forty kilometres from St Jean de Losne. The *Johanna Grietje* was slipping through the water leaving scarcely a wake from her fine hull.

Buschy appeared from the double doors at the back of the wheelhouse. He was gesticulating wildly. Yes, I know it has taken a long time, and we're glad to see you too, I waved back, and ran right over the log he'd been trying to warn us away from.

Verdun-sur-le-Doubs was difficult. Heavy rain had turned the Doubs into a torrent. We swept downstream on the Saône and caught a glimpse of water foaming around bridge piles as we steered around the hairpin bend leading into the Doubs then battled the current into Verdun's little harbour.

Houses whose foundations fell vertically into the river towered above us on one side but the port was a pleasant place shaded by old trees with a newish *capitainerie* built over the water. Madame la Capitaine emerged and told us we must tie up at right angles to the jetties or be charged for three boats. But she was an amiable soul. We did as she said, then helped in a skipper struggling to control his rental boat against the current. In the end he threw us lines and we towed him in backwards. He was from Denmark.

Next morning he berated us for blowing smoke over the river as our DAF engine warmed up. 'I thought New Zealanders were environmentalists,' he said. Well, I thought Danes were once such expert sailors they ruled the seas, albeit raping and pillaging.

In the warm evening we walked the narrow streets of the old town and admired the church and visited the bread museum whose curator had been about to close its doors but ate into her dinnertime by keeping them open for us. Sally loved bread, the feel and smell of it, the baking of it, the taste.

The French loved bread too. Our bread bin was always full of square loaves, and round ones, and oval, usually so nutty even the smallest towns had a dentist or two, and heavy enough to take a body straight to the bottom if you should fall overboard after lunch.

But a bread museum? Certainly some of the bread we had aboard tasted old enough to be on its shelves. I demurred. Sally went alone. She emerged elated, as if someone had added yeast and sat her in a warm place to rise.

I slept uneasily that night, my dreams full of our boat being swept helplessly on the current and smashed against the bridge piles as a galley-full of Danes rattled their tin hats and chorused verses which turned out to be complaints to the European commission on atmospheric pollution.

In fact we woke up and chugged off in company with nothing more dramatic than a few dead branches.

What a difference a day made. This morning the Saône seemed wide as the Pacific, free as the black kites soaring and swooping along its banks.

The morning sun frolicked in the spring green of the passing trees, young sunflowers rose high on stalks which sometimes exploded like fireworks into great clouds of black crows, and we crowed over the cameo appearance of a white heron, so thin that when it turned to face us it almost vanished. The sky was deep blue, clouds plumped and the world was wide and bright as a South Island summer. Fishermen waved merrily from the shore as if they'd all just feasted on fat perch for breakfast.

Chalon-sur-Saône rose ahead of us. An island split the river and boats in the town's port bucked against the current. This was the most expensive port we'd been in. Villages were quixotic with their mooring fees. Some charged up to $20 a night, some nothing at all. Chalon was the second-dearest of the trip, not much cheaper than Paris at $44 a night.

The hot showers were *en panne*, out of order. Two fat workmen returned from lunch and began keening over the innards of a boiler. An alleged mechanic shook his head over our bow-thruster and delivered his verdict: *en panne*.

Who cared? The island in the river had a street jammed full of restaurants and bars. Chalon was a magnificent city, and its splendid eleventh-century Saint-Vincent Cathedral looked even better through a glass of Bordeaux from Chez Louis across the square where we sat in the sun and watched the promenade.

An Australian yacht lay beside us in the port. When we'd arrived, a man had emerged from its cabin, introduced himself as Peter, and helped us tie up. He was friendly and cheerful. His blue eyes laughed as I grumbled about the current. His wife, Jan, grinned. Her eyes were a deep, thoughtful brown.

The Australian stars flew from the stern of a Laurent Giles-designed Salar class yacht, a renowned ocean cruiser, yet it did not look as if it could handle a storm. This was not because of its condition, which seemed good enough, or its gear, which looked excellent.

There was just so much of it. Jerrycans, bikes, planks, wire, boxes, spars, crates, lumps of unidentifiable machinery and things of unknown origin and purpose were packed solid on the deck. Wherever there was something capable of being tied to, something was tied to it. Sometimes, in the evenings when the setting sun cast long shadows over the assembly, I wondered at the physics principles which allowed the boat to stay upright. Clambering around and through all this stuff required the determination of a Hillary and the agility of a monkey.

Its crew had neither. Pete was, well, stout. He might have preferred burly, but stout would do. His face was that shade of pink which springs from within rather than without. His thinning fair hair was usually stuck to his scalp by drops of sweat which appeared after the smallest exertion. His wife Jan was of a build which suggested that Pete had not got stuck into dinner alone.

Deep-sea sailors are not famous for weight problems. Grim determination, self-confidence, independence, mild to serious insanity, yes. Dieting, no.

Perhaps both clutter and weight disappeared at sea. For these two were not just sailors, but ocean cruisers extraordinaire. They'd first left home for adventure on the high seas seventeen years before. The boat had every right to look weatherbeaten. So had they.

They'd sailed from Australia through the Red Sea and the Suez Canal, across the Mediterranean and through the French canals to Britain. They had escaped storms and pirates. They were a couple of paladins in plain clothes. They spoke of all this as if it were a toddle across an estuary, yet without any false modesty. It was something they did. The *River Queen*, formerly pride of my life, suddenly looked pasty as a custard square.

Now they were planning to return to the Mediterranean and prepare their yacht for the voyage home across the Atlantic Ocean with their son as crew. Then they'd sail through the Panama Canal and across the Pacific Ocean. A merry jaunt. Where to then?

'Home', said Jan, firmly.

'Hum,' said Pete.

She gave him the Look. He studied his knees, or what he could see of them. They'd talked of their little house in the suburbs. He could see the picket fence around his life.

'Pete's not keen,' said Jan, in case we had missed the drift.

Sally asked Pete why he liked the life. He thought for a while.

'Because I'm good at it,' he said, 'and I'm not good at much else.'

Jan said, 'He says he's going home to die. I'm going home to live.'

Sally chimed in, two clocks striking the hour. She loved France; but it just wasn't … home. Leaving home to follow me had cost her dearly in the past.

The iron hills in Denis Glover's song of Mick Stimpson had ringed our house in Port Levy, the quiet tides whispered below. Stimpson lay in his grave in the old Māori cemetery above the pa on the other side of the bay.

Scenes still glowed in my mind: of a picnic on the stream bank, the water shaded by the huge wattle. The creek rustled gently to the sea, touched silver by sunlight. The scent of heavy white hawthorn blossom hung over us, the grass lush and sweet-smelling. The oldest of our elk stags ambled over curiously, then grazed nearby, his shiny summer coat glistening. The vast animal standing so calmly exuded peace, the dog lay at our feet and ducklings squeaked from somewhere in the rushes.

I'd found happiness, peace, contentment in the tiny community. We were so lucky, I'd said, for the thousandth time.

It didn't feel like that when the boys came home, around seven. Simon was quiet, sad. Both of them were still grieving for our old home. They could not believe we'd given it up, for this.

I'd sat on the sofa that night and thought of our beautiful old house on the hill above the sea in Sumner and the picture was so clear and familiar I started to weep. Sally was sad too. She went to bed and we didn't talk again that evening. My god, I wrote in my diary, I hope this works. The awful loss if it didn't.

The boys and Sally had commuted at first, in the farm's Toyota truck. It cost a fortune in petrol and was hard to drive. They bought a Holden stationwagon and roared into town with Sally, Sting's *Fields of Gold* on the stereo.

The boys' absences grew longer. They stayed with friends. They spent more and more time in the city, less and less at home. Finally they moved into a little house in Sumner and left home forever.

Sally packed cartons of food, cutlery, crockery. We gave them sofas and beds and a TV. They stacked everything on the truck.

Sally kept coming out and giving them more. Her face was pinched. Then she and I drove over to Akaroa for a bowl of hot chocolate. We stared over the pretty harbour. We were on our own now.

We went back and lit the fire and ate leek and kumara soup, which the boys loathed. Outside the cherry trees were afire with autumn. Flames of bright red, brilliant orange and yellow filled the panes. The lime tree was pale yellow. I went outside and sat beneath it, in a room full of light.

The sycamores filled the little wood beside the house with colour. I stood at the edge of the front paddock. A gentle breeze slipped down the hill and over the water, warming the twilight, but speaking of sadness.

Pete and Jan cast off next morning. I took their photograph before they went. They stood in front of their boat stiff as 'American Gothic'.

We caught our last glimpse of Jan as she waved from the foredeck. She looked wistful. I thought Sally did too. Jan faced a couple of oceans and a lot of living in very small spaces. But at least she was pointing towards home.

We crossed all fingers for both of them. Next morning I crossed a couple for us. We set off for the Canal du Centre, which would, in 500 kilometres, 155 locks and four changes of name plus the River Seine, take us to Paris. Pete and Jan had put our journey into perspective, but it still looked serious enough from here.

The first lock on the Canal du Centre was going to lead us into another world, but was an unlikely looking-glass. It was a huge, dark thing, eleven metres deep, and going through it promised a less-than-magical experience.

We huddled in the bottom of the lock, the *Johanna Grietje* in front. Glenn liked that possie, which was all right with us who still believed in Mr Benny's dictum: the water boiled in from that end and set whatever was floating on it banging this way and that with the crew trying to look as nonchalant as possible while hanging grimly onto lines, fending off concrete and trying to keep the whole assembly facing the front.

The lock-keeper hid in a glass box somewhere far above, sometimes yelling commands which would have been incomprehensible even if he had not sounded like Robocop with the 'flu. The lock gates rose and lowered like guillotine blades, and we had the same expectation of emerging in one piece.

Like Alice, though, we reappeared in another place. We were in picture-book French countryside, full of pretty houses and smiling people. The lock-keeper laughed. His pretty daughter took our lines and laughed. The locks went wrong and wouldn't work. We all laughed.

We worked hard all day, passing through several five metre locks, waiting for locks that were out of order, waiting for other boats that had waited because the locks were out of order, and at the end of it arrived in Chagny in fine spirits although we could have biked the same distance in not much more than an hour.

We tied up in a great brickyard where once navvies loaded barges with rock from the quarries, by hand. We unloaded our bikes and set off for Santenay, pedalling down the canal in the soft evening with the light falling on vineyards turning the hills to velvet, past a hotel boat whose guests seemed entranced by their new world, down a rough track to a road which took us over a bridge almost buried in pink roses, then across a railway line — no, two railway lines, warned a sign, and don't forget there could be a train sneaking up on the other one — then up narrow streets into a town filled with wineries.

Signs pointed to dozens of them, many owned by members of the same families. We climbed to the fifteenth-century château built by Philippe-le-Hardi, Philip the Bold, the king's son; its intricately tiled roof zig-zagged in the Burgundian fashion, the sunset now so luminous the vines seemed lit from the inside.

I bought a bottle of wine made by one of the Clair family, for a special occasion. The young woman in the shop reeked of knowledge. She wanted to share it. She pointed me towards dusty shelves. I checked the labels. No, the ones on the shelves, $30, $40, $100. Mine cost $15; well, you had to splash out every now and then.

We bought chocolate éclairs for dessert, their delicate pastry cases filled with thick chocolatey cream so delicious a single bite seemed sinful. The wine was soft as the night.

Next day we sailed to St Léger sur Dheune on a canal winding through the sparkling countryside, accompanied by an *éclusier* in a truss.

A car with two men and a woman stopped as we were going through a lock. They hopped out for a chat. Where were we from? And the boat? Did we like it? How much had we paid for the *vignette*? Did we get a discount when *l'éclusier* was in a truss? No? My, it was dear: '*Cher, oui?*'

'*Non, non,*' I protested. The *vignette*, the certificate in the front window which gave us access to every canal and lock in the country, along with the help of every *éclusier*, was the best value of all.

Besides, the lockie might be in a truss, but he was handsome. Except I could not remember the word for handsome. *L'éclusier* laughed.

'*Joli?*' Sally ventured.

He didn't mind being called pretty. He laughed some more. He clutched his truss. His hernia was included in the *vignette* too.

Until St Léger we had not met many New Zealanders. We had heard of them. Almost-permanent canal dwellers from New Zealand were reputed to be in residence all over the canals. The Dutch, the Germans, port captains, *éclusiers* and all marvelled at how many New Zealanders took to the canals each summer, from so small a country, where only old people and children must be left to look after the only other known feature of our South Pacific paradise not counting the All Blacks, its sixty million sheep. Only forty million? *Ooh la la la.*

We doubted the Kiwi count was any more accurate than the sheep. For how did they know we were New Zealanders? In a continent where everyone spoke with an accent in every language but their own, no one could recognise a Black-and-Decker twang, except Australians, who had us figured in a trice. Fush-and-chups they said. Feesh-and-cheeps we said back. These intricacies went over the heads of most continental voyagers like the blackbirds and starlings: they all looked the same from any distance, and if one sang, and one croaked, only the participants cared to dispute which was the more musical.

No one could tell the difference between the flags, either. To them it was a mess of stars either way. And wasn't that the Union Jack? These must be English. '*Pas Anglais*,' I got tired of saying, as if anyone cared much about that either.

New Zealanders had their own recognition signal, reliable as a Mason's handshake. 'Gidday,' you both said, and fell into each other's arms. For the rest, we relied on our little black ensigns with the silver ferns, and the battle for a change in the national flag was already well-settled among travellers sick of being taken for any one of three nationalities, if they were recognised at all.

The kiwi was the most instantly-recognised symbol. But the kiwi ran second to the All Blacks in brand recognition, so most Kiwis favoured silver ferns. Some, like ours, carried the words 'New Zealand' underneath. Others wanted locals to be absolutely certain of their country of origin, so their flags said, 'All Blacks'.

We had the Australians beaten hands-down. Plain green-and-gold didn't go far with the French. They were just colours. All those stars? Could be either country.

Some Australians had their city of origin painted on their boats' sterns in large letters. I liked the *Robert,* from Melbourne. Now there was a no-nonsense name. But the sophistry had the French asking, in a puzzled way, how they'd sailed around the world in a boat so plainly unsuited to the voyage.

So many Aussies reverted to the good old kangaroo. This had advantages. Most people recognised the kangaroo. It was the only word of Australian known to the French despite the rest of that language being a great deal shorter and easier to spell.

The disadvantage was that to be recognisable the kangaroo had to be big. Regular flag-size, it might as well be a squirrel, or a rat. Some Australians tried to get around the problem by super-sizing their kangaroo flags. This only reinforced their reputations as a nation of skites.

We were very pleased to spend an evening or two with all the New Zealanders we met, which might go without saying had it not been for our experiences on our several trips around Europe in a van.

Then, we learned to treat fellow-New Zealanders like unexploded bombs. In those days some had reconstructed themselves as Europeans, or English (such was the degree of cultural cringe). Others had bounded off in the opposite direction and emerged fully formed from the fusion of Fred Dagg and Barry Crump.

Some would ignore you altogether; and some you wished would ignore you altogether. One quiet evening we were camped on a lovely beach in Corfu when down the road came a purple VW with 'Stan's Van' written large in yellow.

'Hey, waaaaanker,' came the call from its window. 'How's it hanging?' The couple inside spent the evening tearfully reminiscing over the delights of Tauranga.

Corfu crossed my mind for a moment in St Léger. The silver fern flew from a rental boat. Its crew were from Tauranga also. They had standard Tauranga politics ('Winston Peters had the right idea about immigration') but otherwise they were nice people. They seemed so affluent, and comfortable, and happy. 'I live this lovely life,' one woman, Linda, said almost guiltily. Once more we heard that famous old expression, and thrilled to it like sheepdogs to a whistle: 'You don't know how lucky you are.' Well, I thought, that showed how far New Zealand had come in thirty years: we do now.

Sandwiched between us and the *Johanna Grietje* lay another New Zealand hire boat. Silver ferns decorated this one front and back. These were devoted Kiwis without a doubt, although there was no sign of them. Two blokes appeared around five p.m. Evidently they'd had some sort of epiphany.

'You missed something,' they called to someone inside their boat. 'You missed a real fuckin' experience. It's so fuckin' *beautiful*.' They vanished into their boat, which for the next hour seemed to gurgle like good stew. Something definitely was brewing or rather, had brewed. I heard a woman talking to Sally: 'It's been a bad day. We lost the sailing, we lost the rugby. The boys are back pissed and they're both pissed off.'

Sally asked the scores. From deep inside their boat something stirred. 'Where you from?'

'Christchurch,' said Sally then, just in case, 'Crusader country.'

Silence for a moment. Then: 'You're not proper people. But I'll tell you anyway. We lost the rugby. In the sailing they beat us by a few seconds.'

Tormented by scores we set off next morning behind Glenn and Trish. The canal seemed abandoned. The lock-keepers' cottages lay deserted or barren. Hydraulics swung the lock gates open and closed, without so much as a hint of romance. At one a brown and white duck begged at the gate. Failing to score (we were out of bread) it swam into the lock with us, dived and emerged with a fish in its mouth. I didn't think ducks fished. This one was a relief. Its cameo performance made up for the canal. Inside the locks little waterfalls sprang from fissures in the concrete, trickling over moss that somehow grew underwater for half its life.

Yet the villages along the way were fresh and lovely. In St Julien-sur-Dheune great slabs of stone marked the boundaries of the tiny port, as if a monastery had been dismembered for the purpose.

A fisherman threw old metal buckets into the canal and dredged its bottom, picking through the mud for worms. A man in a white shirt arrived at the boat and stood politely outside until I realised he wanted something: he was the lock-keeper, and he asked what time we wanted to leave in the morning? We told him we might leave sooner, for St Julien was very quiet.

A heron's nest stuck out of a dead tree so haphazardly I could not imagine such a large animal landing in it without toppling the lot to the ground. A dead water rat floated by. Did water rats drown?

I studied the patterns of Burgundian roof tiles. Diamonds, crosses, checks in gold and deep Burgundy red and green. A canal museum just outside the village featured a *peniche*, high and dry. Faded signs announced lost enterprises.

But the church was still alive. Inside, a painted blue sea floated around its walls, bright as a Pacific island. A youthful bearded Jesus in what might have been a lava-lava laid out loaves and fishes. The walls were the colour of sun. It lacked only a barbecue. Fresh flowers sat on white lace, smelling of community, and intimacy. Sally discovered more of that when she walked around the back of the church, into a grassy churchyard enclosed by stone walls.

A young couple were making love. The girl stared at the sky while the boy pumped away. Neither saw her and she stayed for a moment, intrigued as much by their confidence that no one would come to church on a Sunday as by their age, for St Julien seemed some way from the font of youth.

So we left St Julien, and went on up to the summit as the canal crossed the first of three ranges on the journey at Montchanin. It was a beautiful stretch of canal. Purple and yellow flowers lined the banks. The sky was clear blue. Then black thunderstorms flicked lightning and rain, and we were both drenched and hot.

My cellphone rang in the small hours of the morning. 'Look, I've told you before …' carped a Kiwi voice. Still, something was to be said for these wrong numbers winged to France. They cost the callers heaps.

Chapter Ten

Montchanin on Sunday was rather like Upper Hutt on the Sabbath: a little depressing and almost completely shut. The chart showed this to be a mooring, but its bollards had a grassy, unused look about them, as if someone had found them lying about and used them for garden sculptures.

We would not have stopped in Montchanin either, but we were on a mission. The *River Queen*'s bow-thruster was still not working. We needed a mechanic.

Finding one was not an easy job. The French had plenty of diesel engines. Diesels powered trucks, tractors, combine harvesters, *peniches*, the smallest of cars. We wished they'd make a tiny version of the mopeds beloved of French youth, painstakingly tuned to wreck an eardrum at five hundred metres.

All of those engines should have equalled lots of mechanics. Yet mechanics were notoriously difficult to track down on canals.

Explaining the problem was trouble enough. The Dutch had warned us that we should get anything that needed to be fixed seen to before we left Holland. 'In France it is hopeless,' they said.

Our ship's surveyor had told us of taking his boat to France and running his batteries flat. It had taken him a night and a day to persuade a French mechanic that what he needed was a jump start; 'How do you say that in French?' he asked. I did not know. How did you say 'bow-thruster', for that matter?

For no apparent reason the engine on the *Johanna Grietje* occasionally sped up, and as engines do, it usually chose to misbehave at the most inconvenient moment, such as entering a lock. Then it was best to slow down rather than race towards a chunk of ironmongery expressly designed to emerge from such contests intact. Several mechanics had investigated and all of them had pronounced themselves, in a variety of languages, defeated.

After one troublesome patch, Glenn and Trish had summoned their resident English expert in St Jean de Losne. He was not an engineer, but he'd arranged for a French mechanic to inspect the engine, and explained the problem to him in a language he could understand: French. The mechanic dived into the engine room, rummaged around for a while and surfaced declaring the engine irredeemably stuffed.

This was bad news and Glenn and Trish were inclined to be glum.

Then the Englishman brought his thirty-year experience of such affairs to bear.

Ah, non, he said, the French mechanic owned an identical engine. He desired to sell it. In fact, he wanted to sell it to Glenn who, however, had no need of a new engine; his own suffered only a minor malaise.

Not all of us were lucky enough to have such a sound adviser as the Englishman on call. Instead, we carried lists of English-speaking mechanics to be found on the canals, with phone numbers, and assessments of their capabilities ('good mechanic', 'will travel', 'never stops talking', 'charges like a horny ram', etc.).

All of them had washed up in France for reasons of their own. We found them to range from different to eccentric. They had one thing in common, however: they were all creatures of patronage. If you found a good one you cuddled him to your bosom like a hot-water bottle on a July night in Ophir.

One of the mechanics on the list lived at Montchanin. His name was Jeff. Trish had heard he was very good. Others seemed to agree. '*Tout le monde cherche* Jeff,' said *l'éclusier*, when he understood our mission in Montchanin.

Everyone might seek Jeff, but not all of us found him.

We scaled a steep, grassy bank to the road above our mooring. Jeff's address lay in an old inlet accommodating a flotilla of boats, most of them shabby, some apparently dead. We passed a rumpty barge, a flaking cruiser, a few sad vessels of no known species.

We threaded through ancient caravans and portable cabins, some of them with clothes on the line and children's toys outside. This place would definitely be visited by social services back home, I thought. Junk lay everywhere.

We came to a house whose fetid depths accommodated engine parts and lots of grease.

I knocked. No one came. I knocked harder.

We heard shuffling deep within, as if we'd prodded something, perhaps a creature that had found a nice dark and smelly place to hibernate, or die of its wounds.

An Englishman appeared. He looked at us suspiciously, as if we were tax inspectors, or immigration officials. He denied being Jeff. He disowned any knowledge of Jeff.

A second Englishman crept out, blinking at the light. He wasn't Jeff either, he said. Well yes, Jeff did exist. But he wasn't home.

Now he began to evince that enthusiasm we recognised as a prelude to discouraging news. Jeff was on holiday. He would not be back for a week. At least.

The man warmed to his theme. Jeff might be a lot longer. In fact, he might stay where he was. Where was that? The man wasn't saying, but his smirk implied a lot of sun and not many clothes.

No, he knew of no one within hundreds of kilometres who could fix my bow-thruster. Jeff alone was my man. No, he could not give me his mobile number. His tone suggested that I'd only use it to make obscene calls.

But, I said, the man was a mechanic, wasn't he? In business?

'Jeff,' he declared, now with immense satisfaction, 'keeps very much to himself these days.'

'I reckon he's buried in the garden,' said Glenn as we walked away. Trish said that anyway, Jeff always looked to her as if he had Asperger's. I said it looked to me as if his mates had Tourette's.

Only the bow-thruster remained silent.

Temporarily defeated, we descended the other side of the hill to Montceau-des-Mines.

The countryside fell softly. When I dreamed of canal boating, wafting gentle as a feather on gleaming waters, and saw in my sleep the delicious mixture of spires and stones and green, green depths, I might have awoken in the canals around Montceau.

Yes, the locks were being converted to hydraulics. When each became automated its soul fled, as if it had died. But the remaining mechanically-operated gates were opened and closed by huge wheels, like a ship's. You yanked the spokes, pulling ancient chains whose grease seized its chance to see more of the world by transferring itself to any parts of your person which had strayed too close.

They were mediaeval but engaging. The lock-keepers were cheerful as their cottages. One was helped by his young sons. Glenn tipped them cans of Coke. Perhaps the French will declare a national day of mourning when progress overtakes the last of the mechanical locks.

Montceau had been, of course, a mining town, and everyone from Nightcaps to Waihi knows what that meant. Mining had kicked the guts out of the place, then abandoned it.

Montceau should have been stuffed, but was not. It had refused to lie down. Now it was a working town, if not an elegant one.

The main street was lively. It ran to an Otago rugby shop selling clothes with Māori motifs. Māori were sparser than mines in Montceau. Still, Māori art was fashionable. Robbie Williams sported it on various parts of his body. Terry Darlington prepared for the canal journey he recorded in his book *Narrow Dog to Carcassonne* by getting a Māori tattoo on his arm. He wanted it to mean he was well above average in sexual prowess and fortunately the British tattooist must have been proficient in Māori, for he said that was exactly what his tattoo meant.

I found something even more useful in Montceau. Unusually, the port had wi-fi. You might say, what did you expect? This after all was rural France, where even in the sixties people were bathing in basins. But when I returned to New Zealand I found that Takaka in Golden Bay, a lot smaller than Montceau, had five public internet places and I could hook up to a wi-fi network in my remote inlet. Probably they were bathing in basins in Takaka in the sixties, too, that being the kind of lifestyle alternative many of the locals then preferred.

In fact, the internet was not the channel of preference for canal news. Canal boaters preferred gossip.Gossip was much more interesting. Ports were always full of it. The French were getting tough on boaties' driving licences. The VNF, the French waterways' managers, were closing such and such a lock and the canals were blocked. Jean and Brian had done this, or that. Brian had hit that, or this. Jean had put laxative in the soup, or Brian had gone off for a sex change operation.

It didn't matter how much was true. The joy was in the telling, and listening, and re-telling. It was the currency of canals. The more you had to tell, the richer you were. If you were the first in with a story, you could take the throne, until someone else broke another news flash and deposed you.

We'd scarcely tied up than a Dane, his face red with excitement, hastened over. Had we heard? No. The red deepened to magenta.

One side of the Canal de Roanne à Digoin, the short no-exit length of waterway which ran off from the canal we were on and headed south, had fallen down. The water had drained out.

A friend of his had awoken to find his beautiful boat stranded on the mud bottom. He would have to remain there until the canal was repaired and refilled. God knew how long that would take. The VNF evidently did not. They said a few weeks. A few weeks? Phew! The French would not even have finished talking about it by then, much less organised the machinery. Meanwhile boats were trapped in Roanne, at the end of this short canal, a favourite wintering-over spot. Were we going to stop in Digoin? Some chance! Digoin was full of boats that had been on their way to Roanne when this disaster overtook them all.

By the time he'd finished he was thoroughly expansive. He had just set forth after two years living in Paris. He'd loved it. And now this! Could anything be finer?

I began to wonder if we should move, immediately, although we were nowhere near the damaged canal, Digoin was still eighteen locks away, and Montceau itself had only ten boats in its large port. But we must be sitting ducks, mustn't we?

The Dane looked at the sky. He said, 'It's going to rain.'

It did. And the side of the Canal de Roanne à Digoin had indeed fallen out. Others soon rushed to tell us the same news, just as we hastened straight over to Glenn and Trish with the tidings. Everyone now knew someone who had been trapped by the disaster, although some played a trump by knowing people who had just escaped it.

Poor Montceau. It seemed depressed by the news, for now Roanne was all the go. In the market beside the port people huddled under the awnings in the wet. Never rained but it poured.

That night Karen and Chris came over for a drink. They were both from the United States. Karen looked at us expectantly. She said, 'Perhaps you recognise me.'

Perhaps we did. We'd seen her often enough before, a blonde woman in her fifties wearing tight white pants and inhabiting the sundeck of a large, expensive boat. Lots of them were to be found looking like their partners: sleek, a little lost, slightly irascible, as if life had treated them so well they could not believe it had thrown such a curly one as age.

'I was on the news in New Zealand,' Karen said. 'In nineteen seventy-six. I was cycling around the world with my husband. We were on our honeymoon.'

We looked at Chris. He must have put on a bit of weight.

'Not him,' said Karen. 'My first husband was murdered.'

'Well, not ...' said Chris.

'The guy's doing life for it,' Karen interrupted firmly.

Chris subsided. I sympathised. You couldn't compete with a former husband like that.

Much later I looked them up. Round-the-world cyclists in 1976 were Americans Jack and Karen Lambie, who had circumnavigated on a tandem, on their honeymoon. Jack had died some seven years ago, although the cause of death was not specified. He'd been a pioneer hang-glider pilot.

Chris, however, was in the fire safety business. They spent four months in France, the rest of the year in Los Angeles, and as far as I could determine no time at all on bikes, probably to Chris's great relief.

Like many Americans they wondered about the hostility they'd encountered in France. Names would never hurt them, the name-callers being misguided, but those sticks and stones might indeed break their bones, and some had had rocks thrown at them.

They seemed puzzled. We were puzzled that they seemed puzzled. Karen said she could never vote for Hillary Clinton, although we did not discover whether that was because Clinton was a Democrat, or a woman, or just Hillary. Probably they were Republicans, we decided, like every American but one we met on the canals. Both of them were disparaging about President Bush, but every American we met reckoned Bush had been a disaster. Why had they voted for him? God knew. Yes He did, really.

Perhaps talking about Bush soured our mood, but we were both sombre that night. Sally said she wished she was somewhere else, such as Brittany. Let's try and make this work first, I said. I am, she said. Yeah, right, I said. I said ten positive things yesterday, she said. I only counted six, I said. It was a mistake to come, she said. Yes, I said, I think it was. Yet I couldn't see why. I'd imagined the journey as beautiful, and romantic, and gentle, and perhaps that was the trouble; when those things go wrong who can fix them? I should have thought more about what *could* be fixed, stopped in a pretty town, set a table under the trees where we could talk and laugh and watch the world go by rather than having it watch us. Instead I thought about writing a manual on how to live in boats and save your marriage, but I didn't know how it would end.

It was still raining when we set out next day for Paray-le-Monial but Montceau held one last delight. To leave, we had to pass under two lifting bridges. The bridge-keepers stopped the traffic and huge, shiny hydraulic rams hoisted the bridges into the sky — and Montceau had painted its drawbridges mauve and purple. They opened before us like rainbows.

Paray-le-Monial was on the pilgrimage circuit.

Here, on 27 December 1673, after a feast which must have been of the kind alarming to neighbours, a nun reported that a vision of Jesus had allowed her to rest her head on his beating heart then urged her to go and tell everyone. No one could refuse an offer like that, so she did, to the great benefit of both herself and the town.

She was promoted to saint.

Paray-le-Monial became famous.

But today the town lay empty as a priest's promise, mercifully free of the thousands of pilgrims who, centuries after the nun had cocked an ear to the holy breast, still flocked to the scene.

We could see where they'd been. Ranks of white tents were formed up like a crusader's encampment. Great marquees where pilgrims queued to be fed stood empty. The open-air chapel was taken over by pigeons which, like the pilgrims perhaps, searched for crumbs. Ranks of seats which could have accommodated the crowd at a Super 14 game were deserted.

The chapel where the sainted nun held sway accommodated only tourists cloaked with reverence over their shorts. In the grotto where some overwrought sculptor had given the Madonna's hand such a flourish she seemed to be flipping the bird to worshippers, there was no one but us.

Beggars were all over the town. Perhaps they'd come to sack and stayed to prey. Pilgrims chastened by such close contact with the Son of God's organ were evidently a soft touch.

Yet piety had its rewards for dilettantes such as us. Public toilets were everywhere, the tourist office offered free wi-fi, and great baskets of flowers adorned bridges, seats, railings, streets, in fact anything that could wear a begonia or a petunia and not look overdressed.

We sat on the deck, sipped wine and watched a duck swim by with nine ducklings in tow. That was a record. Even the ducks seemed to prosper in Paray-le-Monial. The various French onlookers who always came down to ports for a look at the boats threw baguettes to the duck and her nine offspring. Then they studied our bottle and smiled.

The French loved watching you tipping a bottle. They wished you *bonne soirée*. They were even happier when they saw you having lunch. They studied the food. They wished you *bon appétit*, and *bonne journée, m'sieur-dame*, a handy abbreviation designed to overcome the difficulty of fitting in the long version if you were, say, passing each other at a brisk pace.

For Paray was a fine town. It was both expansive and expensive, its shops selling the kind of gear usually only found in much bigger towns: Gucci, Louis Vuitton, Armani, Prada. Like the beggars, and the ducks, *les négociants* did well out of pilgrims, and the Basilica now faced stiff competition from Leclercs, the giant supermarket operators.

We biked up a hill to the big new shopping mall and wondered, again, why in France all new shopping developments were always uphill. And why was there a sign on a roundabout announcing 'Bad Durkheim, 590km?' I looked it up: Bad Durkheim was on the German wine trail but otherwise undistinguished. Why did citizens of Paray-le-Monial need to know its whereabouts? In that town, not only the Almighty moved in mysterious ways.

Scepticism did me no good at all. The weather stopped messing around. As we moved on, the heavens opened. Within minutes we were drenched. Both of us wore winter gear, poly undershirts, fleece jackets, heavy parkas, and still we froze.

Each new squall arrived in a great gust, usually when we were entering a lock or in the middle of some tricky manoeuvre best executed in complete stillness rather than being picked up bodily and thrown around. The lock-keepers shuffled out of small, comfortless sheds beside their locks, gesturing despairingly at the sky.

Sally went inside, sensibly, and emerged only when we arrived at locks.

But I liked steering from the outside wheel rather than the inside one. The helm on the after-deck gave a better view, which included whatever the sky threw at me. Today, that was quite a lot.

My wide-brimmed hat gave me the illusion of being dry at first. Then its brim began to leak. In the end it gave up the struggle and turned downwards like a Roman emperor's thumb.

At exactly the same moment my parka, donated to me by my son Simon, who had in turn been given it free by a vodka company at a skiing event, went back to its roots and became a soak. To say I was miserable would hardly diminish the trials of such fellow-sufferers as Captain Oates, although we'd both foolishly stepped outside for a while.

In the *Johanna Grietje* ahead I could see Glenn and Trish reclining comfortably in their snug wheelhouse, occasionally sucking on hot coffee, emerging at the locks with the wide breezy smiles of dry people observing wet ones.

They called, 'Why don't you go inside?' Sally called, 'Why don't you come inside?'

Why didn't I? Hair shirt stubbornness, the notion that you can't go boating without getting wet, the idea that you take the rough with the smooth, for otherwise how could you tell one from the other, the base fear of being a wuss; in short, male stupidity.

I hate wet clothes. Watching kids swimming in jeans makes me grit my teeth as if someone were screeching fingernails on glass, not because they might drown, but worse, because I can feel the soaking things clinging to my own legs back on shore, stiff and dripping and completely horrible.

The water dripped through my hat, gushed through my parka, soaked my trusty Earth Sea Sky fleece and hit pay-dirt: quivering epidermis. My skin promptly reported to my brain that the very worst had happened and everything lying between it and the elements was now thoroughly wet.

I slunk inside and dripped gloomily on the carpet. Sally put down a towel, without a word.

We passed through Digoin. Sure enough, it was crowded. A notice at the entrance to the Canal de Roanne à Digoin announced that it was closed for repairs. The stories were true.

We stopped at Pierrefitte. A bright old man from York emerged from his cheerful barge. He'd been living in it, in France, with his wife, for eleven years.

Why? we asked.

The bright old man turned dark. The geraniums on his barge drooped. Because, he said, there was nothing in the United Kingdom for them. 'It's no good now,' he said. 'Everything's a rip-off. It costs too much to live there. We can afford to live here, and we like the life.'

By now we were used to ageing British expats living on boats and grizzling about home. Curiously, given that Margaret Thatcher had executed the reforms which rendered their home uninhabitable, most of them were Thatcherites. Their ideas had stalled in the eighties, and grown hairy, like a Southland policeman's moustache.

We wondered what would happen to the couple from York when one of them died. Would he or she cling on alone? How would the survivor survive? Creatures of their home town fable, they'd marched up to the top of the hill, and marched down again, and now there was nowhere left to go. Not even Pierrefitte, we thought.

The old château near what used to be the town centre was fine, but looked barely maintained; the gatehouse, now a garage, sat broken-windowed, the magnificent gates locked with rusty chains. Some second-storey shutters were open, revealing a nursery with a row of teddy-bears and dolls.

It was a gently mouldering paradise. The houses in many French villages were shuttered, secret, silent, impenetrable to outsiders and tourists alike, hoarding the French way of life like museums, forever mysterious. Pierrefitte seemed to be on its uppers, the boulangerie closed, the bar up for sale, the only store inhabited by a fierce species of shop-keeper not conducive to human life.

Diou was better. A cruiser arrived, full of varnished wood and white leather, captained by a handsome Dutchman flying a Swiss flag. He vectored into the women with all systems locked on. He boasted of his house in Monte Carlo, of his wealth, of the new hotels he was building in Vietnam.

'I have to go now,' he said. 'I must chill the wine for dinner.'

When he'd gone I foolishly noted that his boat was rather small, exposing myself to much female jeering. The New Zealand blokes voted him a champion bull-shitter. Sally and Trish thought him charming.

We cycled along to the thirteenth-century Abbey-des-Sept-Fonts which was being redecorated in what Sally called a spare style but which I thought was more New York apartment.

Sally wanted to see the new stained glass in the chapel but an old monk guarding the gate refused to let us in. Instead he sold us fig and port jam. He turned around and bent over to pick it up from a stack. To my horror I found myself looking up his habit. Force of habit, I supposed. I could report that what old monks wore beneath their robes was not worth reporting, although he sported a fine pair of long woolly socks under his sandals.

I tried out my French on a younger monk. If we really wanted to see the chapel, he said, we could return at six p.m. and pray with them. Alternatively we could go to the flash new *salle des expositions*, through much exposed wood and white plaster, and watch a video on the monastic life.

The film showed monks getting up at three a.m. I may have been biased, but their day only seemed to get worse.

Next day it was clear that our own day was getting better. The sun came out. The clouds turned to silver. Grass sparkled, trees shook themselves like puppies and smiled. It was the kind of day when nothing could go wrong.

One of the lock-keepers spoke perfect English, probably to save himself from tortured conversations about the weather with people like us. He proved to be the unhappiest lock-keeper in all France. He'd moved to this remote place from Paris and although he was married he and his wife lived with his mother and father. When his parents moved from Paris to a house near his lock, he moved with them. This he regarded as just a fact of life if he was to get along in a world where jobs were scarce. 'I had no choice.' He did not elaborate and although I wanted to ask why, I did not.

'Why are you in France?' he asked.

'Because we love it.'

'I do not love it. I do not even like it.'

We left him morosely turning his handles and churned along the canal.

At first we thought we were being raced by a moorhen. Two tiny wings stuck out of the water. They kept pace ahead of our bow. Boy, that moorhen was determined, we told each other.

Slowly we closed in on it. The form took on a familiar shape.

It was not a bird. The wings were not wings. They were ears. They belonged to a tiny fawn.

We were horrified. We'd seen dead fawns drifting in the canals, along with dead rabbits, cats, dogs, a fox, even the water rat. Most had probably slipped into the canal and couldn't climb its banks. The canal sides here were lined with steel, often for kilometres at a time, and the smooth vertical surface offered no hope of footholds for a panicking beast.

The walls were also very hard on a boat's paint if a skipper got too close, but that seemed not to matter much as we tried to rescue the poor animal.

I sped up, passed it and nosed into the bank to cut it off. Clunk, went steel against steel. The fawn panicked. It all but climbed out of the water, sensed the escape route behind it and with huge effort, launched itself out and away. I tried again, with the same result.

I knew how quickly an exhausted fawn could die. Two had died in my arms back on the farm as I untangled them from fences. This one could have few reserves left. Perhaps it would find its way to a section of unlined bank, maybe on the same side its mother was no doubt hiding even now; climbing out on the wrong side would just be another death sentence.

Reluctantly we left the terrified creature to itself, just in time for the occupants of an English barge to round a corner, spot the fawn and give chase in the same forlorn spirit. Imagining the tiny thing slowly drowning cast a pall over the shiny morning.

For Beaulon was beautiful. Pierrefitte had been lovely too, but in a decadent sort of way, whereas Beaulon was the picture-book village. Its château was superb, with no sign of struggling owners. It sat pristine on perfect lawns. Fat frogs plopped into the water as we strolled the riverbank. The lock-keeper dead-headed his petunias. Pale green spiky plants like toe-toes lined the canal. It was a tiny paradise. At any moment we expected Beatrix Potter to pop out, pluck the deer from the water and chastise us for spoiling the picture.

We dozed in the warm sunny afternoon, which turned into a scented evening. We watched old men playing *boules*, envying their easy companionship and sense of timeless community.

The night turned easily into a sunny morning as we set off for Decize.

The locks were alive with flowers, pink gladioli and paler pink dahlias, fiery geraniums and exuberant clumps of lavender. Wisteria was so in love with life it was well into a second flowering.

Four locks short of Decize we stopped. Clive worked here. Clive was on the list of English-speaking mechanics we carried next to our hearts. We tied beside a trim lawn and Glenn and I went searching for him.

We found him in a back room of the rental boat company he managed, having coffee and talking in animated French. He was long-haired and looked piratical, an appearance I hoped would not influence his bill.

Typically English, I thought.

His manicured companion watched through lowered lids and burst into a long reply with many complicated gestures. Typically French, I thought.

'*Vous êtes Clive*?' I ventured to the typical Englishman.

'*Non*,' he said.

Instead: '*Je m'appelle Clive*,' replied the typical Frenchman. 'I'm English. My friend here' — he waved a hand — 'is French. He speaks no English.'

I told Clive we'd heard he was an excellent mechanic, perhaps the best in all France. He repeated this to his friend. The friend laughed, not ironically I hoped.

Would Clive look at my bow-thruster? Clive frowned. Yes, he said, but not immediately, for he was very busy. Perhaps later in the afternoon.

We retreated to the boat and made coffee. Scarcely was it poured than Clive appeared. I'd forgotten the English insistence on appointments. We couldn't expect him to down tools and come immediately even if he carried no tools to down. We had to give proper notice.

Now that the formalities had been observed, Clive warmed to the task. Coffee? He looked at his watch with a worried frown. Well, yes.

Clive told us about his life. He'd been in France for seven years. Ah, Trish guessed — correctly — a broken relationship.

He told us about it. He had another cup of coffee. Now he lived in Gannay-sur-Loire, a village not far from his work, but so quiet! A visitor would imagine it deserted. Clive lived there and often *he* imagined it deserted. Sally and Trish went into Gannay and returned saying the only sign of life was a funeral.

Worse, said Clive, there was one unattached woman in his age range — I guessed late thirties — for every fifteen unattached blokes. All the rest were either sixteen or sixty (a little indrawn breath here from the two women).

Gannay was inhabited entirely, said Clive, by generations of families. The town's bar was like the lounge in a family home.

But Clive preferred it to England. He would never return there. His only family there now was his father, who lived in a town near Brighton. It cost $1000 to get there and back. Clive visited only once a year.

He put down his third cup of coffee. 'Well,' he said briskly, 'can't sit here talking all day. Let's have a look at this bow-thruster.'

He picked up a box of tools and complicated instruments. He unscrewed this, tested that. He pulled, poked and prodded. He scratched his head.

'There's nothing wrong with it,' he said.

'Except that it doesn't work,' I said.

'I reckon there must be something stuck in it outside,' Clive said. 'A stick or something.'

I looked at the canal. I wasn't going to dive under that water, even for my bow-thruster.

Clive considered.

'Let's run it up the slipway,' he said, pointing to a ramp. 'We'll be able to stand on the concrete and feel if there's anything there.'

I thought of eleven tonnes of steel crunching onto concrete.

I thought of the bashing the anti-fouling was going to get.

I thought of getting the boat off the slipway again.

I thought of having no bow-thruster for quite a long time.

'OK,' I said.

'That bow-thruster looks just like a big starter motor to me,' said Glenn.

'That's just what it is,' said Clive. 'A big starter motor.'

'I had a Ford 10 once,' said Glenn. 'When the starter motor wouldn't work I just belted it with a hammer.'

'I was just about to suggest doing the same thing,' said Clive.

He went into his shed and returned with a blacksmith's hammer and a piece of wood.

He belted the bow-thruster. It started immediately, and never played up again.

Decize was an important canal town. It lay at the junction of the Canal Lateral à la Loire, along which we were travelling, and the Canal du Nivernais. The Loire River threaded through the junction, the whole thing forming a knot of waterways.

A wide port basin lay guarded by locks at either end. It was crowded, for this was both a popular stopping place and a rental boat base.

We looked at the jammed jetties. The *Johanna Grietje* was longer than the *River Queen*, but shallower, and squeezed into a space by a bank. For us, there didn't seem enough room to park a Mini.

Suddenly we heard a familiar shout. Herman the German was waving at us from a pontoon.

We'd been tracking Herman, his wife and brother ever since Revin, he in his big converted barge, his brother in a cruiser as small as he was. We'd dubbed him Herman, of course, only because it rhymed. We never knew his real name, for our grasp of German and his of English ran only to the occasional word, one of which he used now.

'Here,' yelled Herman, pointing at a space big enough for a dinghy.

We were flattered. Herman was famous for being brusque. In Verdun a Dutchman had wanted to raft up to him on the crowded quay. Herman had turned him away. He had complained that the Dutchman would spoil his view. At least, that is what the Dutchman said.

Herman's wife was much more fun. She stopped for long conversations, especially with Sally, who hurdled language barriers as if they weren't there. She understood what Herman's wife was saying, and vice versa. And she let Herman's dog be itself: a drooling, clumsy mutt.

Now Herman and his brother shoved boats here, pulled them there, then grabbed our lines and levered us in sideways before any of them could spring back.

'Ho ho ho,' said Herman, which exhausted his English, and we slapped each other on the back (which exhausted my German) then went our separate ways.

I made coffee.

Herman brought out a vast hunting horn and blasted a volley over the port.

A faint note sounded in reply.

In a little while another man appeared. The two were obviously old friends. They ran towards each other and hugged. The effect was rather like two beach balls in a stiff breeze, as even Herman's paunch was eclipsed by his friend's tribute to steins beyond count. The two vanished downstairs and soon we heard the happy clink of glasses.

So this was Decize, we thought, looking around. Beside us, high-rise apartments loomed over the countryside. Alongside those was a new-ish hospital whose architect had tried for something different and come up with a collection of swoops and boxes which may well have worked, from the inside.

On the other side was one of the huge supermarkets we'd come to rely on for everything from *terrine de canard* to diesel. The first we carried in heavy plastic bags which we'd bought and re-used dozens of times, for the French were wisely discouraging that confetti of plastic bags flung out by supermarkets back home.

The second we carted in a black twenty litre jerrycan which fitted neatly onto the carrier of my bike and made riding it interesting, for the front wheel tended to lift off the road and the whole collection wobbled in a crazy top-heavy fashion. That was the New Zealand way, though: better risk your life than pay another fifty cents a litre at the canal side.

Decize itself lay over the River Loire, on a hill, with its church at the centre and remnants of its old fortified wall dotted around. Green parks ranged alongside the river, where jaunty boaties tied their rental craft and young people lay in the sun.

It was the weekend, and Decize staged the biggest *vide grenier* (literally, clear the attic) we'd ever seen.

Trish was our expert on *brocante*, second-hand stuff, or junk, and the *vide grenier*. When she came into a town with one or the other, she'd point like a setter, and off we'd go to a *brocante* shop and scour piles of furniture, clothes, pots, pans, vases, plates, tools, posters, models, hats, pictures, washing machines, fishing gear, football boots, radios, calendars, motorbikes, windows, wheels, scythes.

We loved those dusty old sheds. Trish was expert at excavating stuff, non-descript junk until she delicately picked it out and it lay in her hand like treasure: a woman's keepsakes poignant with tickets to balls; invitations to weddings; an old postcard whose sender had written of lost love in a fine, exact hand. In Montargis, where there was a hypermarché of junk, she bought a card of very old but perfect magenta buttons and a little album of photographs from a village concert in the fifties, each act carefully recorded in a single photograph on each page so that when you flipped through them quickly the album had the jerky movement of a silent movie.

In a *vide grenier*, people set up stalls in the town streets and Decize's was *le plus grand*. Stalls upon stalls wound around every corner, filling streets and alleyways: hectares of old tools and bad paintings. They'd even set up restaurants in a local hall, for who could survive such a day without cafés? I fancied a post-war Mobylette moped, full of struts and curves, but couldn't imagine how to get it home as hand-baggage.

Sally disappeared into the ocean of junk like a seal, emerging every now and then to frolic with some morsel before submerging again.

This time, she scored. She slithered through the crowd towards me waving a heavy, square-cut vase which looked like sea when you peered into its depths. 'Murano,' she said triumphantly. So it was: a fine piece from the Venetian island glassmakers. It cost $40. She bore it back to the boat with the air of a Viking looter, along with a white china dove, and fretted over the Miró print she'd left behind.

In the evening Alan and Lonnie came over for a drink. They were winemakers from California, so they brought the drink. I shoved the supermarket wine out of sight, although together with a bottle of red Sancerre they had a good bottle of Maçon white which I later found on the supermarket shelves for $6 and almost kept the $5 rule afloat.

We'd met them days before; they were travelling in a hire boat with a former fireman called Vinnie. Lonnie had run an advertisement asking for someone to supply grapes to their small winery. Vinnie answered. He grew grapes for fun.

They all made cabernet sauvignon together and decided that if the wine was good, they could make a pretty fine holiday too. So they had, although the laughter floating from their boat in the evenings might have owed as much to the wine as friendship.

Hire boats, or bumper boats as the real boaties called them, provided much entertainment. They went aground, crashed into locks, wobbled and zig-zagged. That was all very well, as long as you were not doing any grounding, crashing, wobbling etc. yourself, for then not only would you be given yet another lesson in humility, but the hire boaters would rush across with help and advice.

Lethal or not, they were more popular in the locks than we were. They bought the lock-keepers' wine, usually at a premium, and tipped the lockies handsomely.

How much did he tip? I asked Alan. Oh, he said, only a couple of Euros. The arithmetic was simple: at two Euros a lock, our lock bill for the trip would be way over 750Euros, or $1500, considerably more than the *vignette*, which was supposed to pay for everything in France.

So we tipped lockies only when they went out of their way, or were exceptionally helpful, which did not include these Burgundy *éclusiers* who merely went out of their way to fit the picture, being colourful and entertaining. One had an ornate organ which ground out music for gypsies to dance to even if there were only four Kiwis looking appreciative but tip-free. We voted him the showiest lockie in all France.

The hire boat crews bought the expensive wine from the vintners in the pretty villages, took the tours, filled the restaurants and cafés. We bought cheap wine from supermarkets, biked everywhere and ate on our boats. They were an important part of the local economy, we were as critical to the local economy as economists. And, they were endlessly entertaining.

We sat under a big tree beside the *River Queen*. Alan told me he'd voted for President George W. Bush not once, but twice. I fetched a bottle of supermarket wine. Winemaker he might be, but I wasn't going to waste good wine on a Bush voter. And I needed a drink. Lonnie was different. Unlike every other American we'd met on the waterways, she had voted Democrat, although she wasn't sure she could vote for Hillary Clinton. Neither could Alan, but he wasn't voting for the Republicans either. 'It was a terrible mistake,' he said, and repeated the mantra of former Bush supporters: 'Iraq is such a mess.'

Sally wanted to talk about it but the subject seemed just too fraught. Yet the world turned on just such nice people as these. 'I was wrong,' Alan said, and laughed, as if he'd just bought a dodgy brand of soap at the supermarket.

Were these people blindfolded, earplugged and gagged? If deep in the South Pacific, in Christchurch New Zealand — in fact, everywhere in our home country — we'd figured Iraq was going to be such a mess even before Bush fired the first shot, why hadn't Alan and his fellow converts? He was an intelligent man, although quantifiably not as bright as his wife.

I mulled over the mystery as we pulled the cork from another bottle of wine (Bordeaux, $5.60), and watched the anglers watching their lines, catching nothing as usual and occasionally passing a quiet remark or two.

'*Les poissons* are not biting, Jacques.'

'*D'accord*, Pierre, they never do.'

'Then what are we doing here, Jacques?'

'*C'est une* good question, Pierre.'

Fishermen remained a mystery to us.

They did not catch very much. When they did, the fish seemed to have been on their way home from a crèche.

We watched one man unhooking a creature the size of a Euro coin (although it would have cost far, far more to catch it) and sliding it into his bucket as if it were a marlin.

If they had caught something, and occasionally we saw very big fish in the canals, what might they have done with it? Hugh McKnight's *Cruising French Waterways* listed a restaurant that served fish caught locally. We made a careful note of it, so that we would not make a mistake and go there. By now we knew what went into the canals. We would never swim in the water, but the fish had little option; they were fish, that's what they did.

Yet every angler we saw seemed lost in happy contemplation of his, and very occasionally her, lot. One, two or even four rods were set up on little steel racks and their bright floats bobbed below, watched by their owners with the same fascination some people, late in the evening when the day is gone and the next one looms, considered the fire in the living room grate while they unwound the secret of life.

One poor fisherman the following day was doing just that.

Chapter Eleven

The day seemed to get up in the morning and dress for a special occasion. Its skirt flowed in the summer breeze and its lipstick was perfect. The trees and the flowers, the dragonflies and squirrels, the swans and the herons bowed to its passage.

They composed themselves into one magnificent tableau, in the midst of which an angler posed. His floral shirt enfolded his girth in its own garden of Eden. He sat under a striped umbrella on a little yellow folding stool, his varnished tackle box, his red bucket, his wicker lunch basket laid out beside him. His four rods pointed over the water as if ready to fire a ten-round salute.

Everything in the assemblage whispered tranquillity. The angler was at peace with human nature, the entire world.

Imagine his shock, then, when they conspired against him.

A large white hire boat popped out of the nearby lock. The skipper pulled into the bank in order, as it proved, to await his friends in two following hire boats. He ran aground. He did so with such speed that the boat reared out of the water and lay panting like a stranded whale.

He shouted. The engine roared. The propeller thrashed the water into a thickshake. His wife shrieked like a klaxon.

The angler started from his reverie. He got to his feet for a better look. He muttered imprecations. *Merde*, mad boaties.

The lock doors opened again and ejected the two other rental boats. They screeched to a halt beside their beached friends. Ropes snaked across the water. One slithered on to freedom, its handler having failed to secure it at either end.

Three engines now roared in unison, three propellers beat the water into submission, three crews squawked and ululated. Slowly the marooned vessel slid back into the canal with a noise signalling that not every bit of it would continue on down the canal that day. Then, with the mad gaiety of a dog loosed from its chain, it leapt off down the side of the canal.

The angler spied it bounding along.

'*Non, non, non,*' he cried.

'*Oui, oui, oui,*' responded every fibre of the boat's being.

It scythed through the first rod without so much as a shiver. Rods two, three and four lined up for execution. Click, clonk, cluck, they went. '*Putain,*' screamed the angler, who now took a dim view of human nature and indeed of the entire world. '*Fou, bâtard, brute.*'

The rental boat made its getaway, the crew ducking as if expecting bullets. Bits and pieces of fishing debris bobbed in its wake.

The fisherman observed them. He took off after the boat on foot. He waved. He screeched. He howled. He disappeared around a bend.

After quite a long time he returned, cutting a dismal figure.

He keened over the wreckage.

He spied us watching him from our mooring on the other side of the canal.

He identified us as members of the rogue breed.

He sprang along the bank. '*Putain,*' he bawled. '*Fou, bâtard, brute.*'

We protested innocence.

He ignored us.

We left, quickly.

Wails chased us along the water, growing fainter until they drifted off into the trees and disappeared, and we were left alone with the hiss of a swan and the angry buzz of a dragonfly.

We were caught behind a fully-loaded *peniche*, so deep in the water only the bow and the wheelhouse seemed afloat. Passing on the narrow canals was fraught. Often the edges of canals hid rocks and pieces of concrete which could make a mess of your boat and even, in the case of an Australian vessel, stop it dead in its tracks. The Australian told us that for weeks afterwards he'd awake sweating in the small hours and could not sleep until he'd inspected his entire boat for leaks.

The *peniche* was going dead slow for fear of grounding, and in turn it had been caught behind *l'éclusier*'s Sunday lunch. Our funereal procession had arrived at his lock at 11.45 a.m. but the lock-keeper would not open up. Madame aboard the *peniche* explained his shortcomings to him but it made no difference. Lunch was lunch and that was that. We all sat there for an hour.

The day wore on.

A few locks on the lunchiest lockie in all France gave way to the slowest.

He was a pantomime of inaction. My new Olympus with its super-fast shutter speed struggled to catch him in action.

The *peniche* minded, but we did not. We were on the canals to go slow, not to water-ski. Besides, the non-start action took place against a cottage which would have graced any calendar, with a garden filled to overflowing with geraniums, dahlias, roses, gladioli and begonias. Obviously it absorbed most of the lockie's energy and in our opinion he'd got his priorities right.

The mooring at Pagny which on the charts offered every facility proved hopeless. Half of it was decrepit and the other half occupied by a rental boat company whose staff forbade us to stop with that classic French gesture, a stiff forefinger prescribing a horizontal arc. So on we went to Le Guétin.

Le Guétin was reached by an aqueduct followed by two deep locks joined together.

On this fine Sunday afternoon we were the entertainment. Crowds on the footpath escorted us across the aqueduct leading into the town, the *Johanna Grietje* leading the parade, the *River Queen* behind. Then they lined the edges of the locks and waited for the show to begin.

This was a double lock. Both were deep, and made even deeper by their sides, which sloped from front to back. The lockie had to lower a hook on the end of a rope, pull up our own ropes and take them around a bollard. Even before the water level began to drop our mooring lines were at an acute angle, not best designed for holding the boats in one place. When you were the spectacle, you carried a heavy responsibility not to stuff up. Plenty could go wrong. With the two boats firmly enclosed in the arena, the crowd awaited the lions.

L'éclusier took on the demeanour of ringmaster. He strutted before the assembly. He explained what was going to happen with many a gesture, all of them closely studied by ourselves; a single chop and we'd, well, something would be said.

The crowd laughed and clapped. Far below we prayed like Paray pilgrims and, bless me, it worked: first one then the second lock dropped both boats to the bottom of a vast concrete pit then spewed us back into the canal. Everyone cheered mightily. Shutters clicked. They pointed to our silver ferns and shouted, All Blacks! We honked our horns, waved, laughed.

One of the men asked Sally to marry him. I thought I saw her consider the offer briefly but hell, after one husband, who needed another? Everyone had a good time.

There was a good mooring beside the canal and we tied up quickly, while we were still on a roll. The crowd followed us down to wish us *bonne soirée*, and as we pulled out cheese and wine, *bon appétit* too. Each following boat was announced to us by a cheer from the crowd. The gates would open in the way the curtain lifted on a stage, and a new crew would be ushered forth.

One of them was a hotel boat we'd first met in Fontenoy-le-Château months earlier, with its crew of three: Robin, a former IT consultant who'd thrown in his drawing-board and converted a rundown Luxemotor barge into the hotel boat; Keith the chef, and Jo the general hand. They were an eccentric crew, but their passengers liked the atmosphere. Robin had found a gap in the hotel boat market: his cruises, he claimed, cost about half the going rate. They took six or seven people at a time, depending on where Robin slept. Ever since Fontenoy we'd been running across them.

Now Jo came along for a drink. Was it a good life? Jo was ambivalent. Only if the punters were good sorts, she said. Mostly they were, but one of the guests on this trip had called her a chambermaid. Jo was offended; she was a university graduate. She'd been to New Zealand. She'd been going to marry a Taranaki farmer. It didn't work out.

We wanted to stop at La Chappelle next day not because it was much of a place — it was not — but it was close to La Charité-sur-Loire, which was. Or at least, it was said to be. La Charité was a heritage town, pretty as every one of the millions of pictures taken of it.

We watched as the sun came up over the Loire, a perfect sphere in the mist. Shafts of gold pierced the silver river. An old Labrador wearing a red scarf hopped along the bank in little clouds of steam.

We passed through Marseilles-les-Aubigny on the way. We did not mean to keep going. We wanted to pause at Marseilles; for here, said Glenn, lived the most wonderful woman in all France, the one who presided over her boulangerie in a negligée.

I had a fair idea that women in negligées would be banned from New Zealand bakeries as health risks. Perhaps that was why French bread was better; and if it was not, who cared? Glenn had told us all about *Madame la boulangère*. We felt we should support her. We wanted to buy baguettes, and croissants, and pâté en croute, and éclairs and, oh, anything else she happened to be selling that day.

But her boulangerie was closed. What's more, it seemed to have been closed for a long time. Its windows were dusty. Perhaps Madame was now collecting her pension, Sally suggested. Or maybe she'd given way to rheumatism caused by exposure, and was sitting in front of a heater in a chenille dressing-gown instead. I could see Glenn felt life had lost a bit of its crust. But he was a stout fellow, and got over it.

It did not take much to crowd La Chappelle. A *peniche* was loading logs of wood in front of two huge silos. An odd collection of boats took up the remaining moorings.

One of them was a Dutch *tjalk*, original from its mast and bowsprit to the huge swivelling leeboards bolted to its sides. Its peeling varnish and old canvas covers fluttered in the breeze.

The only place we could find to moor lay across the mouth of a disused dry dock. I tied to the steel of an old gantry. It shuddered precariously.

A man arrived to help us. His name was Gus. He was an Englishman. He owned the *tjalk*. He also owned the big new house beside the canal, where he and his wife lived permanently.

Gus looked and talked like a remittance man. He should have worn a cravat, although he did not. He doubled with laughter when he heard my name. 'Bruce!' he chortled. Monty Python has much to answer for in the antipodes. I told him the last Gus I'd met had four legs and mounted anything that came its way.

When Gus got over this, he said 'It's a sort of club here, you see.'

I did not. He started again. 'Look,' he said, 'It's nothing official. Do you want water? No? Good. There is none. If you want power, it will be three

Euros (six dollars) for the night, and I'll have to give you a receipt — the more unofficial it is, the more official the receipt has to look, if you see what I mean.'

Again, I did not. I was mystified. Gus gave up. 'My wife Ruth will be over to see you shortly,' he said, and left.

I called after him. 'My mooring line seems to be across your path here.'

'Don't worry old chap,' he replied. 'No one ever uses it.'

Ruth appeared. She fell over the mooring line.

'Oh dear,' I said, as I helped her to her feet. 'I'm so sorry.'

'Oh, I'm always doing things like that,' she said.

She went back to her house and returned with a length of red plastic tape, the kind the police used around crime scenes. She arranged it around our mooring. She wrote a long, very official-looking receipt. The wind picked it up and deposited it in the mud at the bottom of the dry dock.

'Just climb down and get it will you?' she asked. 'It's perfectly safe.'

I climbed down. I stepped onto mud. It sucked in my leg with a kind of starved gurgle.

'Oh dear,' she said. 'I'm so sorry.'

We were quits, although I thought the old country was ahead on points.

A huge dog with the kind of crumpled face that advertises toilet paper lunged from the neighbouring boat and was stopped short by a length of rope on its collar. 'It's OK,' said Ruth. 'It's friendly.'

Remembering the mud, I wasn't so sure. The animal's French owner came over and let it off its rope to show me. The dog charged like a hippo. It knocked me over then slobbered over me. I hoped La Charité was worth it.

Gus came back. 'See that spot behind my house?' he pointed to a rise. 'That's where Joan of Arc camped before she attacked the town.'

La Charité grew around a priory built by monks on one of Europe's main pilgrimage trails, and the church became the second-biggest in France, after Cluny's, thus the third-largest Christian church in the world. It had been a wealthy place, so rich that the town and priory were protected by a huge wall defended by ten towers.

The wall, and the winter, defeated Joan of Arc, but over the centuries the place was ruined anyway. The Nôtre-Dame church was restored later, and bits and pieces of the old priory too, and in 1998 was registered on UNESCO's world heritage list.

Off we went into town with a long list of instructions from Guy, and the old priory was worth it. It must have been vast, once; it was still big. We wandered along its alleyways, climbed twisty stairs, passed cells.

But something else was going on. A bike race. It started after some of the interminable speeches French officials go in for on such occasions, while the riders preened.

They raced round and round the town, headed by a man on a pale-blue Harley Davidson motorbike. A car cut him off as he tried to shunt it out of the riders' way. He ran into it. Much argument followed.

We watched from a café. The waitress served us coffee then marched up and down the pavement shouting to the riders: '*Allez*! *Allez*! *Allez*!' In between laps she turned on pedestrians. '*Allez*!' she shouted. A woman with a kitten draped around her neck like a stole promenaded up and back.

We returned to the *River Queen* and found two people, Karen and Paul, wandering around the dry dock. She was a chef. He worked as a ship's engineer, month on, month off, then he hurried home for dinner. 'I've never had the same meal twice,' he said. 'She's good in bed too.'

She blushed. 'Oh, you.'

The two of them lived on their luxurious barge. They were thinking of buying the old dry dock and basing a marine engineering business there.

We all drank too much wine. We wondered what Karen did for a whole month in France on her own. She spoke little French. They told us how cold it became in winter, how even the fog seemed to freeze, so then we wondered if we were doing the right thing, not leaving until mid-November.

We sailed on, past mansions slumbering by the canal, and farms with so many outbuildings they looked like hamlets.

In Herry we had dinner at Herry's Bar, of course. I don't think Humphrey Bogart would have recognised the place. We were ushered to the special dining room on a dais at the back. While the locals ate on the floor below, the four of us sat alone in a space as well-preserved and as little lived in as a Winton front room. Madame would not hear of us moving: we were her guests. So we sat regally, eating pizza.

Trish talked of the sea and the beaches back home. Tears began rolling down Sally's face. She longed for the clear water and golden beaches of the Bay. Trish and Glenn felt only the magic of France.

Sally said, 'If you follow your dreams you can lose your heart; everyone needs a place of the heart.' Dreams are full of romance and beauty, or they would not be dreams. Beauty stands alone, but romance takes two. I felt my own dream dulling, cold breath on a mirror. I wondered whether it was a dream too far.

I'd gone back to Fiordland a couple of years before. Officially I was writing a story on going as far south in New Zealand as you could go, then as far west.

They were places few people ever saw. The weather could be terrifying, I wrote, and there were no shops. Really, though, I'd wanted to feel the magic of those lonely days when every cell pined for Sally.

Bruce Connew, the Wellington photographer, shared the cost of hiring the fishing boat *Argus* taking us there. He wanted to photograph muttonbirds. Colin Gavan was the captain. He had a long face and long curly hair. The captain's chair was done in tattered red velvet and when he sat on its shaky pedestal he looked like a Victorian rake on a bad night out. When the boat rolled the chair rocked and Gavan orbited around the wheel with his long curls shaking in the aureole from his smoke. He'd lost a leg after an oil rig accident and in his home port of Riverton they'd started calling him Collywobbles then shortened it to Wobbles in deference to the way he walked. He and his crew, Mark Eramiha, grooved along to Creedence Clearwater Revival.

We set off down the east coast of Stewart Island. According to the weather forecast the barometer was falling like a stone but the mixture was too heady for worry, the beaches and bush forming an intricate coastline, cape pigeons and blue penguins circling the boat. The first great clouds of sooty shearwaters appeared, the titi or muttonbirds, dark on top with slashes of light beneath their thin wings, wheeling a few centimetres above the waves.

We sailed along a coastline where even the rocks had names: here the Sisters, there the Orphan; then Eramiha went up front with his torch picking up a black cliff streaked in foam as waves crashed against it with a sinister grumble then everything went quiet and we were in a narrow hallway cut out of the rock, in still water, picking around islets in the dark and coming to rest in a cove deep within Port Pegasus and just about to run off the end of New Zealand.

In the morning the coast was different, rock smoothed by seas meeting their first land mass on the long roll from the Antarctic. South Cape appeared ahead. It was an anticlimax: a low headland, a lump of rock in the grey mist of morning.

We threaded past the Titi Islands. The spell of the place settled on the boat. The tupari and dracophyllum scrabbled for a living in the peat. Wires for the gutbuckets carrying the muttonbird chicks' innards to the sea in the short autumn season webbed the rocky faces.

My father had loved muttonbirds but the greasy, fishy, rancid smell of them made me sick. The house would stink of muttonbirds for weeks after he'd return from a trip down south. To the southerners the stench enhanced the delicacy, like the aroma of vintage cheese. 'Oh, I can feel the fat running down my chin,' said Eramiha.

In the morning's calm the waves rolled gently against cliffs, perfect white fading to aqua then to deep-sea blue. The sun struck sheets of pale-grey rock on Gog and Magog on Stewart Island, giving them the glitter of snow.

The *Argus* steamed northwest, towards the entrance to Foveaux Strait guarded by the mysterious Solander Islands.

The southernmost Alps loomed, then reefs.

A little to the north was West Cape, least remarkable of the capes marking the four points of the compass. At North Cape you can feel the spirits fly. East Cape looks innocent but is malevolent. South Cape has the vile temper of a small beast. West Cape was just a point on the map, another forested spur dropping into the sea amid ranks of headlands so similar that the westernmost point of the land was almost indistinguishable.

The sea stilled and we were in Preservation Inlet. In this dark wilderness we nosed up the sound to a tiny cove. For me it was like coming home.

The sun set down a winding silver channel lined with layer upon layer of headlands and islets and, as a change from blue cod, we ate crayfish with asparagus for dinner. I thought of Sally, the desperation and eagerness and hope of decades before. Connew sat on the boat's rail and contemplated the wilderness. 'What I'd really like,' he said 'is a soy latté.'

I didn't think much had changed. Love caressed and cut. We were both more bewildered than angry about what was happening to us over such a simple difference: I liked living on the canals, she did not. All those years, all that love, all at risk over a *boat trip*? Yet dissonance was turning into something fiercer. That night I slept in the front cabin, alone.

But, as *Gone with the Wind*'s Scarlett O'Hara once observed in circumstances I thought not nearly as serious as my own — after all, what was a lost home, a dead child, and a truculent partner? — tomorrow was another day.

So it was, for it started to rain. Mist curled through the vineyards. Rows of grapes appeared on a flowing hillside and vanished. It was like looking at the world through lace curtains rustling in a breeze. Sometimes the curtains opened to reveal the fabled town of Sancerre high above us on its hill, commanding the countryside.

We passed under a bridge and ahead the *Johanna Grietje* turned sharply, its long, low hull angling across the canal. It disappeared into a hole in the bank. We followed.

We slid under a low bridge and passed into another escape tunnel leading to a world of curious boats. *Peniches*, ancient vessels of no known origin, a fine old wooden cruiser dreaming of its hey-day in the fifties, all lined the banks, some of them works in progress, some like old actors resting.

We passed a beautifully varnished cruiser and next to it a man covering his boat in sheets of clear corrugated plastic, turning the whole assembly into a floating garden shed.

We were in St Thibault.

The marina owner,. François, operated a taxi shuttle service running up the hill to Sancerre. The rental boat crews took it. Even Sally and Trish did, for the hill was very steep. Over the centuries it had made whole armies work hard for conquests.

Glenn and I biked, of course. Halfway up we wavered. Three-quarters of the way we wondered who'd want to conquer the place anyway. Up there, at last, we decided that armies marched on their stomachs and repaired to a café for a long rest.

Sancerre was famous for its sauvignon blanc and fumé blanc. As South Islanders we were sauvignon blanc experts. We agreed that the French had made a worthy attempt at keeping up.

Once, this place had commanded the countryside. It was sacked and the locals slaughtered in the great war of 1563. It was still open for sacking by tourists, but now locals did the slaughtering. We watched a haughty British quartet loading their BMW with cartons of wine then we went and bought a bottle each and sat on a seat overlooking the Burgundy country, fields and vineyards and villages gently laid on soft hills, the kind of picture we'd seen in children's books but could never quite fit into New Zealand's raw landscape.

Then we flew down the hill on our bikes, yelling like little boys.

In the dangerous hours of the early morning my cellphone rang. I thought about throwing it overboard; but it might have been important, so I picked it up instead. The caller said she was from an Auckland garage. Just a reminder, she said; my Mercedes Benz was booked for service tomorrow. I didn't have a Mercedes Benz, I said, and I was not in Auckland, I was in France. Nice place, she said, pity about the car.

Chatillon-sur-Loire lay six hours up the canal. We moored under trees. We climbed to the top of the hill to visit a kind of *brocante supermarché*. Not even Christchurch's Supershed, that great hall of junk diverted from the city dump, could match this one.

A rambling old warehouse was packed with tools, prams, books, glorious rubbish. We spent a happy hour there and bought nothing, of course, one of the characteristics of *brocante* being that it was too big and heavy to take home, except if you were Trish, whose fine eye could pick a gem.

In Briare there was to be a huge *vide grenier* stretching for almost a kilometre along the canal bank. I liked some old photographs of the 1948 Tour de France, the riders with their young-old faces and their desperation. One mysterious picture showed a woman dressed to kill and looking as if she might, for she was holding a revolver as she embraced a cyclist whose patronising smile marked him as a winner; or perhaps he just hadn't spotted the gun.

Chatillon was pleasantly unremarkable.

We stopped near two Canadians. They'd bought their boat in Holland, as we had, but unlike us had hired a broker to find it for them. It sounded as if the broker had seen them coming. The boat had been expensive. It cost them about $350,000. By the time they reached Belgium a few hundred kilometres away they were having major engine troubles.

We planned a big night, for it was Sally's birthday. I gave her a little red leather handbag I'd bought in Sancerre. She liked it. I made veal in a creamy shallot, garlic and thyme sauce. Glenn and Trish made a birthday cake with a candle which played 'Happy Birthday' when you lit it.

The Canadians came over and stayed for dessert. They loved the life. He was an academic on a year's leave; she'd stopped working in preparation for their future life on the waterways.

They were astonished when Sally told them we'd sell the boat after only one year. I was only slightly less surprised, not so much because Sally was going public but because Glenn and Trish did not seem surprised at all. I thought of that commonplace about divorce, the way people could get there without really knowing how, or why. It was like ageing, perhaps: you didn't notice you were getting older until something happened to make it obvious, such as discovering hair in all the wrong places.

Why were we giving up canal life? asked the Canadians. Because Sally was homesick, said Trish.

If only that were completely true. Homesickness was simple. You could cope with homesick. It hung around like a headache and you fixed it with a dose of something interesting. Sally's unhappiness had seized the common ground of decades and left a blank space. She felt alone and lonely, and for once, so did I. We retreated into the desolation of two people who once knew each other well and suddenly did not.

We were sombre as we left for Briare next morning. It was a short trip of two hours. We'd booked our moorings, but even so we thought we'd better get there early, just in case. Briare was popular, although to reach its port on an old length of canal you had to turn off the main route and go through two sharp little locks, or three if your berth was inside the inner basin.

The trip took us over the most beautiful aqueduct in all France. Lions threaded with serpents guarded its ends. Vines entwined its lampposts. Far below, the Loire glistered like gold then left us, winding away in the direction of Orléans until it was no more than a mind's gleam. We wanted to stop for a while in the tight little harbour in the middle of such a splendid town and we did, for it was the weekend of the fourteenth of July, Bastille Day, and nothing moved.

The cabin temperature rose to 42 degrees. We lay in our patches of shade panting like the fat black Labrador which sat on the bank, wagging its tail. A sign around its neck said, in three languages, 'Do not feed me. I have a heart condition.' Its body language said, 'Ignore this sign. Feed me. I want to die happy.'

I had a flat tyre on my bike and no one had a pump. The port captain told me there was a pump at the Champion supermarket. It was only a short walk away. *Très facile*, he said, which should have warned me, for the walk took thirty minutes and when I got there the pump was out of order, *en panne*, and when I got back the port captain produced a pump after all. *Je suis désolé*, he said, sorry.

The wind blew softly through the flowers.

Lamp posts carried so many blooms they looked like blossom trees. The little arched bridges all around us seemed bowed under their loads of colour, so thick that they seemed in danger of collapsing into one great kaleidoscope.

On the thirteenth, fireworks began at eleven p.m. We sat on the riverbank with hundreds of others. A coquettish young French girl performed for her parents, grandparents and the rest of us. She pouted and pirouetted, and everyone loved her even if we New Zealanders from a more forbidding regime felt slightly squeamish.

A band marched by, with brass, flutes, clarinets, flutes, a saxophone, anything that could be played and carried at the same time. They played the theme tune from *The Muppet Show*. Fireworks lit the town and countryside culminating in a *pièce de resistance* set to the tune of Disney's 'It's a Small World'.

Then on to *le bal*, where people danced desultorily, at least until a little after midnight, when we gave up. Next day Keith from the hotel boat, said, 'We danced until three in the morning. Everyone did. It was great. You should have been there.' That was the story of my life.

Next day, Bastille Day, the town band formed up ahead of the fire brigade, the mayor, war veterans and assorted dignitaries. They all marched off to 'It's a Long Way to Tipperary', and arrived on the riverbank alongside my boat whose bunting consisted entirely of underpants hung out to dry. They flapped dismally through the short ceremony. Everyone marched back to the town hall to the theme tune from the film *The Longest Day*, and the mayor invited everyone to a glass of wine.

Sally and I sat inside the fine nineteenth-century church. Yellow and gold stained glass played light onto aquamarine, like the sun on sea. We soaked in the gentle silence. The bright tiled floors reflected a country life, rabbits, ducks, wheat, vines. It was quite modern, built in the late nineteenth century to replace a low, graceful twelfth-century church on the site. We were spending more time in church than French churchgoers, although there didn't seem to be all that many of those. I sneezed. The sound echoed around the pews, chased itself around the tiled lilies and marigolds, ah-*choo*!

Rogny, only fifteen kilometres away, took more than six hours to reach.

Lots of locks. The day was very hot. No sooner would we leave one lock than another would appear, ending in a steep staircase of them which lowered us into the little village. Beside us, stepping down the green hillside, lay Les Sept Écluses, the old Napoleonic staircase of seven locks now empty but preserved, for the modern replacements were more efficient but less interesting.

Rogny was tiny. A single brasserie struggled for business, but you could get your boat overhauled by the port's owners who had bravely started an engineering business and seemed to be making a go of it. Some mornings a woman sat at a sewing machine in their shop, stitching up upholstery and cockpit covers.

The hotel boat pulled in behind us. Keith the chef, who always looked as if he were recuperating from something debilitating, found quail to wrap in panacetta and serve to his guests, two ex-SAS men and their wives.

He didn't say where he got the quail. You could not buy anything in Rogny except the most basic food, although the town had two *brocante* shops. One of them was open, if you rousted the owner out of bed. He stood at his counter, sleepy and suspicious, as we inspected his antiquities, most of them junk, and all of them expensive. He didn't mind that we bought nothing. Nothing was what he wanted to do right then.

Why are New Zealanders so fascinated by second-hand stuff? Is it a generation thing, born of post-war frugality? Couldn't be. Second-hand clothes are *de rigueur* and Japanese imports have booked their own pages in the government accounts. Buying *brocante* was like catching a snapper. When you hooked one, it sparkled like your very own rainbow. When you got it home, it had changed to dull grey. By the time we left, the *River Queen* could have set up its own stall at a *vide grenier*. Singapore Airlines would certainly have had something to say. We kept the stuff Sally loved most, her Murano vase, white porcelain dove, a French lace curtain embroidered with butterflies. We gave the rest away.

Montargis was beautiful and eccentric. Its narrow canals, lit by flowers, threaded through a busy town dominated by its crumbling château. The town was full of boats. The *Johanna Grietje* tied to a pile of steel just outside the port. We pulled into what seemed to be a vacant space, helped by the captain of a hotel boat moored ahead of us. Behind, a tired-looking golden spaniel submitted to a trim and perm on the dining room table of a luxurious canal boat.

We'd scarcely tied the last knot when a large Dutch cruiser, with a name that sounded like someone being strangled, arrived honking. That space was theirs, cried the skipper. No it wasn't, I called back. It was demonstrably ours, for here we were.

I went inside. The Dutch boat stayed where it was. The harbourmaster arrived. We'd have to move he said. The Dutch boat had booked our space. I wouldn't shift until he found us another mooring, I said. He did. I untied, took down the sun umbrella, put away the deck furniture, started up, and moved away from the bank.

The Dutch skipper shook his fist. I flipped him the bird.

His jaw dropped. The impertinence. He abandoned his big spoked wheel and ran to the after-deck, shouldering his passengers out of the way.

He roared at me across the water. I told him to fuck off. He told me I was not an Englishman. I told the New Zealand government to do something about that bloody silly Union Jack and stars. Sally told me to calm down. The Dutchman told Sally she was absolutely right. She told him to fuck off.

An old woman in a wheelchair saw our flag and confirmed the Dutchman's accusation. I was not an Englishman.

'Eh,' she said, 'you are from New Zealand. That is a long way away. I come from Paris. That is a long way away too. I was a *chanteuse*, a singer. Now I am an old woman in a wheelchair.' But much better off than Captain 'addock, we thought.

Captain 'addock lived alone on his barge and was apparently barking. He claimed to have trained horses in Hong Kong and so was an expert on farming. He hated EU farming subsidies. It made lazy buggers of them all. He hated the Dutch. He said one of them had rammed him in the course of running hash to Marseilles, and had bent his rudder. He did not say what his barge had been doing to get in the way of a Dutch drug-runner. He gave me a courgette. He said he was going to sell his boat and grow courgettes instead. He gave me a letter for *l'éclusier*, saying he would be arriving at his lock tomorrow. When I gave it to the lockie, he said 'Ah, Monsieur 'addock, he speak. He speak speak *speak*.'

My brother Craig and his wife Erica joined us in Montargis for a few days on the canals. I met them at the station, called a taxi and told the driver where the boat was moored.

Ah oui, he said.

I'll race you on my bike, I said.

Ah oui, oui, he said, and tore off.

I crashed a red light and passed him. He overtook on the straight. I shot through a pedestrian precinct. He complained to his passengers. Your brother breaks the rules, he said. I was waiting when they arrived. I win, I said. It wasn't fair, he said, and went off in a huff. The golden spaniel saw its owner approaching with scissors and curlers and wearily climbed back onto the table without waiting for the command.

Temperatures rose into the forties. In Souppe we swam at *la plage*, a beach painstakingly reconstructed on the shores of an artificial lake, with lifeguards, swimming pools, fenced swimming zones — a precaution against tide rips and sharks? — *pedalos*, bouncy castle, a library without books. We watched the young studs running up to a rock and bombing into the water. They posted a woman at the edge to signal them when there was no danger of hitting anyone. They took social responsibility seriously here. The sand was fine as talcum powder. It turned us all white as we lay there in the hot, hot afternoon.

On we went to the beautiful walled town of Moret-sur-Loing. The hotel barge pulled in behind us. Jo immersed herself in the latest Harry Potter, just released. Robin, its owner and builder, came to talk. He was Oxford-educated and his long hair and skinny frame gave him a wild look.

Robin did not run a tight ship. 'It's a loose one,' said Keith.

He seemed never to know, quite, where he'd be going that day. The boat bore the scars of many encounters. The crew complained of leaks which kept the water pump running and them awake, of winds blowing through the floorboards. Robin said he was in it for the lifestyle. His guests seemed to like the lifestyle too. They sat under the awning and talked, and laughed, and told us they wouldn't have it any other way.

Herman passed us one last time, going like the clappers towards some destination of the mind. He was everywhere. 'I beat you to Paris,' he yelled as he went by. His wife smiled timidly. For a while I couldn't see his brother, then a little cruiser sneaked into view, like a shadow, and slipped past silently in his wake.

My brother Euan and his wife Gabrielle arrived; now there were six Ansleys in one boat. Once the mixture would have been explosive; now, we were delighted to spend time with each other.

New Zealanders collected in that odd way they do, not haphazardly but not much planned either. They persuaded a café to turn on the sports channel, and watched the All Blacks beat the Wallabies. The café owner kept the sound off. His clientele were supremely indifferent to this critical moment in the affairs of two South Pacific nations. Only an outbreak of cheering, or booing, stopped them talking; then they'd peer curiously at the screen, shrug and go back to their conversation.

We all agreed the All Blacks were looking good for the World Cup. Good? What a euphemism! The All Blacks were going to cream them all. I gave the little flagstaff carrying the silver fern an extra coat of varnish for good measure.

We were very close to the Seine by now and we had a last, long picnic on the riverbank. We ate rare roast beef and duck terrine and spicy sausage in pastry, salads of tiny tomatoes and feta, little chocolate cakes with gold flakes on top, apricot and plum tarts, Brie, Roquefort, curd cheese and crusty bread, huge nectarines and big green cardboard boxes of strawberries. We drank quite a lot of wine. *Bon appétit*, called the French passersby.

My family left in the morning, a little heavily, and the boat seemed empty as we ran the short length of the Loing and turned into the Seine. The civilised river seemed big as a lake after the tight canals. Cultivated banks allowed glimpses of summer homes, some little more than sheds, some suburban, some follies complete with turrets, towers and parapets.

It was two days to Paris and the first was long, wet and cold. We travelled with a cavalcade of huge barges, squeezing into locks with one cumbersome creature of four vessels locked together and pushed by a tug steered casually by Madame, who blew smoke and smiled at us while her husband huddled in the rain and pointed to the heavens in disgust. We felt like Scruffy the Tugboat arriving in the big bad world.

A boat was moored outside one lock. It looked familiar. As we drew closer, we recognised it: Paul and Carla's cruiser. We honked the horn. Paul appeared on deck, sleepy from his after-lunch siesta. Then Carla, then Chica, their dog, the reason they were in this lonely spot in the first place: Chica liked the lifestyle, they said. They planned to sell their boat, but not until the dog died. They threw off their lines: 'We'll come with you.'

Luckily for us, they did. At the next lock *l'éclusier* closed the gates as we approached, to let through a barge coming the other way. He could equally have let us all in and done the same thing, but oh well.

The barge emerged on our side. The lights turned green. We entered the chute, the approach to the lock.

The lights went red, and stayed that way. We went round, and round.

Carla saved us. She called the lockie on the VHF. He was waiting for a barge to come through from our side; he wanted it in the lock first. The barge proved to be the cavalcade steered by Madame. But, we said, she'd wanted us to go first into the lock in the previous locks. Carla and the lockie consulted. The lights turned green. We'd been circling in the rain for more than an hour. We were wet and cold. But, oh well.

Late that afternoon we tied up outside another lock for the night, alongside two Australians, Kev and Yvonne.

Paul told us of being thrown out of his Arnhem home in the last war by Germans who cleared the town. They had been given only a few hours to leave and his parents carried what they could on their bicycles, and on his pram. It was not very much.

After the war they returned. They were lucky. Their house was intact but empty. The Germans had taken what they wanted, then the British, but, said Paul, it was probably the Dutch who stripped it completely. A friend of the family had found her curtains hanging in a neighbour's house. Paul was only two when they became homeless, but he still had nightmares filled with harsh voices and the noise of aeroplane engines.

We were engrossed in his story. That night I dreamed of planes, and invaders, and nearly went into cardiac arrest when we were shaken out of bed before five next morning by the noise of battle which resolved into a blast of hip-hop.

I peered through the curtains. A black Mercedes stood on the path outside, a few metres from the boat, its doors open. Three youths and a girl were dancing in the rain, with a looseness and lack of rhythm that suggested they'd had substances other than croissants that morning.

Dutch youths always looked as if they were searching for old ladies to help across the street. French youths looked as if they would biff you on the head for half a Euro, or for nothing on public holidays, yet we found them friendly, even when they were convinced we were not from this planet. In neither country had we felt any aggression, nor felt unsafe for even a moment.

As it grew lighter, the Mercedes showed signs of a rough night, and so did the youths. They vanished when we appeared, abandoning the car, probably stolen, and leaving one pale survivor who thought it might be a good time to try his English.

'Take me with you,' he pleaded. 'Please.'

Paul was furious, Glenn and Trish friendly as always. Our last impression of rural France was his thin frame, dressed in black and bent like a question mark as he argued his case over the water: '*Pleeeeese*?'

The Seine gave up its airs and graces and turned ugly. Summer houses gave way to industrial theatre. Silos, crushers, foundries, warehouses, dust and barges lined its banks. Roars, hisses, bleeps, blasts — all the noise, in short, of people making a living — drowned even the diesel's purr. The bridges changed from grim to utilitarian to old to elegant.

In the last lock Kev gave us some advice on Paris. We had to go to the Moulin Rouge, he said, although not before nine p.m., otherwise we'd have to pay for dinner. The stage was empty when he and Yvonne last went, he said, so the two hopped onto it for a spot of the light fantastic. It was great, said Kev, and it gave Yvonne a chance to try out her new knee.

At Chinatown, where a hotel, restaurants, pagodas, dragons, lots of green tiles and red paint hung over the Seine, the other two boats branched off into the Marne. The river would take Kev and Yvonne back down the middle of France, and Paul and Carla back to Holland.

We last saw them standing on their after-deck, Carla waving Chica's paw goodbye. For much of the year we'd shared each other's lives; we knew as much about them as of some of our close friends at home. Probably we'd never see them again. It was one of many small endings. They were taking part of our adventure with them. We waved goodbye, we hoped not at Chica.

Now we were amid another city of lost dreams. Barges were being converted into tourist boats. Some of their builders had knocked off for a while, say, two or three years. Many barges had been turned into tourist boats in schemes that had foundered as surely as the rusty hulks surrounding them.

It wasn't hard to see why. A Mississippi river boat and a floating bamboo café must have caused endless ethnic confusion, compounded by the Chinese junk, or the boat that might have started as a junk but ended up looking something like Cook's *Endeavour* shrunk to the size of an Auckland launch. One looked like those shoeboxes we made as kids, with dioramas inside and a hole to peep through at one end. Another seemed to be a half-sunken Oxford caravan, and possibly was.

We passed a high-tech floating swimming pool, closed despite the heat. A new city was springing up on the left bank: new roads, flyovers, supermarkets, malls, apartments, warehouses.

And suddenly we were in front of a cranky old lock which let us into the Arsenal in the Place de la Bastille.

We tied up beneath the Colonne de Juillet, the July column celebrating the revolution and mourning the dead. From our mooring we could see the golden girl atop her pedestal, the *Génie de la Liberté*, the spirit of freedom.

Paris!

Chapter Twelve

The Tour de France ended the day after we arrived. I'd done my time at such places as Eden Park and Carisbrook, but enthusiasm for the bike race made the home crowds look like the Kirwee Bowling Club veterans' tournament. Paris had some two million residents, and in late July tourists had doubled the population, and all of them seemed to be intent on watching the grand finale.

That year's Tour de France was supposed to have been spoiled by drug scandals. Spoiled like Kate Moss. Everyone wanted a look. The finish line was invisible beneath the press of bodies.

I chose a spot near the Champs-Elysées. Cavalcades of team buses went by, looking as if they accommodated rock stars, which of course they did. Fleets of official cars rolled past. A posse of motorcycle police in green helmets got a cheer. An hour passed, then another. At last, the crowd roared. I spotted flashes of colour, moving at incredible speed. That, for me, was the end of the Tour de France.

Later we watched on TV the winners being crowned and the losers smiling lemony smiles and everyone going home vowing they'd be back next year. I wished I could say the same.

For we had found the ideal way of living in Paris. The Arsenal, where we were moored, was once a real arsenal serving the Bastille demolished after the Revolution. Now it was a perfectly safe harbour, a lock at one end from the Seine and a tunnel at the other leading to the tree-lined Canal St Martin, crossed by lacy bridges. It had good showers, washing machines, dryers. Best of all, it was right in the middle of the city, beside the Place de la Bastille, an easy walk down the Rue de Rivoli to the Louvre or across the river to the Ile de la Cité and Notre Dame, although we didn't want to go to either; it was peak tourist season and queues stretched for blocks.

We could hop on the Métro at the nearby station and stroll anywhere in Paris, and we did. One of the Paris markets was two minutes' walk away. We bought big red prawns and peaches, and bottles of wine whose labels were torn and disfigured, covered in dust as if they'd lain in a cellar for half a century. Much discussion between buyers and sellers flowed, little understood by the eavesdropper *moi.* I picked a bottle at random. I can report no more than it was red.

We became strollers, *les flâneurs*. All of this cost $56 a night. It was the dearest mooring in France, in both senses, and the cheapest way we knew of staying in Paris without joining the tent encampments of homeless along the Seine. We spent hours in the Horseshoe Bar in the Marais watching the world go by at full tilt, eating the canapés of ham and olives and avocado and talking about nothing very much. Glenn and Trish left to sail down the Marne River then the Canal de la Marne to the Saône River and back to St Jean de Losne where they were leaving their boat for the winter. They loved life on the canals so much they were framing their future around it. They offered nothing but support, forming a solid substance we leaned against. The day they left I thought the filthy old lock was gurgling even more than usual. The Arsenal seemed dead without their laughter, and now Sally and I were without buffers.

We went down to our favourite bar on the Rue du Lappe, a few minutes' walk from the Arsenal in a less fashionable part of town, at least for tourists. The barman saw us coming, filled two glasses the size of mugs with rich red Bordeaux, and had them waiting by the time we'd found a seat. Happy hour, he said, 4 Euros ($8) a go.

The tiny bar was always crowded, smoky, noisy, friendly. They squeezed up to make room for us to watch France play England. We got marks for being New Zealanders. We were the favourites for *le World Cup*. We owned the secret of life. I tried to live up to it, making knowing remarks about tackling and rucks and the ref's bullshit. Bullshit, they agreed, and everyone laughed. *La France* had not the chance of a meringue in a maul, they said. They were playing badly.

There was a pause. Wait, said our companion at the next table. Wait. A huge long-haired man ran onto the field. Any number of old Biblical epics could have used his stern beard and fierce eyes. A tatt peeped below his shorts. The bar was delirious. *C'est le* bear! they shouted. *C'est le* caveman. It was the first we'd seen of Sebastien Chabal. He scored the winning try. Drinks were on the house.

Our son Simon and his partner Sarah came over from London for a weekend and when they left we felt dark in the city of light. We went aboard the Australian boat nearby. The owner, a retired doctor, lived aboard with a couple of nurses. It used to be a partnership boat, he said, but one partner died, one divorced, one went to jail and one went bankrupt. He didn't say which partner he was, but he was the sole survivor. His boat had sunk five times, he said with considerable pride, and he pointed to brand-new carpet as evidence of the latest misfortune.

On the wide stone walkways other boat-owners were taking their cats for walks, on leads.

Sally loved staying in one place, especially when the place was Paris. She devised a Le Corbusier tour of her favourite architect's work in the city, putting together a circuit of buildings she wanted to see. Off we went on our bikes. French drivers ran true to form: they treated us with respect and courtesy, and never honked once.

First on the list was a Salvation Army hostel buried deep in a street of tenements. The concierge welcomed us. We made a change from the flow of African refugees, he said. Himself, his father was Spanish and his mother Moroccan. He would visit us in New Zealand at the earliest opportunity, he said, and he must have our address.

He was proud of his building. He showed us the offices, and the cafeteria. Sally asked if Le Corbusier had also designed the stylish seats. No, he said, they were for Africans. Sally tried again. She pointed to the architect's name on the commemoration plaque. Ah, he said. He'd never noticed that before. Le Corbusier? Was he French? His workaday life of stress and wreckage had no room for the finer points of architecture. The architect probably would have approved.

Chastened, we went to an artist's studio with a flaking facade and two Japanese students who evidently got sick of just looking from the outside. They rang the bell, took fright and fled like naughty kids, leaving us to take the rap. There was no response from within.

Then another set of studios, like a wedge, in a private street full of the prettiest houses I'd ever seen; and the Brazilian students' accommodation at the International University, painted in bright primary colours with an attached house Sally photographed from every angle in case she could ever replicate it back home.

We saw the Eiffel Tower from la Place de Mexico near a Le Corbusier house. The tower was perfectly framed at the end of a street, for Paris knows the secret of space. From there it looked clean and pure. The winding line of tourists below it was invisible.

In the bar in the Rue du Lappe that night we drank a couple of buckets of red wine then went next door for a Thai meal.

The weeks went by happily enough although in the end we knew little more about Paris. How did you unlock a city like this? You did not. Adam Gopnik, author of *Paris to the Moon* still floated on its surface after five years and a small son, children being the best way we knew of getting under a place's skin. In the end, though, I didn't care very much; we lolled in the beauty, thawed in its warmth.

I could live on a boat forever. Perhaps I'd have to. Ashore, I hated small rooms, little houses, things to trip over. On a boat I loved them all: the order, the easy way one thing flowed into the next — the spartan order of the deck into the glow of cabins below — the neatness, the place for everything and everything in its place. I could lie in bed and admire the joinery, the way the designer had fitted everything in, the sheen of wood in the yellow light.

Sally simply thought it small. She needed to step out of the boat, feel the grass and trees around her, go into town and buy food without having to ask the way.

I'd thought seriously about selling the boat when we reached St Jean de Losne. She'd thought about flying home, but knew that if she did, I would be stranded without a crew. So she'd persevered, and I'd hoped that when we reached St Jean de Losne and our friends and their contagious love of the canals it would get better. It did, for a while.

Sally loved some of the towns and cities: Verdun, Gray, Fontenoy-le-Château, Briare, Montargis, Moret-sur-Loing, Paris. But it wasn't enough, and we lopped off the second year of our planned life on the canals as you'd prune a diseased limb. We sold the boat to a group of New Zealanders who were to take it over when we laid it up for the winter.

Sally said, 'If you think I'm coming out of this with any sense of righteousness, or victory, you're wrong. I have nothing but a sense of failure. I wish we hadn't done this. It's just too hard. But that's what they said about childbirth. I hope next year I'll look back on the bits I liked, living in Holland, the villages, friends, being with Glenn and Trish and Simon and Sarah, Paris.'

Later, she said she thought the rest of the trip might be salvageable. If she thought so, I said, I'd work hard at it. The *trip* might be salvageable, she said.

We left Paris as summer ended. We watched jousting at St Mammes, where *peniches* were drawn up waiting for work in ranks ranging from hopeful on the outside to hopeless on the inside.

Two opposing crews wearing black and yellow shirts and looking like bumblebees planted their most stalwart members in body armour in the bows of punts, one red, one blue. The jousters mounted platforms, brandished their poles and struck poses while their mates made chicken noises from the bank and girlfriends called for care. Then the two boats revved their outboard motors and belted towards each other and the knights levelled their poles. To much shouting (*Allez!*) each set about knocking the other from his perch.

This was serious business. St Mammes on Sunday was quieter than Bulls and this was not only the best game in town, it was the only one. No one laughed except me and soon, not even me.

Once 24,000 vessels a year had passed through this town, most of them the smaller *peniches*. But other forms of river transport, including giant bulk carriers, had changed all that. At last count, several years before, the number was down to 16,000, only 6,700 of them *peniches*.

George owned the boat tied next door. He was an ex-policeman from Liverpool. He quit the force, couldn't get a job, went to university, got a psychology degree, became a hypnotherapist and was waiting for his wife to join him in taking his yacht to the Mediterranean where he hoped to offer jaded executives sailing cruises with therapy thrown in.

George was mild and surprisingly liberal for an ex-cop but yes, fed up with the UK. It was too hard to live there he said, the taxes, the crime, the government he once supported but which now disgusted him because it had changed nothing and because it was shedding nurses from hospitals and his wife was a nurse.

We went back to Moret-sur-Loing for a few weeks. Red squirrels chased each other through copper trees. Two of our oldest friends, Anne and David McPhail, still waving from the shore decades after they'd farewelled me at Taiaroa Head, joined us there.

An odd community of expats gathered. George and Toby arrived. They intrigued me with their air of completeness. They met when they were very young, they'd been married for around half a century. For years they'd lived between the Bahamas and France. They met each other's needs, they were physically able, charming, made friends easily. Their visits home were brief. They seemed to have less need of friends and family, the weft and weave of a community or neighbourhood than, say, we did.

But Roger and Jenny needed community. They were taking their sailing catamaran home to England after three years sailing around the Mediterranean. They lived in a seventeenth-century house in a little village in Kent. Roger had been in the oil business. They'd been well-off. But he'd been made redundant in his early fifties. He'd gone inside his house and had scarcely emerged for eighteen months. He'd thought that everyone knew, everyone would laugh at him.

They were very British, almost caricatures. He was the son of a naval officer and had inherited the manner. She, Hobbit-like, spoke with the chopping sound of a motor mower, he with that English drawl you could tie knots in.

We walked along the grassy riverbank, past families picnicking and fishing in the evening quiet. A little restaurant was built into the old town wall beside a tower where, past a portcullis and up winding stone stairs, lay a tiny wooden cell where miscreants once languished. The restaurant, a crêperie, was tucked into a gallery above the river, unchanged since it was painted by the town's former resident celebrity, the impressionist Alfred Sisley. It lay beside the town's old church, a gunpowder factory during the French Revolution although it had taken almost three centuries to build and was so old that one side of the apse had to be walled up to stop it collapsing. Had the armaments' manufacturers been a little careless with their tobacco they might have disappeared into the ether along with bits of revolutionary.

I ate crêpes filled with beans and egg and *andouillet*, French tripe sausage so pungent it carried a whiff of farmyard. Sally's were stuffed with ratatouille and poached egg.

Roger, asked for his order by the waitress, barked it out in English and saw me watching. 'Name rank and serial number,' he said.

He told the table, 'My parents were well to-do.' Next morning George was outraged. 'Wow,' he said. 'Did you hear that? Who would ever say a thing like that?'

Each night Roger regaled us with tales of corporate derring-do. Once he'd gone to a hotel in India and asked for his usual room. To his horror, they'd given him a standard one. Worse, when he went to the hotel pool, the attendant had given him only one towel; 'One towel is all you get for that room number, Sahib.'

The indignant Roger soon fixed that. He called his mother back home. She was the big boss's secretary — they'd call her a PA now, he said. On his very next trip to the hotel lobby the manager had hailed him. There had been a mistake: 'For you, Sir, the presidential suite.' And next trip to the swimming pool — why, he got three towels. One small step for mankind, perhaps, but for Roger … He'd drop remarks into conversations like bombs. 'We're of an age when sex is not an issue,' he said once. 'And on a boat it's either non-existent or a floor-show.' Well, possibly, but only Roger was going to talk about it.

Yet they were both honest and vulnerable, and anxious about their return. Roger thought he might serve on the vestry committee, Jenny that she might volunteer for hospice work, and they chorused the by now-familiar theme of the English, things at home were not the same; they were much worse.

Going home was more mysterious than worrying for George and Toby. She wanted to go, he did not. She said rather wistfully, 'I just want to go back home for a while. But I wonder what George will do.' Yet I felt home for both of them, like so many of their companions, was the transient community on the canals.

Clive and Di simply seemed displaced forever. They seemed to have nowhere to go, nowhere to call home. They'd arrived on their cruiser and launched straight into canalside society. Clive had bought, by his account, possibly the world's best cruiser, built by a man so busy making himself rich he never had time to use any of its vast array of toys.

We were talking about the film *The Queen* when Clive arrived. 'I was in it,' he announced, by way of introduction. He had our immediate attention.

He'd been a cop on a motorbike in the film's documentary footage. Clive was an ex-cop, although you needed a very sharp eye to spot him. We'd met so many of his fellows we thought we had the answer to Britain's crime rate: all the cops were on the canals.

Clive had been in a protection squad and was full of stories.

Cherie Blair, wife of the former Prime Minister: 'She once wanted to send one of the squad for milk and bread.' Clive stood firm on this misuse of police personnel.

Labour government generally: They made excessive use of the Royal Flight. 'Maggie Thatcher only used it once.'

The Queen Mum: She'd tapped him on the shoulder one day when he was fishing near Balmoral. 'You should try over there,' she said.

The famous butler: Didn't do it.

Clive had loved his job, he said, but when he'd done thirty years he took the money and ran and some seven years on was still telling the tale. Clive's partner Di said, 'You get his whole life story in the first thirty minutes.' We reckoned that in Moret he made it in twenty. Sally fed their dog Harry (yes, named after the prince) a piece of sausage from the BBQ. Di was aghast: 'He's a *vegetarian*.'

Di went back to England for a few days. Sally detected a spring in her step, but she might only have been sympathising. Clive was morose. He came over for a drink. He was talking (about propellers) as he climbed over the rail. Sally found a novel she urgently needed to read. David received sudden inspiration for a column he wanted to write. Anne just disappeared. To cook dinner, she claimed. Later we ate sausages stuffed with Roquefort and potatoes fried in olive oil and rosemary.

We all caught a train to Fontainebleau, the magnificent palace restored by Emperor Napoleon Bonaparte. At Fontainebleau Napoleon bade farewell to his Old Guard and went into exile in 1814. We stood in the little room at the table where he'd signed his abdication, climbed the steps where he made his farewell speech on his way to Elba.

Then we went back to Moret and met two wistful boys and their collie dog. For French kids they didn't seem to have much French. That's because we're Irish, they said.

Their mum and dad had started a café in an ornate building in a town square, full of spires and garrets and decorated with carvings of artisans at work. Their dad served us coffee there next day, under a wooden stonemason chipping blocks, woodcarvers brandishing chisels, blacksmiths beating iron.

He was a vet who'd decided to move to France, but not for the usual reasons. He was not disillusioned, just adventurous. 'If you don't do it now ….' he said. He and his wife wanted to buy some land and farm it. Land was cheaper in France than either Britain or Ireland, he said. I asked the boys how they liked it here. 'It's a bit boring,' said the older one. The younger said nothing.

David and Anne settled into all of this very well for people not yet acclimatised to the passing parade. They even took the ship's bathroom, if not in their stride, then at least at a shuffle in the middle of the night.

Next door, Christian and Julia had come to stay with George and Toby. The couple were French. George had met them when his engine broke down in St Mihiel, the Ardennes village where we'd stopped months earlier. He'd gone into the Citröen garage owned by Christian. '*I* have a problem,' he'd said.

'You no longer have a problem,' Christian had replied, 'I have a problem.'

They'd been friends ever since. Christian and Julia had wanted to retire for the past two years and had at last found a possible buyer for the garage. If it did not sell this time, said Christian, he'd have to walk away from it, partly explaining the huge number of locked and closed-down businesses in parts of rural France.

Christian insisted on the panoply of courtesies at the start of the day, lots of *bonjours*, earnest discussion of the weather and the beauty of the day, a handshake for me and a kiss on each cheek for Sally, who was soon promoted to three kisses.

Once, Christian said, a customer had rushed into his garage with a problem he thought desperate enough to be worth dispensing with the formalities. The client was mistaken. Christian made him go outside then come back and start again, this time properly. When he and Julia left, Sally's was a four-kiss farewell. I stuck with the handshake.

'I'd rather say goodbye to your wife,' said Christian.

New Zealanders arrived. 'We're from O'Rewa,' announced the captain, a man named Austin.

'We're from Christchurch,' we said.

'Oh my god,' they said.

'At least we know how to pronounce Orewa,' we said.

'Gerrruph,' he said.

'Austin is obsolete isn't it?' someone else said.

We called it quits. Why waste good lines when there were so many Australians around? But instead, a French couple found the only vacant space. They had a huge chow dog on their little boat. The dog was grumpy and the couple quarrelsome, especially in the early hours. The dog would bark in chorus.

George and Toby left to travel east and find a winter mooring. They intended spending the first part of winter in France instead of the Bahamas. Then they'd travel to New Zealand for our summer. We'll see you there, they said. Sure, we said. We wondered whether the Ministry of Tourism was ready for the numbers of canal travellers who'd said the same thing.

That November they sent us an email. They'd stayed overnight in France alongside two Aucklanders, John and Rosemary, they said. The pair invited them to look them up when they arrived. They did. The Aucklanders had fixed them up with a house to stay in and a mobile caravan to travel in. George and Toby were overwhelmed. They were more astonished that we knew the Kiwis. 'Wow,' said George.

They drove down to Golden Bay after Christmas that year and visited us. George looked at the emerald water tinged with gold at its edges. 'Wow,' he said.

They were at last going back to their home in Connecticut. It was a dream of its own, deep verandahs and white lace on the edge of the water, yet they seemed frightened by the prospect. They told us Christian and Julia had not sold their business in St Mihiel after all. They'd walked away from it, just as they said they would. Now it was another closed shop in the little Ardennes town.

Roger and Jenny sailed for home, she happily, he diffidently.

David and Anne packed up and left early one crisp autumn morning on their way to meet their family in Spain. They accidentally took my mobile phone with them and posted it back. The French bureaucracy was cumbersome, but it always worked. The trains ran on time and so did the post. My phone was waiting at the next port.

The noise and laughter died away.

We went back to Briare and settled among the flowers. Now white and mauve autumn crocuses formed bright little islands on the canalsides. Flecks of red and gold tinted the trees, lighting the way into a new season. Fields of corn ripened beside us, clouds of crows bursting above them like smoke. The faintest breeze shushed in the oaks.

A hotel boat opened its windows to reveal another life: polished wooden floors, a deck set with chairs and tables, plush white chairs and sofas inside and a table set with white linen and silver and cutlery all gleaming and playing the sun around the room.

We sat amid the bright tiles of the Briare church. The glass now shone with the colours of autumn. That night was the opening match of the rugby World Cup, although we were not praying for that, or for anything else; we just liked sitting in churches. They soothed us, smoothed us. Their endurance seeped into our bones.

Pascal, the port captain, had good news for us. He'd scouted the town. The nearest brasserie was also the best. They would have their TV set tuned to the opening World Cup game. We should book a table for dinner, said Pascal, for it was bound to be crowded.

We'd already met Madame, who ran the brasserie, but we'd planned dinner elsewhere. So we went along afterwards, and found only one table occupied, by Madame's large extended family. Sally and I sat at the bar, listened to the speeches, sang along to '*La Marseillaise*'. The men of Madame's family slowly got interested. All Blacks number one, they said. France also number one, but All Blacks more number one. Kids yelled, women went home, France lost. The men quickly got drunk. All Blacks number one, they said, but France still number two.

Bill the mechanic came aboard to check over the boat in Decize. He had innocent blue eyes and missing front teeth. He sucked on a roll for lunch. He'd done a degree in modern languages in Scotland and had come to France to perfect his French. That was around three decades ago. He'd stayed. After a few years his father, his only family, came to France and the two of them shared a caravan. Then they'd bought a house in Decize.

Bill arranged for a crane to lift the caravan over the wall of their new house and into the back garden. When the crane arrived his dad was still asleep. Bill didn't like to wake him. Besides, it was well before eleven a.m., when his father usually got out of bed. So the crane picked up the caravan, dad and all, hoisted it into the air and deposited it on its new site. Bill went back to work.

In the evening when he returned home his father had not emerged. Bill opened the caravan door. His father was still in bed, quite dead. He'd died the previous night.

I'd given Bill a roll of tissues; he'd taken one piece, wiped oil from the engine, carefully folded it and put it in his pocket. Now he pulled it out and wiped his nose.

Bill had perfected his French and become a mechanic, although he could fix computers too, and oh, the odd musical instrument. Lately he had been unemployed, but he'd discovered that the French allowed him to capitalise his benefit to start a business, so he'd gone out on his own.

Bill had an unusual way of billing us. He decided to charge $20 for every point Scotland scored against the All Blacks in their World Cup game. Scotland failed to score anything at all. Bill wanted to stick to the bargain. We argued; we compromised.

We returned to St Jean de Losne through the black stalks of sunflower fields. A few raindrops fell, then more, and suddenly it was very cold. For the first time since Holland I turned on the boat's central heating. With wi-fi throughout the harbour I went to the BBC website and downloaded Radio 4. News, comment, politics, world affairs were sucked into the boat as if it were a vacuum. We were happy, laughing at everything like children at a birthday party. All around us people now said 'hello' rather than '*bonjour*,' for the canal community was settling in for the winter.

After two freezing days to let us know summer was over the sun returned.

I heard a 'gidday', in a Welsh accent. My god, Beni. He'd come back like a bad peni. Worse, he'd read my account of him in a series I'd written for the *Sunday Star-Times* in New Zealand. Both Beni and story had returned to haunt me.

But wait. I'd wronged him, badly. This wasn't the blowsy Beni of Fontenoy-le-Château. He was the new, no-nonsense, polite, friendly Beni, a Beni who observed the proprieties and did not abuse anyone, much less the woman he had aboard, Gillian's friend Carol from Auckland.

We trusted Carol. Beni behaved himself around her. He was a new man, or perhaps just the old one with the corners knocked off by a good woman. He told us of more adventures, of restoring the old olive oil mill in Spain, of a house restoration business he'd run alongside a B&B, of derring-do in Argentina, of sailing before the trade winds across the Pacific, of the Galapagos, and this time we knew he was not a bull-shitter because Carol had been with him a lot of the time, and while he was telling of the Marquesas she was talking about leaving the same boat and sailing on another through the Aleutian Islands to Alaska, of cold and fog and running out of food.

Beni said the best moment of his life was at Marfells Beach, in Marlborough. Once, he and Carol had been walking on the little beach gathering mussels when they'd heard a faint splashing in the kelp. It was a baby Dusky dolphin, entangled. They'd lifted it free, run along the beach and released it in clear water and knew they were alive, a single moment for the lucky. And some others on the beach gave them crayfish, and they ate it for dinner with their mussels and drank local wine, and God was in his heaven.

Not many have been to that distant beach, much less had the best moment of their lives there, but Beni had. He'd been to Blackball on the West Coast too. He'd loved both places. You could not hold anything against someone like that. So Beni and Carol and I went to a bar to watch the All Blacks play France in the World Cup quarter-final. Just a formality, we thought, on the way to glory. Sally stayed on the boat and listened to Radio 4. Perhaps we should have done the same.

The bar was full of locals, and all of them had a little French flag painted on their foreheads. We ordered *vin de maison rouge*, the house red, which came in thick green bottles. The French ordered pizza in heavy square slices.

The All Blacks went into their early lead. The French bent over their dominoes. The balance shifted. *La France* was gaining ground. The French ordered more pizza, enough for us too. We ordered more wine. Dan Carter came off crying. The French were crying too. We knew it was over. I went to pay the bill. 'Pouf,' said the bar owner and waved it away. One disaster a night was enough for anyone. I presented him with the fat All Black pen Maurice and Denise had given us long ago in Toul, although it had just lost some of its cachet.

France began filling up with displaced New Zealanders. Evidently our love of rugby did not extend to someone else winning the cup. They made alternative arrangements. They sold their finals tickets, now fetching inflated prices among the British. They wandered around France looking dazed.

Later that month we took the boat to its winter haven at St Symphorien, a few kilometres and one lock from St Jean de Losne. It would be looked after there by Roger, an Englishman so long in France that his velvety whippet was as much a memento of home as it was a pet.

We went through that last lock as carefully as if the boat were glass, although we didn't escape without collateral damage.

The lock-keeper asked, 'Do you want a Kleenex?' I puzzled for a moment. Perhaps my French was not up to this.

'The last New Zealand boat came through the week before the All Blacks played France,' he said. 'The captain said I'd be crying that Saturday night. He asked if I wanted a Kleenex. So now I'm asking you. Do you want a Kleenex?'

Our glory days were over. We were yesterday's heroes.

We lowered the silver fern that night, and that other one with the Union Jack and stars. Sally listened for the 'Last Post' but heard only grunts: the flagstaffs had been so long in their sockets they'd stuck.

One foggy morning we left the boat covered in tarpaulins, awaiting its new owners like a badly-wrapped Christmas present. Fog lay thick as a blanket over the port.

We were looking forward to driving across France, for we were travelling from quite close to the Swiss border, through Burgundy and the Château district all the way to the west, through sweet countryside to the wild armoured coast of Brittany.

In the event we drove through fog and saw only roadside, emerging into clear sky at Rennes. We drove up to Dinan then negotiated half-remembered lanes to the hamlet of Le Bois Meen where my brother's house sat, as it had done for three centuries, in its tiny farm at the end of a row of peasant cottages. After almost a year in the *River Queen* the house seemed wonderfully luxurious. We lay in the bath, stacked dishes into a dishwasher, slept in a bed so big we called to each other as if we were loose in a meadow. We gulped the sharp sea air, fresh as the spicy green apples we picked from trees in the garden.

Nearby Dinard, the seaside resort fashioned for Victorian British holiday-makers, hunched over pale sand, its blue-and-white striped bathing tents packed away for the winter. Picasso had taken long holidays here with his mistresses and his palette in the 1920s, painting plump women dancing with joy. The blue autumn sun warmed us.

We drank cider in a little bar in Dinan, among ancient houses leaning towards each other like *les vieux* gossiping in the autumn sun, and perched on the thick walls of St Malo eating half apples baked in sweet pastry rounded like breasts and watching tanned old people brave the cold Atlantic water.

Signs warned of being swept away by currents around cliffs looking over capes and reefs and islands dotted with forts and castles. We bought scallops and watched fishing boats unloading huge red crabs glowering in boxes. We sat under ancient oak beams in the fissures Bretons call harbours and ate bowls of tiny mussels, picking out the orange flesh with the blue shells. We ate two-hour lunches with lorry-drivers in Les Routiers restaurants, four courses of salads, sausage, potatoes, prawns, pâtés, cold meats, pork, spaghetti, calf's liver, panacotta, crême brulée, crême caramel, chocolate mousse, Camembert, Brie, Port-Salut, Roquefort, with all the wine you could drink, all for $20. We found huge boulders which rang like bells when you hit them with stones. We explored the shattered ramparts of castles, climbed capes and leaned against the wind. We walked on beaches and kicked our bare feet into their fine gold sand and gazed over a sea whose colour washed into the sky. We marvelled at a lighthouse keeper's house that looked like a palace. We met five men who'd been together in a seminary, turned away from the priesthood and now shared holidays together. We farewelled a man who proposed to row alone across the Atlantic. We listened to violins played by two women who sat under a tree, wine and glasses and a vase of marigolds set on a gingham cloth.

We smelled the salt water and the sea breeze cleansed our souls. We began to heal in the pale blue light.

But the light was fleeing, the nights drawing in, lonely hedge birds trilling a late dawn chorus. We sat above a pearly beach in the port at St Malo one last time in the crisp air, white sails on the sea, new pansies and chrysanthemums replacing the petunias, the French eating and talking all around us, and next morning we packed a car, drove to Paris and flew home.

The Takaka Hill went on forever, especially when you were in a hurry, or anxious, or excited. We were all three.

The thin road squeezed through bush, broke into the open, brushed by a limeworks, wound through weathered marble, ignored overgrown driveways leading to fanciful houses built by people escaping from lives known only to themselves, and, perhaps, their kindred spirits in converted barges and *peniches* lying along the waterways of Europe.

It glided past an abandoned quarry with its manager's house still staring forlornly over desolation, but this was a ploy; it only seemed to be descending. Just as you were shifting your bottom with that smug feeling of being over the worst, the road kinked left and began toiling upwards again. It widened into a passing lane where, if you were quick, and knowledgeable, and adventurous, you could even pass. It ran through country which once had carried sheep, although any survivors were now outnumbered by hermits.

Here I once drove my vintage Jaguar, its grace then unrecognised, and was startled to find one of its wire wheels passing me. The car's corner hit the road with an awful grinding sound; but we fixed the wheel back on with No. 8 wire cut from a fence and drove away feeling guilty. Broken fences now lay everywhere. Knobs of marble jutted from tougher scrub and quite suddenly, the road broke out onto a summit.

Golden Bay unfolded below. The last of the winter's snow traced its peaks. Bush purpled in the evening light; queer valleys turned dark. Far off, the sea sprang light, like a new dawn.

The way was now steep, through four hairpin bends, as if it had done all it could to slow us, to sharpen our anticipation, and now it was rushing us home. We seemed about to fly off the mountain and land on the beach. Instead it led to what had been the Rat Trap Hotel, before it burned down. When we were kids the hotel meant we were almost there. Mum and Dad would go inside; he for a beer, she for a shandy. The Zephyr would cool in the carpark, ticking deep in its innards. In its blue seats the five brothers — my sister was not yet born, and when she was, I was far too old at seventeen to commit social suicide and travel with them — would sit quietly, for once. We knew what would come next and oh, the cacophony when it did. Raspberry and lemonade, in trumpet-shaped beer glasses. The trick was to be last to finish, for then you'd have four pairs of envious eyes upon you; fine if you were the eldest, dangerous for the young.

Golden Bay had a final trick. It kept the sea till last. Instead the road ran through a little town, lingered in a valley, dallied with a river and threw a few one-way bridges at the unwary until at last Tākaka, the bay's only town of substance, blocked the way. Then you swerved to the right before anyone had any fancy ideas about stopping at the Telegraph Hotel and headed back into the country. But now the skyline cleared. Patches of estuary appeared beside the road, then a camping ground and motels and at the end of it, we burst upon the sea, so blue, the limestone cliffs dotted with palms and trees, the sand the palest gold, so fine I felt dizzy.

Tuis sang on every side, kereru swooped low. I caught an oystercatcher's desolate cry, glimpsed a dark rock heron hunched over the water. The eerie grey silos of the old cement works rose from the cliffs above Tarakohe harbour. What strange craft moored there today? Once it was a ship being dismantled, then a square-rigged sailing ship, then a high-bowed fishing boat painted bright blue, whose owner would tell you it was once owned by Jacques Cousteau while he made espresso under a sign announcing, 'Pirate Coffee Ship'.

We drove up the little rocky peninsula with its tall white monument to Abel Tasman's dismal adventure here. And at the top, our lovely bay appeared as bright as new, as wondrous as never seen before, as exciting as a present. The tide was out. Still ponds of seawater lay on its yellow sand. At the far end lay a natural harbour, its stone breakwater pointing like an arrow to our tiny green house almost hidden in bush.

I stopped the car. We walked on the beach, hand in hand, fused into a single ball of delight.

Adventures are not simple events. They are complex things, filled with satisfaction, and moments of complete happiness, and danger, and shards of hardship, and fright, and despair. Otherwise they would not be adventures. They would be ten days in Fiji.

I'd hoped our journey would show us, or even just hint at, the way we might spend the rest of our lives. Perhaps that was too ambitious. Perhaps too much change shifts or breaks the patterns that keep people whole. Ours worked in a way we did not expect; it narrowed the options by revealing starkly what was important and even more urgently, what was not.

Neither of us imagined for a moment that it might put our marriage in danger.

How could it? Break-ups only happened to other people, like air crashes.

We were living on the French canals in villages and towns that were said, by everyone, to be the most romantic in the world. We had one hundred different kinds of cheese at the smallest village shop and all the croissants we could eat. We were so lucky. Everyone said so. Not to enjoy every minute of it would be kicking luck in her teeth.

Yet we did not belong in someone else's country, no matter how much we tried. It was theirs. They made us welcome, or at least tolerated us, and some of their good things were ours, but not the critical elements of knowing and fitting that make home.

On balance, though, throwing in my job was a roaring success. Moving to the French canals had a collateral benefit: no one ever mentioned retirement, nor did I think of it myself.

Our lives did change. In some ways for the good, in others … well, let's just say we're still working on that. If you're going to change your life you must first know those parts of it you want to stay the same.

We lived in Golden Bay for a time then moved back into our house in Sumner. Sally did what she always did: lived her life as best she could and was satisfied with what she had. I had no real idea of what I wanted to do, other than write.

I don't know if we're better. Both of us are different people now, not for a year in France, but for having nowhere to hide.

Our marriage took a bad knock. Perhaps we were complacent; being surrounded by wreckage makes your island too much of a refuge. But we peeped into the abyss, teetered on its brink, and we both took a step back.

It is very hard to grow older without having regrets, and if you have none, what sort of life have you lived? It is a close-run thing between living life and losing something, and not living life and regretting what you have not done. If you're going to throw your cards in the air you can't expect them always to come down into something nice and neat, or even recognisable.

When people asked where we'd been, I said, we spent a year on the French canals. They said, oh how wonderful. And I said, yes, it was.